Crisis
Vision

Crisis
Vision

Torin Monahan

RACE AND THE CULTURAL PRODUCTION OF SURVEILLANCE

Duke University Press *Durham and London* 2022

Cover design by A. Mattson Gallagher
Typeset in Whitman and Trade Gothic
by Westchester Publishing Services

Library of Congress Cataloging-in-Publication Data
Names: Monahan, Torin, author.
Title: Crisis vision : race and the cultural production of surveillance /
Torin Monahan.
Description: Durham : Duke University Press, 2022. | Includes
bibliographical references and index.
Identifiers: LCCN 2021056771 (print) | LCCN 2021056772 (ebook)
ISBN 9781478016113 (hardcover)
ISBN 9781478018759 (paperback)
ISBN 9781478023388 (ebook)
Subjects: LCSH: Electronic surveillance—Social aspects. |
Surveillance in art—Social aspects. | Art—Political aspects. | Art and
race. | Social practice (Art) | Art and society—History—21st century. |
BISAC: SOCIAL SCIENCE / Privacy & Surveillance (see also
POLITICAL SCIENCE / Privacy & Surveillance) | ART / History /
Contemporary (1945–)
Classification: LCC HV7936.T4 M66 2022 (print) | LCC HV7936.T4
(ebook) | DDC 363.2/32—dc23/eng/20220528
LC record available at https://lccn.loc.gov/2021056771
LC ebook record available at https://lccn.loc.gov/2021056772

Cover art: Hank Willis Thomas, *Raise Up*, 2014. Bronze, 112.2 × 9.84
inches (285 × 25 cm). © Hank Willis Thomas. Courtesy of the artist
and Jack Shainman Gallery, New York.

For Mom

CONTENTS

ACKNOWLEDGMENTS

As the refrain goes, this book has been a long time coming. From my early exploratory interviews with artist-activists as I transitioned from graduate school to my first academic position nearly two decades ago and throughout the many research projects since, I have been drawn to artistic forms of resistance to surveillance. Perhaps owing to my humanities roots, I felt a need to grasp the resonances and potency of artworks beyond their surface provocations, to approach them as vibrant forms of life. Many colleagues generously pushed me forward in this inquiry. I have had enriching discussions with scholars and artists, have received countless suggestions for artworks to consider, and have been granted many forums to present and develop this work. In short, I have had a genuine scholarly community and encouraging friends within it; for that, I am both lucky and grateful.

Especially generative were the invited talks I gave on preliminary versions of the book's chapters. These events afforded the kind of improvisation, musing, and dialogue that significantly honed the book's overall argument and shape. In 2016 Kelly Joyce and Susan Sterett invited me to an amazing workshop on Collaboration as Big Data Ethics at the Virginia Tech Research Center, where I fondly recall animated discussions with Karen Levy, Solon Barocas, Katie Shilton, and Meg Leta Jones. The Institute of Geography at the University of Neuchâtel generously invited me to present a large overview of this work in 2017, and it was my host and friend Francisco Klauser who mirthfully prodded me to "make it a book." As part of the Big Data Surveillance project spearheaded by David Lyon, I presented a chapter at a workshop on Security Intelligence and Surveillance in the Big Data Age at the University of Ottawa in 2017. Austin Sarat, Lawrence Douglas, and Martha Merrill Umphrey invited me to present to Amherst College's Department of Law, Jurisprudence and Social Thought in 2017 and gave me the added challenge of connecting my work to legal studies. One of the most pivotal moments in the development of the book was an invitation by longtime colleague and ally Mary Romero to participate in a special session on Surveillance and Emotion at the American Sociological Association conference in 2018; along with fellow panelists Simone Browne and Ruha Benjamin, the rich synergy among our presentations on race and surveillance, along with the audience's enthusiastic reception, affirmed for me that the book was on the right track and galvanized me to finish it. Closer to home, my sharp and delightful colleague Tori Ekstrand invited me to present a portion of the book to the University of North Carolina at Chapel Hill's Center for Media Law and Policy in 2018. Finally, the most flattering invitation came from Anders Albrechtslund and the other organizers of the Eighth Biennial Surveillance Studies Network Conference—held at Aarhus University in 2018—who asked me to deliver the conference's keynote lecture and allowed me to convene a special plenary panel on critical surveillance art.

In addition to invited talks, I have benefited from the input of many other interlocutors at seminars and conferences. I thank the participants of the Surveillance Studies Summer Seminars held at Queen's University in 2015 and 2017, and especially my co-organizers of those events, David Murakami Wood, Valerie Steeves, and Scott Thompson. The meetings of the National Communication Association have been particularly fruitful for receiving critical feedback on nascent articulations; I thank my many brilliant fellow panelists at those conferences, including Lamiyah Bahrainwala, Ingrid Burrington, Rachel Dubrofsky, Mia Fischer, Radhika Gajjala, Racquel Gonzales, Rachel Hall, Mél Hogan, Nathan Hulsey, Chris Ingraham, Gary Kafer, Lisa Parks, Joshua Reeves, Tamara Shepherd, Jennifer Daryl Slack, Armond Towns, and J. Macgregor Wise. Finally, the members of my fellowship cohort at the Institute for the Arts and Humanities at UNC in 2020 truly went above and beyond in providing a close, caring reading of the book's introduction and helping me weather the intellectual unmooring of the COVID-19 pandemic; thank you Jocelyn Chua, Michael Figueroa, Maggie Fritz-Morkin, Philip Hollingsworth, Tim Marr, Susan Pennybacker, Aleksandra Prica, Victoria Rovine, Rebecka Rutledge Fisher, Petal Samuel, and John Sweet.

Beyond the people already named, many others generously gave their time to read drafts, provide comments on presentations, or share resources. Foremost, my life partner, Jill Fisher, read everything closely, through multiple drafts, with awesome patience and perceptiveness. Others I am indebted to include Toby Beauchamp, Fareed Ben-Youssef, Clare Birchall, Susan Cahill, Julia Chan, Krista Craven, Benjamin Fleury-Steiner, Stephen Graham, David Grondin, Atilla Hallsby, James Harding, Marina Levina, Randolph Lewis, David Lyon, Shoshana Magnet, Tobias Matzner, Elise Morrison, Isabel Ortiz, Robert Pallitto, Dennis Pauschinger, David Phillips, Matthew Potolsky, Carrie Sanders, Gavin Smith, Karen Louise Grova Søilen, William Staples, Tyler Wall, and Jennifer Whitson.

The importance of my larger academic community, particularly the Surveillance Studies Network, cannot be overestimated, for it has provided a sense of home in what can otherwise feel like, and be, an isolating profession. Some of the core members not already namedropped include Louise Amoore, Mark Andrejevic, Kirstie Ball, David Barnard-Wills, Colin Bennett, Philip Boyle, Julie Cohen, Karen Fang, Chiara Fonio, Martin French, Pete Fussey, Gemma Galdon-Clavell, Oscar Gandy, Kelly Gates, John Gilliom, Amanda Glasbeek, Daniel Grinberg, Kevin Haggerty, Hille Koskela, Kathleen Kuehn, Manu Luksch, Debra Mackinnon, Aaron Martin, Gary Marx, Mike McCahill, Adam Molnar, Michael Nagenborg, Bryce Newell, Priscilla Regan, James Rule, Mark Salter, Minas Samatas, Alana Saulnier, Keith Spiller, Emmeline Taylor, Özgün Topak, Daniel Trottier, Pinelopi Troullinou, Rosamunde van Brakel, Kristin Veel, Kevin Walby, James Walsh, Jutta Weber, William Webster, Dean Wilson, Catherine Zimmer, and Nils Zurawski. I also thank my editor, Courtney Berger, and the two anonymous reviewers at Duke University Press who offered amazingly astute and constructive comments that helped me ground the book in larger scholarly debates while also connecting it to the tumultuous political present.

Furthermore, the project has been intellectually enriched by the many exchanges I have had with colleagues and graduate students, both past and present, in the Department of Communication at UNC. I give special thanks to Codey Bills, Carole Blair, Bill Brown, Ben Clancy, Renée Alexander Craft, Christopher Dahlie, Cori Dauber, Andrew Davis, Margaret Franz, Larry Grossberg, Julia Haslett, Ken Hillis, Sonny Kelly, Alice Marwick, Ashley Mattheis, Steve May, Alex McVey, China Medel, Amrut Mishra, Dennis Mumby, Ali Na, Mike Palm, Zac Parker, Will Partin, Tony Perucci, Courtlyn Pippert, Della Pollock, Susan Ryan, Joyce Rudinsky, Elaine Schnabel, Aaron Shapiro, Sarah Sharma, Kumi Silva, Eric King Watts, Megan Wood, and Heather Woods.

I must also give my heartfelt thanks to the artists who let me reprint images of their work and particularly those who provided feedback on my interpretations. Exchanges with artists, more broadly, have helped sensitize me to some of the key differences—and tensions—between critical scholarship and critical art. Although we may disagree on certain criticisms or conclusions, I hope that they recognize my deep appreciation and gratitude for their work. Not all of them are represented in the book, but those who nonetheless deserve special mention are Rose Butler, Paolo Cirio, James Coupe, Dries Depoorter, Heather Dewey-Hagborg, Hasan Elahi, Jakub Geltner, Andrew Hammerand, Birgit Johnsen, Stéfy McKnight, Hanne Nielsen, Marco Poloni, Leo Selvaggio, Julia Scher, Dread Scott, and Kai Wiedenhöfer. For any people I have forgotten to include in these acknowledgments, I offer my sincere apologies, for my debts are many and sometimes exceed my memory.

My university also generously supported my work on this project. In the 2020–2021 academic year, which was a year of upheaval marked by the coronavirus pandemic and radicalized white supremacy, I was provided with something like a life raft in the form of an Ellison Fellowship from the Institute for the Arts and Humanities and a research leave from the College of Arts and Sciences, which together gave me protected time to write and revise the book while sheltering in lockdown. The stresses of the world frequently succeeded in interrupting the work I was trying to do, but writing also provided an outlet, a way to process events and sublimate anxiety. Until it couldn't anymore. Nonetheless, I am grateful to have had these vital forms of institutional support, and I recognize my privilege in receiving them.

Early versions of some of the chapters appeared in various other venues. As the book evolved, the primary argument shifted a few times, and many new examples and interpretations were added. In other instances, entire sections were cut or radically reworked. I appreciate having had the opportunity to iterate earlier drafts in this way and to benefit from the insights of other peer reviewers.

Sending a book out into the world is always an unsettling experience, at least for me. It is a moment to reflect on the sacrifices made and the time invested, a moment to question one's choices and to hope that others will find the work valuable. On a personal level, publishing this book is especially bittersweet because it was something I looked forward to sharing with my mother, from whom I acquired, at a very young age, my love for books and my activist streak. She passed away in the weeks before I submitted the final manuscript, leaving both an immeasurable void and an abundance of wonderful memories. I know she would have been proud, just as I am of all she accomplished and all she was. My family remains the weave that holds it all together. Thank you Monahans, Fishers, and honorary family members (that's you, Christy and the Walsh clan).

Finally, my most profound gratitude is reserved for Jill, who infuses every day and every moment with vibrancy and meaning. Thank you for being the rock star that you are and for choosing me to share your life with. Along with our often-inscrutable pup, Addie, I couldn't imagine a better lockdown crew.

Let us start with two visual scenes. The first is of a street-art mural spray-painted on the side of a London building (see figure I.1). In large font, the piece proclaims, "ONE NATION UNDER CCTV," with drips of white paint running underneath the letters, a testament to the work's hasty production. A stenciled figure on a ladder, a boy raising a paint roller to one of the letters, simulates the act of creation; his red hoodie covers most of his face, but he is nonetheless watched. Below and to the left of him stand additional painted figures: a gray-attired policeman holding what appears to be a camera and a Doberman pinscher police dog sitting at the man's feet, mouth open and ears up. Both man and dog assess the scene, the authority and implied threat of their attention nudging the interpretive frame toward one of judgment. Above them all, to the right, an actual video surveillance camera clings to the wall, potentially documenting the scene as evidence for unknown observers in an unknown location. A final unrepresented viewer is the person absorbing this entire panorama, either someone physically present, such as the photographer, or distantly removed, such as you or me. Notably, the CCTV video camera—which is obviously an intentional, appropriated prop for this artwork—points outward, directed toward those who might be consuming this scene, as if to demonstrate the veracity of the textual claim of ubiquitous surveillance.

The second scene is of museumgoers playfully flowing through the darkened rooms of an art space in New York City. As they run, dance, or lie on the grid-lined charcoal-colored floor, discreet video surveillance cameras and drones capture their images and project them back onto the grid (see figure I.2). Thus, participants' digital ghosts follow them and echo their movements, evidently encouraging interaction as groups of people flirt with their feedback loops and take selfies with their digital doubles. The underlying algorithm further communicates its tracking and processing ability by drawing red boxes around represented faces, arms, legs, and torsos. Participants watch one another and their ephemeral traces; they watch themselves in the act of being watched. In this work the ominous police threats of the first artwork fade into the background, lost in the hum of ambient monitoring and the thrill of technological capability. Watching is pervasive but diluted, totalizing but fleeting, at least in its representation. Near the exit, the museum gift shop plies visitors with various privacy-enhancing paraphernalia, such as radio-frequency-blocking mobile phone cases, suggesting consumption as a viable means of reducing exposure.

The first scene was staged in 2007 by renowned street artist Banksy. The second, provocatively titled *Hansel & Gretel*, was an installation created in 2017 by artist Ai Weiwei and architects Jacques Herzog and Pierre de Meuron. Both of these art projects engage with surveillance themes but in different ways and with different messages. Spaced ten years apart, what might they reveal about changing perceptions of surveillance and its threats? What different problematics are they addressing, and what

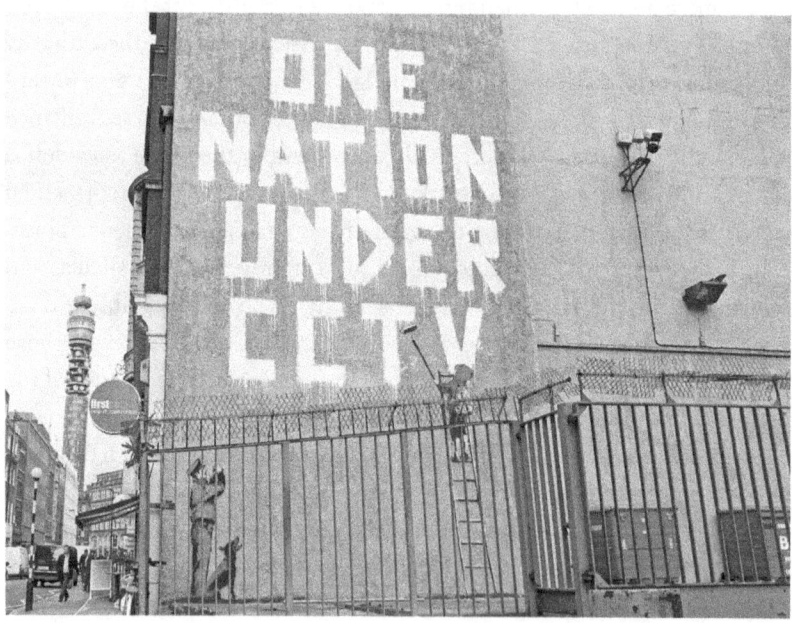

FIGURE I.1. Banksy, *One Nation Under CCTV* (2008). Courtesy of Pest Control Office, Banksy, London, 2008.

gets left out of each? Appearing during the height of the War on Terror, the Banksy mural followed in the wake of revelations of widespread state surveillance by the US government. These revelations included information that telecommunications companies and allied countries such as the United Kingdom were collaborating with the National Security Agency (NSA) to illegally monitor phone calls, emails, web browsing, and text messages of citizens.[1] Banksy's mural critiques this culture of generalized suspicion, where multiple sources routinely amass evidence on individuals and pass it on to state agents for possible investigation. The threat is one of a totalitarian state operating in relative obscurity while it stifles creative expression, civil liberties, and sociality.

By the time that the installation by Weiwei and colleagues materialized, social media and smartphones had become commonplace, Edward Snowden's disclosures of even more pervasive, illegal NSA surveillance had come and gone, and critical public attention about technology was routed toward areas like social media's threat to democratic processes. The emphasis had shifted away from the state and unambiguous surveillance devices, moving instead toward private digital platform companies and the compromising—but seemingly unavoidable—data trails produced by

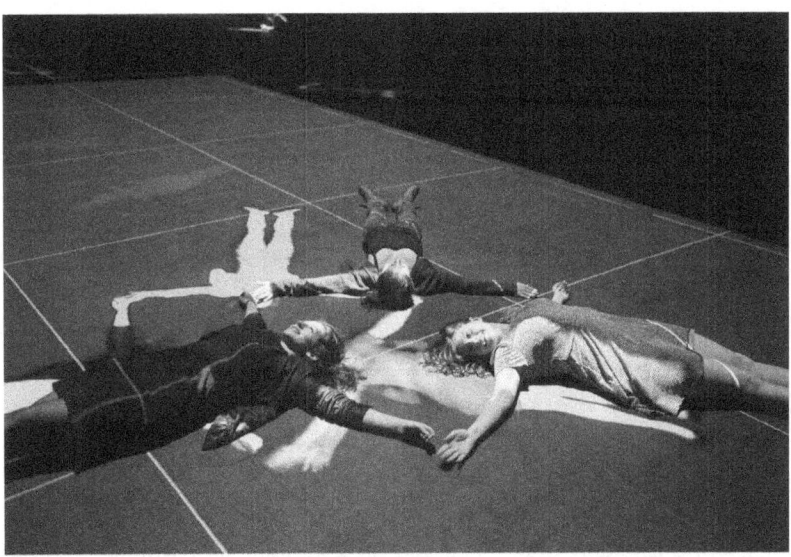

FIGURE I.2. Ai Weiwei, Jacques Herzog, and Pierre de Meuron, *Hansel & Gretel* (2017). Photograph by Agaton Strom for the *New York Times*.

websites, personal devices, and ambient sensors. *Hansel & Gretel* illuminates some of these usually hidden data trails to cultivate awareness in museumgoers.[2] Unlike Banksy's work, which symbolically pointed toward an Orwellian dystopia of repressive state control, thereby painting a clear target for progressive intervention, *Hansel & Gretel* offers no external object for denunciation. Instead, the piece enjoins participants to take responsibility for their digital exposure and mitigate it through practices of personal privacy hygiene. Viewed through the lens of the Hansel and Gretel fairy tale, the confection-like allure of technological products represents a danger that individual ingenuity may be poorly equipped to counteract.

Themes of visibility animate both of these works. With *One Nation Under CCTV*, visibility represents vulnerability, on one hand, converting all observable acts into evidence for possible correction, and empowerment, on the other hand, serving as the mechanism by which one can draw attention to and undermine these repressive logics. Banksy's own conscientiously guarded identity operates as a subtext to this critique, whereby his anonymity grants his works mystique and him relative safety: he relies on a robust network of supportive artist and activist colleagues who know his identity and keep it hidden. With *Hansel & Gretel*, largely concealed conditions of ubiquitous exposure are represented, haunting participants with their own digital ghosts while encouraging interaction and play. For all its ostentatious technological mediation, though, the underlying code remains as opaque as the external parties who routinely capitalize upon digital exhaust.[3] The individual, conversely, lifts to the surface, rendered hypervisible against the dark backdrop of technological mystery. *Hansel & Gretel* performs the seeming inevitability of individual exposure and subjection to the interests of remote others.

Something crucial, however, remains invisible in both of these works. For different reasons, neither successfully engages with the differential ramifications of state and corporate surveillance. Banksy's piece draws its power from the universal: everyone in the nation is under surveillance, and society as a whole is imperiled by latent totalitarianism. Weiwei and colleagues distill exposure to the individual who may move with others but must confront privacy threats alone, if at all. This is not to discount how these works resonate with and educate viewers, but the reasons for their appeal notably blunt their radical potential. As I will show, these works, like many others in this vein, illustrate broader societal constraints in contending with surveillance problems. By embracing the symbolism of universal threats or individual responsibility, such interventions can create blind spots to social inequality, racialization, and violence, to the ways that liberal social orders depend on and propagate exclusions, often through visibility regimes. Nonetheless, art offers a profoundly generative and enticing way to apprehend surveillance dynamics, as well as to better understand the challenges of activating change.

The Trappings of Visibility

The past decade has witnessed an explosion in surveillance-themed artworks. Whereas previously there may have been dozens of art projects grouped together in infrequent exhibits or in the rare academic book,[4] today there are hundreds of works presented at major and minor museum exhibits, implemented in activist movements, staged in theaters, published in books, circulated across social media, and marketed as anti-surveillance consumables. What is it about this particular conjuncture that catalyzes such artwork? What does it signify? And what are its potentials?

Although Snowden's 2013 leaks about the NSA's massive telecommunications surveillance apparatus proved, again, that government security agencies were committed to collecting every data element, no matter how small, relevant, or legally protected,[5] this was only one important galvanizing force for artists and activists. This renewed awareness merged with growing concern, more generally, about concealed yet consequential vulnerabilities emerging from data circulation and use. Police agencies routinely deploy drones, cell-phone tracking systems, and social media surveillance to monitor and interrupt Black Lives Matter and other activist movements.[6] Algorithms are programmed to assess the worthiness of individuals for jobs, housing, university admission, or reduced criminal sentencing, among many other obscure code-based determinations affecting people's lives.[7] Smart devices such as virtual assistants, televisions, and other appliances infiltrate homes, silently amassing and acting on personal data.[8] Facebook and other social media sites continue to be harnessed by foreign actors to manipulate election processes and fuel hate groups.[9] The list can and does go on, but what it reveals is a move toward relatively invisible, ubiquitous surveillance systems that rely on data to alter social systems in fundamental ways. Most of the recent surveillance-themed art projects attempt to render this invisibility visible and subject it to critique.

Surveillance implies much more than just watching: it is focused observation infused with judgment and yoked to a purpose.[10] Surveillance is a key mechanism of influencing, directing, and regulating the behavior of individuals and groups in society. In short, it is a principal mode of governance deployed by institutions and individuals, through both technical and nontechnical means, to assert control over domains and the bodies within them. As recent scholarship in the field of surveillance studies has argued, surveillance activities—regardless of intention—are perforce ideological exercises that support systems of oppression and domination, whether symbolically or directly.[11] The judgment implied in surveillance normalizes hierarchical relations and enforces unequal treatment of populations based on their perceived value or threat (e.g., the tourist or refugee, the consumer or criminal). As such, surveillance is hegemonic in that it can appear rational and reasonable even while it reproduces undemocratic and discriminatory social orders shot through with gender, racial, class, and other inequalities.

Although many artists may be committed to visibilizing the hidden worlds and effects of surveillance, visibility projects are far from neutral endeavors. If one thinks of visibility not as a representation of reality but instead as a complex social process that orders the world and establishes relationships,[12] then efforts to change—or maintain—visibility regimes are always political and contextually dependent. What is perceptible and knowable at any given moment is a product of dominant aesthetic arrangements, or what Jacques Rancière calls "the distribution of the sensible,"[13] so efforts to disrupt those arrangements can never simply be about unveiling the truth of their partiality or unjustness.[14] Redistributions of the sensible rely on alternative-visibility projects that undermine the legitimacy of the dominant while manufacturing possibilities outside or beyond the trammels of political authority and the status quo. Experimental creative practices hold great promise for destabilizing prevailing forms of visibility, but they are also inseparably woven into existing social structures and orders, making degrees of complicity unavoidable. Interventions emerge from and are dependent upon dominant distributions of the sensible, which constrain potentials for fundamental change.[15] When artists take the politics of visibility *as* the subject of art, frames for difference become even more fraught because typical visual grammars and metaphors—such as "shedding light" on abuses—mobilize, and reinforce, scientific registers that undergird the aesthetic order being critiqued.

Modern forms of visibility are ultimately violent, reductive, and exclusionary. This orientation finds its roots in the Enlightenment and subsequent scientific revolution, where depictions of a more organismic, female conception of nature that should be safeguarded gave way to a mechanistic view of nature that should be conquered and exploited. This new culture of science rested on visibility—both in the method of inquiry and the political order granting science a privileged position. As Carolyn Merchant graphically recounts, proponents of science such as Francis Bacon invoked analogies of women being tortured, raped, and enslaved to explain how one should harness nature's secrets.[16] Rather than a demonstrable shift from values of subjectivity to those of objectivity, social stratification infused scientific knowledge production over the course of the seventeenth century, ushering in a period where aristocratic white gentlemen trusted the honor of their colleagues and served as "modest witnesses" to their discoveries.[17] European women, who previously ran science-themed "salons," were excluded from these professional viewing practices by the eighteenth century.[18] Early scientific vision was therefore founded on themes of violent subjugation and social exclusion, which gradually acquired the trappings of objectivity and placeless, unmarked knowledge. Such knowledge, as Donna Haraway explicates, disavows its responsibility for the sordid outcomes of its visualizations—"militarism, capitalism, colonialism, and [white] male supremacy"—while executing "the god-trick of seeing everything from nowhere."[19] Objective vision is a violent parsing of the world that constructs elements as separate from context and subject to manipulation.[20] Even if its modalities shift over time,[21] objective vision is a political achievement masquerading as a disinterested scientific posture.

Because visibility is a way of ordering the world, it has symbiotically developed with and infused many state and colonial governance projects. Modern state efforts to police and administer societies strive to make people and their activities legible, simplifying social and ecological complexity in the process. As James C. Scott explains, even when grand state projects fail, they nevertheless succeed at imposing reductive frames and remaking the world, at least partially, in the image of bureaucratic and imperial apparatuses.[22] The impact of such state projects is especially apparent in urban planning, as with the grid structure imposed upon cities like Chicago or with the cold, rational design of cities like Brasília, where material infrastructures reflect the models of city planners and force people to adapt.[23] In the contemporary context one can trace related logics with, for instance, state-industry schemes to implement global supply chains, facilitate the flow of goods across national territories, and criminalize any impediments to those imperatives.[24] Visibility is integral to rationalization efforts, whether of states, corporations, or institutions more generally.

These processes of "governing through visibility" have deep roots in social systems founded on white supremacy and antiblack violence. As recent black studies scholarship in the Afro-pessimism tradition has productively insisted, slavery and colonization should not be dismissed as exceptional, if shameful, events in the histories of modern liberal societies but should be viewed instead as constitutive features of such societies, as foundational racial hierarchies and violences that continue to shape the present. Thus, for scholars such as Frank Wilderson and Jared Sexton, full incorporation and inclusion of marginalized groups into civil society is a definitional impossibility because civil society is predicated on the erasure and disavowal of black subjecthood.[25] Black and brown bodies were—and are—subjugated and controlled through visualization and containment processes that deny their personhood and reduce them to malleable "flesh." Hortense Spillers characterizes this dynamic as one of "pornotroping," where nonwhite bodies are presented as objects for dehumanized manipulation and possession while white subjecthood is simultaneously centered as the position from which one could perpetrate such violence.[26] To this conversation, Amber Jamilla Musser adds an important focus on the sexual dimensions of such exercises of racial domination: "The pornotrope allows us to see that violence toward black and brown people is inextricable from theorizations of sexuality. The violence and projection that produce the pornotrope require at their core a subject who desires and who thereby objectifies and possesses others through this desire."[27] Put differently, there is a profound and troubling intimacy involved in exercises of racialized power that can be detected in visceral form, for example, in graphic scenes of white police officers grappling with, dominating, and killing black men—with the knee on the neck, the chokehold, the hood placed over one's head.[28] In these embodied performances of racial domination, visibility regimes informed by white supremacy position nonwhite bodies as out of place, as unruly, as dehumanized targets for masculine police aggression.

In sum, schemes to make people legible have ignoble racial histories that permeate the present and continue to shape contemporary politics. As surveillance studies scholar Simone Browne puts it, "Racism and antiblackness undergird and sustain the intersecting surveillances of our present order."[29] Whether with the management of enslaved people on plantations, the arbitrary segregation of populations by racial markers, or the fabrication of photographic archives of supposed criminal types, scientific or bureaucratic visualizations of human difference have served to justify and normalize violent, discriminatory practices.[30] Today, racial profiling and neighborhood "hot-spot" policing reproduce some of these dynamics, where for some, being visible is synonymous with being in danger. If one is perceived as a threat, one's visible presence can be interpreted as an invitation for correction, potentially with fatal results. If these are the valences of modern visibility, then appeals to visibility to correct social problems run the risk of shoring up visual economies that have decidedly harmful encodings even if—or perhaps because—they present themselves as impartial or objective.[31]

Critical Surveillance Art

The current preponderance of surveillance-themed art indexes growing concerns with power and visibility in a technologically mediated, data-dominated world, one marked by ambiguity, vulnerability, and violence. Though acknowledging the pitfalls and double binds of using creative visual media to contest deleterious state-corporate visibility regimes, inspiring and emotionally powerful art projects nevertheless suggest ways to sidestep or work differently within the constraints of modern visibility. Typically, the term *surveillance art* refers to art or performance projects that either focus on surveillance problematics or incorporate surveillance technologies into their aesthetic production.[32] By adding the word *critical*, as in *critical surveillance art*, I signal that the works in question also tackle issues of domination, oppression, and inequality. As my analysis will make clear, not all surveillance art aspires to or achieves this standard, but the works in question still provide ample opportunities to reflect on aesthetic limitations and their implications for other modes of engagement.

What can art teach us about visibility and surveillance today? Art theorists have long observed that technologies, art forms, and modes of perception codevelop, allowing one to read societal mutations through art.[33] For example, Jonathan Crary relates the emergence of "subjective vision" during the nineteenth century, where increasing mechanization coincided with scientific understandings of the body as a technical apparatus that actively produced perception, as opposed to simply receiving visual stimuli passively.[34] Artistic forms echoed these ideas, such as Muybridge's motion slides of horses or Seurat's pointillism paintings, both of which referenced the *process* of perception by making explicit the mechanistic links between discrete visual components and the whole. More than that, such art forms referenced the formation of new subjectivities aligned with capitalist logics, as people strove to focus their attention to be productive and disciplined. Similarly, by engaging with contemporary surveillance art, one can discover new problem areas, such as new articulations of state violence, while also detecting emergent subjectivities, sociopolitical formations, and methods of interruption.

Accordingly, critical surveillance art can reveal and challenge current configurations of visibility and violence. By resisting the impulse to reduce art to its practical application, the aleatory opens up, allowing the imagination to run and emotional connections to form. As Néstor García Canclini poetically writes, "Art is the place of imminence—the place where we catch sight of things that are just at the point of occurring. Art gains its attraction in part from the fact that it proclaims something that could happen, promising meaning or modifying meaning through insinuations. It makes no unbreakable commitment to hard facts. It leaves what it says hanging."[35] Art can tease apart relationships to contemporary visual economies and present them for contemplation.[36] It conjures the demons of the political present, refracted through their past incarnations and future potentialities. As Ronak Kapadia relates in his incisive work on creative responses to imperial warfare, "Attention to art and aesthetics as forms of sensuous knowledge and critique can make available alternate ways of knowing and feeling the social world."[37] Particularly for the task of tracing the outlines and implications of the invisible worlds of surveillance, such creative expression may be uniquely equipped to communicate threats and shape political sensibilities because the point is not to identify a single problem but to describe a pervasive assemblage with significant, if uneven, consequences for entire populations and ways of life.[38] Elise Morrison therefore describes surveillance art as inviting "critical spectatorship" and encouraging audiences "to interact with surveillance technologies in new and different ways and to examine anew their habitual relationships with the matrix of discipline and desire in contemporary surveillance society."[39]

In a sense, this is a book about invisibility. It follows artists who strive to render visible the hidden vectors of social, political, and economic power, particularly those vectors that are technologically mediated and instantiated. Drawing upon Merleau-Ponty, Andrea Brighenti portrays the invisible as "not simply something visible that happens to be contingently away from sight. Rather, the invisible is what is *here without being an object*. The invisible is *intrinsic* to the visible, is what makes it possible."[40] The cultural logics of surveillance, those of pervasive, unassailable assessment and control, function as such intrinsic scripts that order worlds and destabilize subjects. Thus, artists endeavor to depict the invisible operations that govern contemporary life. Rather than posit solutions, per se, critical surveillance art seeks to agitate, to fashion situations that expose visibility regimes and challenge audiences to reflect on their places within them. In keeping with a general shift toward performance-based approaches to art over the past few decades,[41] many of the works I discuss in this book can be read as creating *situations* that enfold audiences into scenes. Whereas individual artistic artifacts or installations are still central, they often operate in the service of the experiences they catalyze and subjectivities they engender.[42] From this perspective, then, consumption gives way to subject transformation as the most potent desired outcome of artistic encounters.

There are dangers in emphasizing the visual, though. The primary danger is succumbing to the escapist allure of transparency, with its attendant traps of objectivity, impartiality, and truth. Transparency infuses state and corporate efforts to make populations governable and profitable; it is a cornerstone of modern scientific rationality, which valorizes legibility and the production of empirical evidence as the basis for decision making. Transparency is a weapon that affords the objectification and control of others, so it is an agonistic method at best and a means of domination and destruction at worst. As such, many of the surveillance abuses contested by artists and activists are motivated in the first place by logics of transparency. If all one does is unearth and shine a light on such abuses, one risks reproducing their underlying logics. Appropriation of transparency, in other words, reaffirms the value and importance of making others visible and controllable when, instead, perhaps such conceptual tools of domination should themselves be discarded to make way for alternative, more ethical arrangements.[43] At the very least, by deconstructing transparency one can stress the partiality and politics of institutional vision that—while well insulated and assiduously maintained—is nonetheless vulnerable to competing representations and collective action.

Crisis Vision

Reading art as a lens into the problematics of visibility today reveals increasing apprehension about loss of control over the conditions of one's life, where even legal and technical frameworks—contemporary governmentalities—are blurred and volatile.[44] From discourses of big data disclosing counterintuitive facts, to fears about living in post-truth and fake-news informational ecosystems, to resurgent nationalisms and authoritarianisms, to conditions of radical economic precarity, to growing awareness of police violence against people of color, a sense of insecurity characterizes contemporary social worlds. A dominant *subjective vision* remains, responsibilizing individuals for their plights as they actively labor to achieve security, but it has mutated into a *crisis vision* that perceives the overwhelming menace of supposedly extrinsic forces (economic, environmental, technological) as filtered through racialized visibility regimes.

Crisis vision is a destructive way of seeing that amplifies differences among individuals and inspires the scapegoating of those marked as Other (the refugee, the undocumented immigrant, the racial minority). It is a type of transference whereby blame for economic and environmental instability and unpredictability, and for the illegibility of the grounds for those conditions, is redirected to the marginalized. This results in demands for increased surveillance, punishment, and exclusion of the marginalized and abject, leaving intact and obscure the underlying systems of crisis.[45]

Crisis vision also signifies an entire field of operation where visual logics structure social and cultural life. It is revealed as much in low-level worries about routine surveillance as in moral panics about immigrants or the poor, as much in bourgeois white uneasiness about privacy infringements as in discriminatory police targeting of minority neighborhoods. In all cases, crisis vision works to position subjects along a *continuum of threat* and, by extension, position others along that same continuum. It solidifies a worldview predicated on threat mitigation through exposure, where one's selective and voluntary self-exposure may perversely normalize the violent, involuntary exposure of others. Crisis vision continuously resecures conditions of privilege—particularly white, male, straight, affluent privilege—through the subjugation and disenfranchisement of others. Therefore, inequality underwrites a pervasive system of crisis vision and is materialized through it.

Crisis vision is racialized vision. It thrives on the pornotrope to reduce racialized bodies to flesh—or to nonsubjects—whose domination occurs increasingly, disturbingly, without apparent compunction on the part of police or other authorities. As Rachel Hall relates in her work on the cultural politics of airport security, racialized bodies can never be sufficiently transparent for authorities because they can never sufficiently achieve white subjecthood.[46] This relative lack of transparency is perforce coded as threat "merely by daring to show something that is not totally visually accessible and immediately comprehendible to the viewer or monitor."[47] In response, Hall continues, nonwhites are disproportionally subjected to performances of "forcible transparency"—strip searches, imprisonment, torture—in attempts to uncover and decipher what are presumed to be hidden truths or at least to discipline the bodies that contain them.[48]

The component terms of the concept—"crisis" and "vision"—each speak to the rationalities of the present. Crisis implies a temporary rupture of normality, an unsettling that motivates emergency measures and extreme actions. It is a condition that compels triage, not a fundamental rethinking of social norms and structures. Vision suggests a neutral mechanism by which one can parse crises and perform the triage necessary to reestablish normality. Vision, in this sense, is a powerful fiction that equates seeing with understanding, and understanding with control. Vision hides more than it reveals, though, particularly with respect to its role in maintaining the racial order through the consistent construction of racialized subjects as threats and white subjects as victims. Putting the terms together, this visibility regime appeals to exceptional circumstances while obscuring the history and obduracy of racialized response. Crisis vision, as a concept, describes a cultural formation that positions people in the world and structures their relationships. The emphasis here is not on specific agents but instead on modes of activation, on the ways that insecurity and uncertainty find expression in vision.

By approaching surveillance in this way, crisis vision focuses attention on the racializing and hierarchy-building effects of contemporary visual economies. It underscores the violent, dehumanizing, and unequal implications of surveillance apparatuses that reify white supremacist and patriarchal normative structures. It affords recognition of the tight historical entwinement of scientific rationality, gender exclusion, and racial subjugation within liberal social orders. Therefore, grappling with the crisis-vision concept may compel scholars to be skeptical about present-day reformist appeals to the rule of law or to institutional transparency as antidotes for surveillance abuses, particularly given that legal structures and scientific rationalities have historically been—and still are—tools of domination.[49] Although likewise enmeshed in the expansive cultural context of crisis vision, art may offer a way to think and feel its dynamics differently. To the extent that art denaturalizes crisis vision by calling into question its terms or truth claims, it holds the promise of fostering different ways of being—and being seen—with others.

Potentials of Opacity

The fusion of crisis vision with contemporary transparency imperatives presents a seemingly unassailable force that resists redirection. In response, many artists present—or perform—*opacity* as a countermove to ubiquitous surveillance. Opacity entails the maintenance of relative illegibility and blurred boundaries to preserve individual potentiality within collective existence. Crucially, opacity in this sense is *not* about invisibility or privacy but is instead an assertion of ethical relations among nonreducible subjects.[50] As Édouard Glissant articulates, opacity represents "a world in which one exists, or agrees to exist, with and among others." In contradistinction to the control logics of transparency, "the right to opacity . . . is not enclosure within an impenetrable autarchy but subsistence within an irreducible singularity."[51] Opacity revels in the entanglement of diverse subjects and knowledges without striving to uncover their essences or impose order upon them.[52]

For Glissant, mandates for transparency—as with the policing of language use—are part of a rearguard action by former colonial powers, such as France, to maintain control over minoritized subjects and protect civilization "against the rash actions of an excessive collectivization of identity."[53] Such state-driven mandates are efforts to contain and purify the potentials of opacity. In the contemporary context of pervasive surveillance systems predicated upon datafication, hyper-classification, and differential treatment of subjects, transparency serves as the master protocol, such that opacity is anathema to digitally mediated existence.[54] Hence, claims to opacity—for instance, on the part of transgender individuals—can be self-affirming but also construed as subversive actions that invite exclusion or aggressive reassertions of hierarchical power on the part of institutional authorities or others.[55] Consequently, opacity possesses both "liberating and oppressive"[56] modalities: it can be liberating when affording conditions of coexistence within multiplicity, but oppressive if taken as an invitation for retaliation or if deployed by institutions to mask dehumanizing violence and abuse.

Opacity also emerges from crisis vision and its enactments. Whereas the racial animus of crisis vision may provoke distress at the supposed unknowability of black and brown bodies, which are read as possessing a kind of ominous opacity, crisis vision also *produces* opacity by dehumanizing subjects and positioning them as Other, and subsequently as illegible and unrelatable by definition. Significantly, such racial opacity resides not only in the realm of the interior, as in the inability to know someone's thoughts or feelings, but also on the exterior, on the unreadable surfaces of wounded skin and flesh. Musser writes about this as "what violence produces and cannot incorporate . . . excess flesh actually hides in plain sight—opacity is found in the inability to take it all in and produce coherence."[57] Such failures to incorporate the excess of violence also signal places of possibility, places where systems of racial subjugation and capital extraction encounter glitches and where liberating articulations of opacity can manifest in survivability, creativity, and sociality.[58]

As I deploy the term in this book, opacity does not stand in direct opposition to transparency.[59] Rather, it is that which cannot be contained by transparency, that which exceeds purification or eradication: (co)existence alongside, within, in spite of modern liberal orders that would deny life beyond their legal and technical parameters. The opaque persists and survives, suggesting both rich meaning beyond hierarchical systems and avenues for activist intervention to nourish its growth. Furthermore, I seek to move beyond a recognition or celebration of opaque subjects to question the ways that *contexts* and *structures* could be transformed to support liberating opacity as a deeper ethical relation. Said differently, the opaque points to conditions of ambiguity, uncertainty, and possibility that foster the emergence of noninstitutionally defined formations of identity, collectivity, and praxis. Thus, in my exploration of artworks I push for readings of the opaque on the level of relations, and I explore the potentials of opacity to serve as an aesthetic counter to the destructive patterns and dynamics of crisis vision.

Practicing Cultural Critique

The creative outputs of artists offer vital projects to think with. Therefore, my focus is not on the intentions or political commitments of artists per se, but rather on the cultural work enacted by their efforts. Creative projects tend to spill over with an excess of signification and affect, pointing toward alterity even when they are stunted, making them especially generative resources with which to engage problematics of visibility and power. This book explores the surveillance vocabularies such works generate, the sub-jectivities and relationships they represent and catalyze, their assump-tions and omissions, and their participation in the cultural production of surveillance as a social category. Following from theorist Terry Eagleton, I understand art to reside in the realm of the aesthetic, which serves as an "amphibious concept" that can both normalize and challenge dominant capitalist forms.[60] Consequently, it is necessary to trace the ideological foundations and resonances of art, or its conservative overtones, even as one explores its progressive possibilities or productive disruptions. Much scholarly writing on surveillance-themed art has simplistically viewed it as laudable resistance, a useful representation of current or future surveillance problems, or a resource for advancing social science arguments—that is, as captivating images justifying the importance of one's area of study.[61] I instead advocate for a more critical posture. *I assert that artworks function as political performances that contribute, for better or worse, to discourses on surveillance, inflecting cultural understandings of crisis vision.* The task is not to valorize or demonize the works in question but instead to carefully *interpret* their layers of meaning and situate them in larger symbolic economies and sociopolitical contexts.[62] This necessitates, of course, approaching artworks both as individual efforts and as part of a broader field of aesthetic activity grouped by aligned concerns with surveillance and its ramifications.

The materials for my analysis come predominantly from discrete cre-ative products and installations that highlight relations of visibility and power. These are works that in different ways explore the ramifications of relatively hidden surveillance systems, practices, and conditions, most with attention to subjectivities engendered by technologically mediated forms of control. I also selectively include performances, such as dance or street protests, that unearth—and trouble—visibility dynamics that link bodies to larger systems of violence and oppression. That said, because per-formance studies scholars have made major contributions recently inves-tigating performance-based critiques of surveillance,[63] I direct my focus mostly to the work of visual artists. I embrace here a cultural studies ap-proach that engages artworks as political performances that contribute to the cultural production of visibility regimes even while they offer critical perspectives for change.

Art projects can either obscure or highlight relationships of power, privilege, and violence. Especially for those works that take watching or visibility as their subjects, they have the potential to confront the relative invisibility of privilege, especially the white, affluent privilege of many art consumers. They can uncomfortably call into question differential experiences of exposure to and complicity with the systems in question, including, perhaps, the complicity and status positions of artists. Not discounting the productive capacity of artistically provoked discomfort, such moments may also serve as interventions in watching. According to artist and theorist Adrian Piper, "Artwork that draws one into a relationship with the other in the indexical present trades easy classification—and hence xenophobia—for a direct and immediate experience of the complexity of the other, and of one's own responses to her. Experiencing the other in the indexical present teaches one how to see."[64] From this position, the question becomes how to stage conditions for seeing and acknowledging the unpalatable (injustice, complicity, racism, sexism). Important as this question is, it is surprising how few artworks about surveillance begin to confront these issues in any depth, let alone explore the nuances of activating change. The reasons for this lie in the conventional framing apparatuses that present themselves for activist and artistic use. Even for projects that do address larger systems of violence, artists and others may be reluctant to explore relationships of complicity and may inadvertently reproduce racialized or gendered hierarchies of value in their attempt to activate empathy or change in viewers.

For example, as I discuss in chapter 4, Hanne Nielsen and Birgit Johnsen's video art project *Drifting* draws attention to the refugee crisis in Europe but does so in ways that reproduce tropes of heroic, masculine individualism. The artists create a scene of a lone figure floating at sea on a makeshift raft: a handsome light-skinned man pitted against the unforgiving elements in his quest for a better life. As the camera follows the man through the bureaucratic process of determining his identity and rights, he may be moving closer to his goal, but viewers see the ways that state apparatuses slowly erode opacity. State systems reduce the man to data and thereby diminish his potential, which was so abundant initially when he was adrift and his situation most dire. Thus, this work tackles a pressing social problem and subtly critiques the bureaucratic systems tasked with managing refugees, but it does so by maintaining a shroud over the historical and contemporary determinants of refugee crises and fabricating a simplified story that ignores the magnitude and racial dimensions of the situation.

Likely unintentionally, it affirms narratives of worthy and unworthy refugees, where those who are the most deserving happen to look white and fit conventional rescue narratives (for example, of the lone castaway or the helpless woman or child). The amphibious qualities of this piece can be detected in these cultural tropes of worthiness, which normalize a form of value-based sorting of populations even as the piece seeks to educate viewers and support humanitarian actions. By critiquing the art project in this way, one can begin to grasp the tenacity of crisis vision—which constrains social awareness and action more broadly—and identify areas where more, or different, work needs to be done.

From this standpoint, critical art projects can be seen as offering a way to organize collective attention to cartographies of state and corporate violence that percolate through social systems and material infrastructures. Surveillance, as a privileged mechanism for regulating the identities and mobilities of individuals, provides a generative starting point for tracing systems of domination as they materialize in a specific application, such as in state-run refugee screening systems. If interpreted beyond their initial surface meanings, such aesthetic projects can carve out space for reflection on the differential ramifications of visibility for different groups. Even when artists ignore their own privileged standpoints or invoke a universal subject whose privacy or autonomy is at risk, in so doing they enact omissions that can be discerned by critics and flagged as sticking points in ideological edifices. Through their creative acts, they constitute problem areas (privacy loss, police violence, automated discrimination), and they script roles for characters (victims, villains, heroes, witnesses). The structure of these dramas reveals and reifies the nature of crisis-vision problematics. It is the critic's responsibility, as I see it, to connect the dots and show how and where these creative works support or undermine the systems or rationalities in question, or how they do both simultaneously.

To summarize, surveillance-themed artworks emerge to critique increasingly pervasive yet obscure visibility regimes that undemocratically structure the conditions of life. Such works provide partial glimpses of control systems and their politics, presenting targets for intervention, but many of them have difficulty unpacking crisis vision's corrosive tendency to amplify social difference and violence. That is to say, the artworks possess their own blind spots, which reveal something about the broader difficulties of addressing surveillance problems while depending upon limiting but alluring frames. For instance, notions of universal threats and individual responsibility, in particular, eclipse the racial violence inherent in liberal social orders; likewise, tropes of transparency and accountability allow artists, scholars, and others to conveniently ignore the logics of domination and exclusion encoded in those historically contingent constructs. These are not insignificant quibbles with art or activism or scholarship. By participating in these conversations, through creative expression or otherwise, one delimits the problem area and contributes to the fabrication of common sense (the distribution of the sensible), effectively diminishing or delegitimizing more radical, as in "root," critiques. In short, the stakes are high.

Artistic Frames

This book explores the operations of crisis vision through critical surveillance art. I illustrate the ways that crisis vision manifests in various economies of surveillance and how artists engage with, capitulate to, or push back on crisis-vision formulations with their work. Through interpretation of artworks, I bring into focus the tenacious ideological underpinnings of crisis vision, which often normalize structural racism and violence through dominant cultural narratives or discriminatory surveillance apparatuses. I develop the concept of opacity across the chapters and assess its potential to destabilize crisis vision, especially through creative means. Importantly, this project enters into conversation with art as a way to generate perspective on *collective constraints* in dealing with surveillance problems, not just artistic constraints alone.

Each of the book's chapters explores a different artistic frame for critiquing contemporary surveillance. The frame of "avoidance" constructs notions of universal threats that can be mitigated through private consumptive acts, which is an approach that consolidates white privilege while ignoring how crisis vision unequally affects marginalized groups. "Transparency" focuses attention on the dangers of institutional archives in an era of crisis vision, where inaccessible archives are often deployed to segment populations and maintain racial hierarchies. "Complicity" highlights the illegibility and ambiguity of surveillance situations under crisis vision to cultivate a sense of shared ethical responsibility among viewing subjects. The frame of "violence" productively recasts surveillance as discriminatory, inflected by both economic forces and cultural prejudices, but it also demonstrates the resilience of crisis vision in valorizing evidentiary modes of inquiry and viewer agency, not the agency of those most harmed by violence. Finally, "disruption" rejects, rather than recuperates, crisis vision's destructive mythology of liberal personhood, opting instead for defiance, resilience, and faith in community that survives despite it. Across these chapters, *I argue that the most productive interventions are those that destabilize the crisis-vision framework by tracing its inherent exclusions and carving out space for collective opacity.*

The book's general arc moves from specific surveillance devices or systems to broader social problems that are reproduced by surveillance logics. Thus, if critical surveillance art aspires to disrupt crisis vision's conditions of domination or oppression, then decentering the technologies appears to allow artists to refocus attention on such deeper concerns. Surveillance logics are woven throughout modern states and their institutions, so starting a critique with technology, while certainly practical and generative, may occlude deep-seated relations of power that are fused to conceptions of objectivity, transparency, and accountability. In a time of perceived ontological insecurity, crisis vision flourishes, motivating further surveillance efforts to reestablish control through means that mask their politics, through visibility projects that marginalize and exclude, once again. The visibility imperative must itself be questioned, explored, and critiqued. It must be felt differently and anew.[65] This is the realm of the arts, not the sciences. It is the motivation that drives this book.

1. Avoidance

Long simmering in the background, the violence of crisis vision boiled over in 2020. In the context of a raging coronavirus pandemic, police killings of unarmed black men and women, racial justice protests, and deep divisions exacerbated by conspiracy theories and a failure of political leadership, the destructiveness of crisis vision propagated quickly, especially in the United States but also in, and between, other countries throughout the world. The politics of exposure, writ large, further entrenched social fragmentation. Many people struggled to avoid COVID-19 through masking and other measures while also joining movements to confront racialized police violence; meanwhile, others, emboldened by President Trump's politicization of masks, flaunted their unmasked and undistanced exposure to the virus, engaged in armed counterprotests, and threatened anyone who would dare infringe on their supposed freedoms, even in the interest of public health and safety. The racialized scapegoating dimensions of crisis vision were brought to the fore with Trump's and the conservative media's xenophobic depiction of COVID-19 as the "China virus" and their portrayal of racial justice protesters as dangerous anti-American, radical socialists.[1] Such articulations operated as code for threats to white supremacy or, put differently, to the distribution of the sensible that would position racial hierarchies as natural and just.

Notions of "exposure" and "avoidance" function as two sides of the same coin when discussing the convergence of crises generated by the growing pandemic and entrenched white supremacy. For racial minorities in the United States, exposure to the pandemic or to the police was—and is— more likely to result in death, yet members of this population are also more likely to serve as frontline "essential workers," depend upon public transportation, or face housing displacement such that their exposure is heightened.[2]

However, avoidance signifies racial and economic privilege: the privilege of having housing, food, and job security, of being able to work remotely, of being ignored by the police.

Crisis vision inflects these social inequalities in seemingly contradictory ways. With respect to the pandemic, crisis vision afforded aggressive assertions of white privilege through the voluntary abdication of avoidance, through the very disavowal of avoidance as a privilege, which could be witnessed in rallies and recreational events of unmasked whites or in angry reactions from whites (the so-called Karens and Kens) who were asked to don masks in public.[3] These were assertions of white supremacy—and often white masculinity—through performances of transparency: naked faces of aggression, bravado, and militarism. "Transparency is the new white,"[4] Rachel Hall pithily observes, but whereas she was describing a situation in which innocence must be proven through willing exposure to surveillance, here it was claimed as an *unwillingness* to submit to the state and its public health dictates. At the same time, pandemic masking was recast as feminized, racialized, and queer by Trump and right-wing commentators, so much so that when Trump finally did deign to wear a mask in public, he chose to defend his (macho) appearance in one: "I sort of liked the way I looked. OK. I thought it was OK. It was a dark black mask, and I thought it looked OK. . . . It looked like the Lone Ranger."[5]

Masks worn by Black Lives Matter protesters, Antifa members, and others symbolically challenged white supremacy and science skepticism during these times by combining techniques of avoidance, to mitigate exposure to the virus or police surveillance, with techniques of exposure, to draw attention to and support for the racial justice movement. Progressive resignification of masks gained salience through the circulation of entertainment-media tropes as well, such as with the hooded and mask-wearing black female protagonist who takes down white supremacist operatives in the superhero show *Watchmen*, which was released by HBO in 2019 and gained popularity during the early days of the pandemic.

These articulations of crisis vision draw into focus what I described in the introduction as a racialized "continuum of threat" that unequally positions bodies as endangered or dangerous, as valuable or expendable. Crisis vision generates differences, antagonisms, and conflict as people bristle at their placement along the continuum or perceive others as upending long-standing racial, gender, or other hierarchies. Moreover, especially with respect to the racial justice movement and calls to defund or dismantle the police, challenges to the racialized normative order amplify the sense of crisis for many of the actual or assumed beneficiaries of white supremacy, thereby fueling perceptions of a deeper existential threat. If liberal humanism and its institutions are revealed to be predicated on racial subjugation and exclusion, not universal rights and individual freedom, then this rightly undermines perceptions of earned white privilege and entitlement. In this chapter I explore the construction and maintenance of crisis vision's continuum of threat by analyzing artworks dealing with various expressions of surveillance avoidance. I ask what "avoidance" means in this context, who is privileged to exercise it, and what we can learn about crisis vision's operations through this particular artistic frame.

Art of Avoidance

Well before the coronavirus pandemic and the intensified mobilization against antiblack police violence in 2020, a curious trend was emerging with respect to pervasive surveillance. Alongside increasing public awareness of drone warfare, government spying programs, and big-data analytics, there was a surge in countersurveillance tactics.[6] These tactics ranged from software for anonymous internet browsing to detoxification supplements for fooling drug tests, but what was particularly fascinating was the panoply of artistic projects—and products—to conceal oneself from ambient surveillance in public places. These artworks, which are still popular and serve as the basis for many other embellishments, center on the masking of identity to undermine technological efforts to fix someone as a unique entity apart from the crowd. A veritable artistic industry has mushroomed from the perceived death of the social brought about by ubiquitous public surveillance: asymmetrical face paint and hairstyles to confound facial-recognition software, hoodies and scarves made with materials to block thermal emissions and evade tracking by drones, and hats that emit infrared light to blind camera lenses and prevent photographs or video tracking. Countersurveillance camouflage of this sort flaunts the system, ostensibly allowing wearers to become opaque and hide in plain sight—neither acquiescing to surveillance mandates nor becoming reclusive under their withering gaze.[7] This is an aestheticization of resistance, whose strength lies in its accessibility and capacity to generate media and scholarly attention.

Through their playfulness, these creative works invite viewers to question institutional surveillance systems that identify and track individuals largely without their knowledge or consent.

These artistic practices should be situated in the context of the state visibility projects that support crisis vision. As discussed in the book's introduction, visibility is about the normalization of state control through techniques of classification, separation, and aestheticization, which enforce a kind of reductive, exclusionary legibility.[8] As Nicholas Mirzoeff relates, state visibility projects manifest in a set of extractive and dehumanizing complexes (plantation, imperialist, and military-industrial) that are institutionalized through bureaucratic and scientific apparatuses that render classifications true and populations governable.[9] These complexes resonate with crisis vision's racist, neocolonial, and necropolitical dimensions, affording the prejudicial allocation and distribution of death for populations deemed dangerous to the state, which could include terrorists, asylum seekers, or the racialized poor in today's capitalist economy. Thus, biopolitics and necropolitics fuse in destructive ways, in the service of neoliberal capitalism, to create conditions of abjection and human insecurity.[10] Therefore, visibility denies the Other the right to legitimate autonomy and agency; it denies the right to look back and challenge the identities ascribed by institutions.[11] As Stephen Graham reminds us, following Michel Foucault,[12] there is also a "boomerang effect" to the deployment of biopolitical and necropolitical technologies in distant territories, leading frequently to their application in the homeland on so-called civilian populations, as can be seen with the domestication of drones[13] and biometric identification systems.[14]

The artistic frame of avoidance seeks to sidestep state and corporate visibility efforts. However, by largely ignoring differential exposure to surveillance-based violence and oppression, the frame reveals the tenacity of crisis vision's continuum of threat. After all, despite popular claims about universal subjection to surveillance, it must be recognized that a host of surveillance functions are reserved for those who threaten the status quo, principally those classified as poor or marked as Other.[15] Racialized identities of dangerousness are encoded back upon the targets through surveillance encounters that are always tied to the threat of state force (for example, the stop-and-frisk search, the video tracking of racial minorities through commercial stores, the scrutiny of purchases made by welfare recipients). These are mechanisms of *marginalizing surveillance* that produce conditions and identities of marginality through their very application.[16]

The field of surveillance studies has laid the groundwork for critical inquiry into the differential treatment of populations and the ways that marginality inflects experiences of surveillance. In particular, the field has had a long-standing concern with discriminatory surveillance practices predicated on "categorical suspicion" of marginalized groups[17] and "social sorting" of populations through increasingly abstract, invisible, and automated systems of control.[18] Perhaps because of the strong voyeuristic modalities of surveillance, scholars have further interrogated the gendered dimensions of watching and being watched and have explored possibilities for gender-based appropriation and resistance.[19] Recently, there has also been a concerted effort to foster engaged feminist and race studies critiques that attend to intersectional forms of oppression, which are often enforced by surveillance practices.[20] For instance, Corinne Mason and Shoshana Magnet show how many policy initiatives and surveillance apps intended to combat violence against women tend to responsibilize victims, fail to target perpetrators, and aggravate conditions of vulnerability, especially for poor women who may lack a social safety net if fleeing from an abuser or who risk assault or arrest if they do call the police.[21] Feminist and intersectional approaches to surveillance studies connect the embodied, grounded nature of individual experience with larger systems of structural inequality and violence. Such approaches investigate the technological and organizational mediation of situated practice, advancing a critique of contemporary surveillance systems and power relations.

Artworks that mobilize the frame of avoidance may activate a sense of possibility for empowering opacity, but this artistic frame simultaneously normalizes a universal stance that makes it difficult to address the discriminatory logics of surveillance societies. Exercises in avoidance allow artists and activists to perform their "right to hide," thereby placing themselves on the white, privileged end of crisis vision's continuum of threat as individuals who believe in a system where rights could be claimed and granted. By unspoken extension, the other side of the continuum of threat is reinforced as well, such that the subjugation or exclusion of racialized groups makes possible the entitlement and inclusion of normative subjects. In these ways, artworks of avoidance exploit the allure of countersurveillance while simultaneously contributing to the cultural production of surveillance.

The Thrill of "Perilous Glamour": Face Paint and Hairstyles

Bold asymmetrical marks on haughty white faces. Pointy blue and red bangs cutting dramatic lines across models' straight noses, plucked eyebrows, and parted lips. These are some of the images that constitute the fashion "look book" for the cv (computer vision) Dazzle project that aims to confuse facial-recognition systems.[22] The lead designer, Adam Harvey, describes this as "the perilous glamour of life under surveillance"[23] and appropriates naval tactics from a bygone era to ostentatiously "dazzle" and confuse electronic observers. An *Atlantic* article explains, "Dazzle takes its name from a type of naval camouflage (and otherwise) used in the world wars. Huge, jarring stripes were painted on ships, less with the intent to conceal them in the water and more with the idea of disorienting enemy weapons and maneuvering. cv dazzle applies the same concept to algorithms."[24] The presumed enemies in the contemporary surveillance context include any operators of automated facial-recognition technology, be they state agents, advertisers, or technology companies such as Apple or Facebook.

Harvey positions his countersurveillance camouflage as consistent with evolutionary models of natural adaptation to environmental threats. As a Roy Behrens quotation prominently displayed on the cv Dazzle website reads, "From all appearances, deception has always been critical to daily survival—for human and non-human creatures alike—and, judging by its current ubiquity, there is no end in immediate sight."[25] In providing advice for makeup application, Harvey makes a similar comparison: "Ideally, your face would become the anti-face, or inverse. In the animal kingdom, this inverse effect is known as countershading."[26] This framing is appealing in that it casts resistance through avoidance as a natural response, as something required and expected, not deviant. At the same time, it is a framing that conflates natural and social systems and—in neoliberal and social Darwinian fashion—responsibilizes avoidance of undesired scrutiny, implying that those who cannot evade the predator deserve targeting and are unfit for survival. If deception is considered normal and unavoidable, this may also have the effect of inviting the production of augmented surveillance applications to circumvent such deception.[27] For instance, the increasing popularity of neuromarketing, behavioral monitoring, and lie-detection tests, each of which claims to circumvent intentional or unintentional dissimulation, illustrates desires to obtain direct, unmediated access to bodily truths.[28]

Not restricted to evolutionary discourses, cv Dazzle's heterogeneous rhetoric echoes a social and political sphere marked by fragmentation and division. The discursive registers invoke the biological ("the animal kingdom"), marketing disclaimers ("results will vary"), scientific experiment ("tested and validated"), practical suggestions ("avoid enhancers"), and participatory enticements ("creating your own looks").[29] This disparate appeal for attention fits snugly with observations about the contemporary era of populist postmodernism, where a surplus of messages vies for recognition and no longer relies on shared adjudication processes to determine which are more factual or true.[30] Likewise, in keeping with a wider culture of entrepreneurial self-branding in online environments,[31] Harvey is clearly invested in promoting himself and his artworks as part of his brand, so the visual elements (photos, diagrams, videos) are given primacy as fungible referents in this aestheticization of resistance.

Dazzle face paint, with its allusions to the primal and overtones of stylized subversion, can be generatively compared to tattooing in contemporary US society. In her work on the cultural politics of tattooing, Jill Fisher writes:

> Fashion, by definition, has a fear of commitment. Consequently, the permanence of tattoos is terrifying. Permanence is a "bad word" within late capitalist economies, which are dependent on and nurture change. . . . Semi-permanent body modifications are ideal in a capitalist structure because there is always already space for the next body modification. Hair grows, bodies expand, clothes fade. Resistance is everything because there are always new (pre-packaged) battles to wage. . . . The postmodern primitive can play at permanence when it is fashionable without any danger of commitment.[32]

With dazzle designs, the face's surface may be rendered unreadable, at least temporarily, granting the postmodern primitive freedom from a radically delimited form of fixity. Although late-capitalist economies may thrive on the protean, the state seeks permanence and precision with respect to the identity of bodies flowing within and beyond its territories.[33] Playing with illegibility draws attention to these control logics in ways that are not necessarily intended, or able, to subvert them. After all, there are many circulating, overlapping, and reinforcing markers of identity beyond the face, so the notion of evading them entirely is always a losing game.

In terms of the cultural production of surveillance, another consideration is the question of who could or could not claim opacity of the sort presented by CV Dazzle. It is the relatively privileged and white who ride the waves of voluntary mobility and whose state-verified identity markers buoy them in their pursuits. Whereas this artistic frame centers on the poses of the privileged adorned with tribal-looking paint, absent are critiques of racialized threat inscribed indelibly on black and brown bodies.[34] Additionally, in her discussion of Harvey's work, Morrison notes that there are troublingly sexist overtones in his presentation of "tall, thin female models in high-fashion couture poses, [which reifies rather than challenges] cultural pressures to conform to standards of beauty placed on (particularly women's) bodies."[35]

Rather than being neutral in any way, biometric systems, such as facial recognition, catalyze symbolic and physical violence. In her work, for instance, Simone Browne elucidates how bodies are racialized and disassociated from what is seen as the normal order of the world when biometric systems mediate the encounters between state agents and those marked as Other: "It is these moments of observation, calibration and application that can reveal themselves as racializing. . . . It is the making of the body as out of place, an attempt to deny its capacity for humanness, which makes for the productive power of epidermalization."[36] The "avoidance" frame advanced by Harvey and others is ill-suited to problematize how markers of difference position one as a threat within the crisis-vision matrix. Instead of such a conversation, journalistic responses to Harvey's work tend to veer toward titillation and shallow quandaries about whether the time spent grooming would be worth it: "Harvey's work is amazing. I adore this male 'do and make-up; I may have dreamt of the day something like it will appear in some thumping, ominously globalized music video. But, like, look at it! Do you know how much time getting downward-facing spikes like that takes in the morning? And that pixelated make-up? Every morning? Oy vey! Maybe it's better to acclimate yourself to the omnipresent eye of Total Surveillance than the daily toil of a blowdryer and göt2B Glued."[37] Such opinions, though not reflective of Harvey's position, nonetheless reveal blind spots with the avoidance frame, specifically where issues of racial identity, difference, and power are concerned. Given that biometric systems already "fail" at a greater rate for racial minorities,[38] effectively nominating those populations for increased scrutiny, what might be the effects of someone marked as Other openly and intentionally challenging state surveillance systems? Could this lead to anything but intensified observation, search, and intervention?

Masking and Weaponizing Faces

Beyond the surface decorations of face paint and hairstyles, physical masks invoke a deeper symbolic order. Used in rituals across cultures and times, masks can convey connections to the natural world, communicate social status and privilege by referencing one's ancestral lineage, or temporarily equalize revelers at carnival events, which in turn may signify the casting out of dark forces from society.[39] Masks can conceal one's identity, affording behavior that transgresses traditional social norms and boundaries. Used by social movements, they can also assert an anonymous collectivity, drawing attention to issues of shared concern while protecting individuals from reprisal; such deployments of masks can be seen, for instance, with ski masks worn by the Zapatistas, Guy Fawkes masks worn by Anonymous or Occupy Wall Street activists, and cloth masks worn by racial justice activists during the pandemic.[40]

In the service of combating surveillance, especially facial-recognition systems, one artistic effort by Leo Selvaggio involves the design of masks that are eerie reproductions of his own face, potentially spawning swarms of expressionless doppelgangers moving through the streets (see figure 1.1). The resin masks created by Selvaggio, which are generated through a process of 3D scanning and printing, are realistic "personal surveillance identity prosthetics" that match his facial contours, skin tone, and facial hair.[41] He has tested the masks with facial-recognition systems such as the one used by Facebook and found that they consistently fool these systems into identifying the masks as his face. His goals are to increase public awareness of facial-recognition surveillance throughout society and to foster debate about its ramifications.[42] The resin mask is but one element of a larger project called URME (pronounced "you are me"), which also includes open-source software that automatically edits video to replace individuals' faces with Selvaggio's face.[43]

Several interesting performances are enacted here, not the least of which is the attempt to assert solidarity among people who may be radically different from one another. In a produced video, Selvaggio says, "Surveillance is here, and it's here to stay. And rather than try and combat that surveillance directly, I propose that we change what's being surveilled, until the

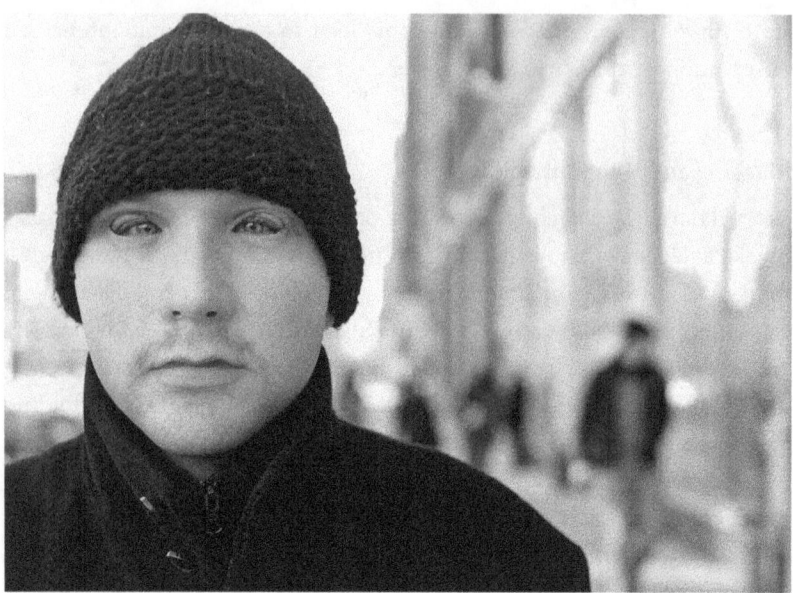

FIGURE 1.1. Leo Selvaggio, URME *Project* (2014). Courtesy of the artist.

reason we are surveilled is no longer relevant. I'm talking about changing us. Help me change us. And what better place to start than, oh, with me. Join me. You are me."[44] The intended message here seems to be that because surveillance is inevitable, people should both accept it *and* find ways to maintain privacy in spite of it, especially by working together to do so. Another, more interpretive read is that the original rationales for surveillance cease to matter as surveillance practices multiply through function creep: the initial reasons for surveillance are less relevant than the fact of it and its effects. A component of this, as Selvaggio understands, is that tenacious systems resist alteration and social norms change through intentional modulations by organizations, for instance by companies such as Facebook gradually stripping away privacy protections.[45] Selvaggio's URME project presents these elements while also creating productive discomfort, challenging viewers to question their uniqueness and to see themselves in his visage.

As with Harvey's projects, though, this artistic frame cannot directly engage with difference, in large part because its power resides in aspirations for connection and similarity. In speaking of the project, for instance, Selvaggio explicitly acknowledges white male privilege but says that his work advances "the utopian ideal" that everyone should be granted the same level of privilege.[46] Still, the empirical differences are vital and stark. For example, police may tolerate the wearing of masks in public by relatively privileged white men in US cities, but meanwhile there is a corresponding criminalization of people of color for wearing hoodies or even daring to look back at (or "eyeball") police in similar urban settings.[47]

Apart from its effective strangeness, the URME mask achieves impact by presenting one's identity as being both under assault and instrumentalized by others. The project suggests that pure or true identities are somehow corrupted by exposure to state and corporate surveillance. As Selvaggio says, "When we are watched we are fundamentally changed. We perform rather than be."[48] Of course, individuals always perform and craft presentations of themselves for others,[49] and as surveillance studies scholars have shown, greater risks may come from individuals being *unaware* of the extent to which data are severed from the context of their production and acted upon in other spaces and times, enabling the invisible judging and sorting of populations.[50] Moreover, technological systems are not separate from social context, somehow tainting authentic individual behavior; rather, they are constitutive and coproductive of those contexts, enabling social action and interaction in ways that are always value-laden, regardless of the system in question.[51]

A different reading of Selvaggio's position on identity and performance could be that he is critiquing the efforts of institutions to render individuals transparent and governable, to force people into identity categories such that their freedoms and potentials are curtailed. His work calls into question the fiction of unique and stable individual identities,[52] which is a point that brings to mind Judith Butler's insights into the ongoing, performative aspects of identity work with respect to gender.[53] From this perspective, as Rachel Hall, Joshua Reeves, and I explain elsewhere, "Gender is never merely a voluntaristic or intentional performance but rather a compulsory citation of cultural and social norms that one inherits and is repeatedly called upon by others to embody on demand."[54] Therefore, there are serious constraints on identity performances, gender or otherwise, and the relative invisibility of these constraints is part of what makes identity constructs seem so stable and secure. In relation to crisis vision, URME could be interpreted as asserting the importance of opacity for providing space for less scripted experimentation with identities or recalibration of power relations. By aspiring to fold everyone into the realm of white male privilege, however, this project effectively recuperates liberal humanism rather than deconstructing it, which is a move that, in my reading, misplaces faith in the capacity of rights-based systems for overcoming their originary conditions.

Following Selvaggio's work, the early days of the COVID-19 pandemic inspired an aligned masking project intended to allow users to wear printed face masks so that they could limit virus spread and exposure while continuing to project recognizable facial features (see figure 1.2). This "Maskalike" project, conceptualized by Danielle Baskin, promised to reduce impediments to using facial recognition to access one's iPhone or other electronic devices.[55] The artist's website advertised this convenience— "Unlock your devices with a surgical mask that looks just like you"—while also playfully appropriating and rerouting sexist descriptions of unsmiling women by initially tagging the project as "Resting Risk Face."[56] Although this creative work emphasized conformity through adaptation to normalized surveillance applications, such as facial recognition on phones, it also allowed for experimentation, where individuals could adopt someone else's face (as with Selvaggio's URME), a fictional face generated through artificial intelligence, or a variation of one's own face that could be intelligible to people but would obfuscate—or multiply—one's representation in facial-recognition databases (as with Harvey's CV Dazzle).[57] Latching onto these alternative uses, Baskin suggested a latent criticism of surveillance generated by these masks: the mask "appears to be working with facial recognition, but it will never actually be your face. . . . The image is something your friends could identify as you but that machine learning can't, and it shows that face recognition has errors."[58]

As with my earlier discussion of masking in the time of a pandemic, privilege is mapped onto positionality in these games of exposure and avoidance. The Maskalike project may illustrate that biometric systems are flawed, that they do not truly capture the essence of individuals or their faces, but that particular formulation still implies a core identity that one could assert ownership of and regulate other's access to. Moreover, the primary intervention of these masks seems to be in the service of enhancing the convenience, privilege, and safety of autonomous subjects so that they can maintain unrestricted access to their devices and unrestricted mobility as they venture into risky spaces. Both everyday surveillance and hierarchical systems of privilege are accommodated, not undermined, in the process. Here we see at best a performance of obfuscation that strives to

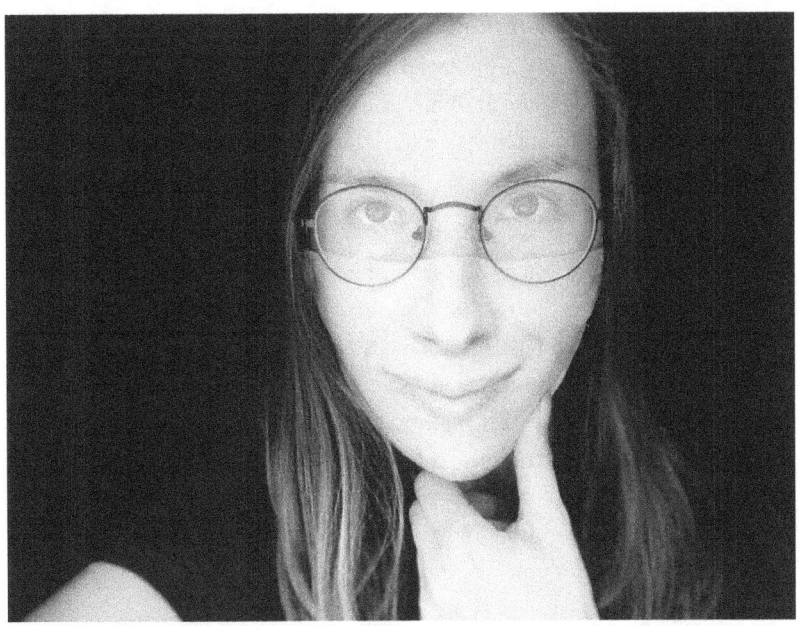

FIGURE 1.2. Danielle Baskin, *Maskalike* (2020). Courtesy of the artist.

maintain one's right to privacy, even if that right is voluntarily ceded, not a performance of opacity, which would seek out ethical engagement with others and would fissure the very grounds for asserting privilege.

A quite different masking project called the Facial Weaponization Suite presents another artistic foray into the production and regulation of identity.[59] Created by Zach Blas, this project captures the images of many different faces and aggregates them into one, grotesque, cellular, plastic mask that confounds facial-recognition systems and defies legibility by people or machines. Blas forges "collective masks" of this sort to critique regimes of visibility that reduce people to static identity categories and discriminate against them. Thus, one of his masks, the Fag Face Mask, responds to scientific studies claiming that queerness can be read reliably on one's facial features, which could lead to automated algorithms for detecting sexual orientation in the absence of any other information.[60] The so-called Fag Face Mask is thus a monstrous merging of the faces of many self-identified queer men, perhaps showing the grotesqueness of bigoted categorization while also serving as a symbolic weapon against the unnamed enemies who would control through stigmatizing visualizations.

Rather than simply substitute one bizarre collective representation for an alienating singular one, the Facial Weaponization Suite aspires to erase identity markers altogether. It denies the legitimacy of a market of discrete identities and the systems that would reduce people to them. Blas and colleagues explain:

> We want a technology that allows us to escape regimes of identification, standardization and control, like facial recognition technologies and biometrics. In response to this, we ask, What are the tactics and techniques for making our faces nonexistent? How do we flee this visibility into the fog of a queerness that refuses to be recognized? We propose to start making faces our weapons. We can learn many faces and wear them interchangeably. A face is like being armed. . . . Today, in our biometric age, existence has become a means of control. . . . Becoming nonexistent turns your face into a fog, and fog makes revolt possible.[61]

This articulation epitomizes the logic of the "right to hide," a right to become nonexistent and invisible to institutions. The envisioned space of fog purportedly frees one from social constraint and expectation, affording identity experimentation and potentially "revolt." Although this project embraces the possibilities of performativity, it draws upon a presumed universal "we" and advocates for the erasure of difference, or at least its markers, in the service of individual autonomy. It performs a kind of post-identity political right to social and political equality without any signifiers of difference, which are themselves seen as oppressive impositions on the part of others. The fog is a utopic nonspace where the artist can speak on behalf of others, not because everyone is him, as in the case with Selvaggio's URME project, but because no one is anyone—people, as defined by difference, do not exist.

The Facial Weaponization Suite explicitly seeks opacity as a challenge to—or weapon against—institutionally imposed identities. That said, in asserting the need for this intervention, the work comes dangerously close to conceding that the identity markers ascribed to us by institutions, including the institution of mainstream science, are accurate, so only by erasing and evading (not debunking) them can we obtain freedom. What does it mean to take seriously such dubious scientific claims about being able to read queerness on people's faces? Critical science studies scholarship has revealed over and over how cultural prejudices are encoded in supposedly impartial scientific measurements of biological difference. This can be seen, for instance, in assertions dating back to Aristotle about the infe-riority of women because of their having "less heat," in nineteenth-century claims that criminality could be read from one's physiognomy, or in mid-twentieth-century research professing to have found bodily markers of homosexuality on women's genitalia.[62] In each case, science reproduces the values of its practitioners and its wider culture. In accepting scientific claims about queerness and the body, this project might unwittingly affirm the validity of constructed truths about measurable biological differences.

Additionally, while this artwork is powerful for being confrontational, it is worth questioning the semantic appeal to militarized action. If faces are already being enlisted in militarized security responses to constructed terrorist threats—through biometric facial-recognition capture at borders or on city streets, for instance—then military logics already prevail and infuse dominant discourses and practices.[63] The hegemony of militaristic framings bounds what is viewed as possible and practical, positioning re-sistance problematically as threatening to the nation-state and deserving of criminalization. Perhaps, taking a cue from Jacques Derrida,[64] a better goal might be to *disarm*, instead of combat, the violence of binary logics. Such a discursive move could inspire a greater tolerance for opaque existence, ambiguous identities, and the messiness of social worlds.

Dangerous Play on the Surveillance Fashion Runway

On a raised stage in a low-lit room, soft azure lights project gyrating patterns on the crowd as male and female models strut across the stage. A mix of house music with drum loops and simulated record scratching sets the tone, creating an edgy vibe to frame the presentation of novel surveillance and countersur-veillance clothing and accessories. Most of the designs incorporate electronic sensors and circuitry, either facilitating or obstructing the flow of personal information. An MC struggles to read the descriptive text for each design, and the models also have difficulty showing off their items without dropping them or engaging in exaggerated miming to communicate their intended func-tions.[65] All of this—which was the Anti/Surveillance Fashion Show presented by designers from the Noisebridge hackerspace in 2010—generates a spectacle of frivolity, where performers poke ironic fun at their mock-serious designs while audience members look on with vague curiosity.

First, there is a demonstration of the Dazzle makeup described above. The voice-over asserts: "This will give you the freedom to travel around in public, free from the unblinking eye of computer surveillance." Next, affecting a secret-agent aesthetic, two men in dark suits and sunglasses model computerized belts that can surreptitiously scour nearby networks, collecting serial numbers, passwords, and other sensitive information. Another belt with "vibrating motors" and a "digital compass" can constantly communicate the direction "north" to the wearer, who is cast as an agent on someone's trail: "So he won't lose track as you try to evade him in a twist of streets." In response to potential desires for restricting one's exposure, the MC opines: "Then, on the other hand, why try? . . . Get in on the game. Share, share. Over share."[66] On cue, a woman takes center stage to present a handbag with an electronic display that constantly reveals the purse's contents, which, the MC explains, will allow her to move quickly through security checkpoints. Each of these designs promises a kind of freedom or empowerment through selective sharing (a face without facial recognition, a purse that enables transparency) or secretive data acquisition (network-sniffing belts). This play with security brings to mind Lauren Berlant's sharp observations about precarity: "Adaptation to the adaptive imperative is producing a whole new precarious public sphere, defined by debates about how to rework insecurity in the ongoing present, and defined as well by an emerging aesthetic."[67] In this instance, surveillance is not challenged or resisted by this aesthetic so much as it is manipulated or augmented to establish a facade of constrained freedom for individuals.

When the fashion show turns toward issues of harassment of and violence against women, the severe limitations of this neoliberal logic of freedom become even more apparent. There are women's shoes equipped with panic alarms to "tell people to stay back and for her handlers to pick her up." As an accompaniment to a hoodie that blinds cameras with LED lights, another design, referred to as a "rear window shade," allows women to see when someone is sneaking up on them; the MC explains: "Of course, as a soloist, no one's going to watch her back but her. . . . [The rear window shade will] allow her to surprise her surprise assailants." Finally, there is a device for dealing with upskirt photographs of women's underwear. As a woman sashays to center stage in a very short skirt and heels, the MC asks: "But what about the common problem of the upskirt? What is a girl to do? Fortunately, she has the 'crotch dazzler.' . . . She simply need not worry. . . . [The reflector on her underwear] will show only flashes of the paparazzi's cameras rather than her privates."[68] The message delivered by each of these designs is a variation on the theme of not worrying about the male gaze or sexual assault. Technological gadgets are presented as exerting a form of delegated patriarchal protection (with the panic-alarm shoes and crotch-dazzler panties) or individual responsibility for detecting and evading attackers (with the rear window shade).[69] The technologies also connect these women to their systems of (white) privilege, where one could envision "handlers" coming to the rescue. Overall, the designs problematically assume both the inevitability of dangers and the vulnerability of women. External security efforts, Hille Koskela reminds us, tend to construct women as passive victims and sexualized objects, whereas responsibilization motifs do little to undermine these hegemonic constructs.[70] Violence against women is accepted as a given with these designs, just as is exposure to public surveillance, which effectively removes from the discussion any question about how to change the underlying cultural conditions of violence and abuse.

Although it is important to note that the Noisebridge group and the artists included in this show are increasing awareness of surveillance by signaling some of its problems, the playfulness of the Anti/Surveillance Fashion Show belies some of the deeper aspirations of the group. As Noisebridge writes, "Constantly under the lens of the camera, fashion is a natural form in which to explore the relationship between surveillance and culture. How are we watched? How do we watch? How do we present ourselves to the eyes of the world? . . . Anti/Surveillance [is] a runway show that explores the role of and our relationship with surveillance in our society."[71] The Noisebridge designs draw upon conditions of ubiquitous surveillance for inspiration, using design to transmute surveillance into something accessible and nonthreatening. The compromise for such accessibility is that the designs fail to achieve any critical responses to these issues. Instead, they normalize unchecked exposure to surveillance in public, especially surveillance that can lead to the objectification of and violence against women. The dominant message of this fashion show is that women and others must take responsibility, through the consumption of countersurveillance clothing and devices, for anticipating and managing dangers. Similar to Baskin's Maskalike designs, a semblance of freedom is secured through such consumptive practices. Clearly, this postpones any engagement with root causes of gendered or racialized violence.

Conclusion

The artistic frame of "avoidance" is compelling. Countersurveillance camouflage and fashion designs, in particular, provide colorful and easily circulated representations that tap into viewers' anxieties about being singled out. They also play into heroic resistance narratives of individuals, or collectives, taking a stand against state or corporate dictates. For these reasons, creative works in this vein resonate with artists and their progressive audiences. This artistic frame also touches upon one of the key problematics with surveillance: the governance of populations through identity, especially through imposed identity categories. Thus, the artists and designers discussed here do perceive the symbolic violence of having one's identity fixed by others and one's movements tracked by objectifying surveillance systems. Some of them additionally recognize how these systems might introduce additional vulnerabilities for women or LGBTQ+ groups. That said, the works obtain purchase among diverse groups of activists, journalists, and scholars by invoking the specter of *universal* exposure to unwanted surveillance, such that anyone and everyone may perceive their risk and the need to mitigate it.

These countersurveillance designs and artworks emerge at this historical juncture because of a widespread recognition of unchecked, pervasive surveillance and popular criticism of government and corporate overreach. The key to the popularity of these artistic efforts may be that they mobilize the trappings of radical resistance, in highly stylized form, but do so in ways that do not compel people to challenge state visibility projects. They offer hyper-individualized and consumer-oriented adaptations to undesired surveillance. To the extent that such efforts can be seen as critical interventions, they rely on an appeal to the pedagogical potential of art to galvanize meaningful political change. "Art is presumed to be effective politically," Jacques Rancière explains, "because it displays the marks of domination, or parodies mainstream icons, or even because it leaves the spaces reserved for it and becomes a social practice. . . . The logic of mimesis consists in conferring on the artwork the power of the effects that it is supposed to elicit on the behavior of spectators."[72] In the case of the examples covered in this chapter, it is clear that although some of the signifiers of critical art are present—for instance, with the Fag Face Mask's blurring of institutionally imposed identities—the primary message is nonetheless one of accommodating pervasive surveillance and inviting a playful dance with it. Recognition of crisis vision's violent, unequal, and marginalizing applications of surveillance is bracketed or denied in the presentation of universal, neoliberal subjects in search of a modicum of (fashionable) control over their exposure.

This is not to say that play has no place in resistance efforts. As Jeffrey Juris has illustrated in his ethnography of the anticorporate globalization movement, play and frivolity can sometimes succeed in ways that oppositional tactics cannot. For example, in spaces of confrontation, people playing music or staging performances while dressed in elaborate costumes are effective because these are symbolically powerful solidarity-building activities that are not physically threatening to the police: "Such playful provocation represents a form of ritual opposition, a symbolic overturning of hierarchy much like medieval carnival. . . . Play, in particular, reveals the possibility of radically reorganizing current social arrangements."[73] In the mode of countersurveillance, earlier groups such as the Surveillance Camera Players similarly embodied a spirit of play as they staged performances for video-surveillance camera operators and spectators in public places like New York City subway stations.[74] Perhaps because of the public setting of these performances, which usually ended with police or security guards escorting players off public property, these interventions may have had the effect of fostering in audiences a critique of policing priorities and the commodification of public space. Play of this sort may be an effective form of resistance that alters public awareness and cultural sensibilities, but it can be a difficult task for such interventions to problematize inequalities that can fester within assumptions of shared rights.

Ultimately, discourses of "the right to hide" are weak variations of "the right to privacy," both of which depend on conceptually inadequate and empirically deficient mobilizations of universal rights. Indeed, poor and racialized populations subjected to the most invasive forms of monitoring are much more concerned with issues of domination and control, along with the practicalities of survival, than they are with legal or philosophical abstractions such as privacy.[75] Privacy is also a deeply individualistic concept, poorly suited to forestall discriminatory practices against social groups.[76] Sami Coll writes: "The notion of privacy, as a critique of [the] information society, has been assimilated and reshaped by and in favour of informational capitalism, notably by being over-individualized through the self-determination principle."[77] The discourse of the right to hide, as with the right to privacy, accepts the legitimacy of state demands for legible populations and offers symbolic compromises to assert degrees of freedom within those constraints.

Instead of being content with forms of hiding, artistic projects, such as some to be discussed in later chapters, could aspire to disrupt totalizing regimes of state visibility. They could seek to undermine the authority of state control by challenging the capitalist and racial imperatives that lend legitimacy to forms of state violence and oppression.[78] They could do so by engaging with "the political," which, as Rancière describes, is always in opposition to the police: "The police is not a social function but a symbolic constitution of the social. The essence of the police lies neither in repression nor even in control over the living. Its essence lies in a certain way of dividing up the sensible. . . . Politics, by contrast, consists in transforming this space of 'move-along,' of circulation, into a space for the appearance of a subject: the people, the workers, the citizens."[79] Artistic intervention, broadly construed, can serve an important role in eroding the authority of the police to structure the sensible, or exclusionary logics in societies more generally. Whether through filming and documenting cases of police misconduct,[80] engaging in culture-jamming activities to raise awareness of corporate malfeasance,[81] or challenging the status quo of rape culture by hacking into computer systems and publicizing attempts to cover up sexual assault,[82] there are many viable prototypes for artists and activists.[83]

As a caution, this is the moment of easy slippage into a reification of transparency and its presumed corrective potential. As soon as one desires to improve upon resistance tactics, the progressive impulse is to turn the tables on the surveillers, to correct asymmetries in transparency by rendering surveilling institutions, agents, and practices visible.[84] Some of these moves might have pragmatic efficacy too. For instance, instead of ostentatious face paint, masks, or fashion accessories to hide from identification systems, alternative projects might "hijack"[85] computer algorithms to identify abusive police personnel or perpetrators of violence against women and hold them accountable. Other projects might make visible data on police shootings, stop-and-frisk profiling, security contracts, drone attacks, or illegal rendition of terrorist suspects.[86] Still, transparency is a crutch that performs only the inverse of the current crisis-vision problematic: substituting one direction of visibility-based control for another. It neither contests the underlying logic of visibility *as* a form of power nor imagines alternative ways of coexisting with others.

The notion of transparency as a universal good ignores the historical system of judgment and politics infusing that ideal. Édouard Glissant relates: "If we examine the process of 'understanding' people and ideas from the

perspective of Western thought, we discover that its basis is this require-
ment for transparency. In order to understand and thus accept you, I have
to measure your solidity with the ideal scale providing me with grounds
to make comparisons and, perhaps, judgments. I have to reduce." With its
roots in Enlightenment thought, transparency is a mechanism of taming
and containing the unruly, of managing opaque populations and territories
by placing them within a reductive hierarchy that diminishes their rich
complexity while buttressing systems of imperial governance. For Glissant,
an alternative response would be to insist on a "right to opacity" that re-
linquished "this old obsession with discovering what lies at the bottom of
natures."[87] Crucially, a celebration of the opaque would not be about hiding or escape but would instead emphasize the fruitful entanglement and
convergence of irreducible elements in nonhierarchical relationships.[88] It
would resist dehumanizing categorization schemes that allow one to see
others as barbaric and to treat them accordingly.

In this respect, the imperative for opacity seems especially pressing in
times of crisis vision. Whereas crisis vision essentializes and demonizes
the Other, who is scapegoated for perceived personal or national insecurities, the opaque resists such reductive categorization. For instance, projects such as the Million Hoodies Movement for Justice,[89] which emerged
after the 2012 shooting death of black teenager Trayvon Martin by neighborhood watch volunteer George Zimmerman in Florida, could be read as
operating in the register of the opaque. The hoodies used in this movement
disrupted legibility by surveillance apparatuses, but their more important
function was to express community solidarity and protest systemic violence against racialized groups, all while enfolding and safeguarding the
movement's diverse participants. Similarly, the widespread adoption of
Black Lives Matter masks during the racial justice protests in 2020 generated a space for opacity and for a collective coming together to confront
racialized police violence and white supremacy in its myriad forms. By
linking these protests to calls to defund or dismantle the police, activists
were effectively challenging the foundations of crisis vision: racial hierarchies that are secured both through state violence and through ostensibly
neutral institutions that are anything but.

By contrast, the countersurveillance designs presented in this chapter offer narrow forms of resistance that are unlikely to interrupt current
crisis-vision regimes. The reason for that has to do with how the artworks
frame problems with surveillance as universally experienced or as needing

individualized and product-based solutions to manage. What gets left out of this framing is a serious discussion of race and gender differences, a critique of surveillance commodification, and reflexive awareness of the possibility that the artistic interventions could contribute to the harmful conditions they seek to change.

To bring this back to the opening discussion of exposure and avoidance during the time of the coronavirus pandemic and racial justice movements, performances of white privilege manifest similarly in assertions of the right to reveal one's unmasked face or the right to hide from facial-recognition surveillance. Both moves shore up crisis vision's racial order by positioning white subjecthood as normative, as the place from which one could claim rights and pretend that they are—or ever could be—universal. Whiteness authorizes not only the right to reveal or conceal but especially the right to be unafraid as a fundamental position of privilege. In these ways the artistic frame of avoidance illustrates how crisis vision maintains a racialized continuum of threat by consolidating and centralizing white subjecthood and, by unspoken extension, subordinating or excluding racialized others.

2. Transparency

Archives—as records—wield power over the shape and direction of historical scholar-ship, collective memory, and national identity, over how we know ourselves as individuals, groups, and societies.—JOAN M. SCHWARTZ AND TERRY COOK, "Archives, Records, and Power"

But if we grant that symbolic systems are social products that contribute to making the world, that they do not simply mirror social relations but help constitute them, then one can, within limits, transform the world by transforming its representation.—LOÏC J. D. WACQUANT, "Toward a Social Praxeology"

As public concerns about state surveillance ebb and flow, with people buf-feted from one revelation to the next, demands for transparency assert a powerful organizing force on responses. Transparency often serves as the initial impulse motivating disclosures, as a way of shedding light on hidden surveillance programs in order to activate change and as an objective in the aftermath of public revelations, when actors seek to discover more details about the programs and practices in question. The predictable valorization of transparency should be interrogated, though, especially given that his-torical precedent provides ample reason to doubt that transparency will au-tomatically lead to accountability or substantial changes in law or policy.[1]

Perhaps ironically, the affective comfort provided by the discourse of transparency can be traced to the dominance of modern scientific rational-ity, which privileges decision making based on observation, quantification, and data analysis.[2] Desire for a knowable and controllable world is coded into the DNA of contemporary institutions as part of the legacy of the scien-tific revolution and its twentieth-century emphasis on efficiency and ratio-nality.[3] In other words, institutional quests for transparency and control *lead* to many of the surveillance abuses that the public seeks to rein in through similar strategies, beginning with making them visible. Transparency efforts usually concentrate on publicizing existing state or corporate archives of monitoring and intervening in the affairs of others. That said, discourses of transparency tend to ignore the politics of archival categories and the rationalities upon which transparency depends.

In her important work on performances of cultural memory and identity, Diana Taylor explains how archives sustain power over time in part through their durability and transmissibility but also through their subordination of cultural repertoires of embodied practice, knowledge, and memory. Secured through myths of being unmediated and resistant to alteration or external influence, archives mask their inherent politics while simultaneously imposing knowledge hierarchies.[4] With respect to surveillance, archival imperatives drive compulsive data collection, with the aim of transforming social or natural phenomena into tractable and categorizable material that can serve as the basis for action. However, the knowledge fabricated through archival processes is biopolitical in that it silences other possible knowledge formulations or cultural repertoires even as it imposes normative conditions and identities.[5] In his book *Going Stealth*, for instance, Toby Beauchamp describes how seemingly progressive expansions of state identity categories to recognize transgender status hinge on transgender individuals' performances of legibility and legitimacy through official documentation to prove that they have "nothing to hide" and are good, patriotic citizens. Beauchamp argues that these assimilation strategies afford "the scapegoating of other marginalized groups, such that the good citizen and the normatively gendered person are produced against the terrorist, undocumented immigrant, and gender deviant."[6] Therefore, by becoming transparent and categorizable within state archives, by persuasively performing assimilable identities, one might mitigate the violence of state exclusion while also enabling its transference to nonnormative and typically racialized others. This is a potent articulation of the continuum of threat under crisis vision, where the state's seemingly stable and impartial archival categories are put into the service of discriminatory social and political systems.

The critical surveillance artworks investigated in this chapter trouble archival certainty and destabilize transparency, thereby illustrating the fractured epistemological foundation upon which crisis vision rests. They offer a general critique of ubiquitous, undemocratic surveillance operations that invisibly and unequally structure people's lives. To draw upon James Harding's forceful framing, "Rather than ushering in an era of increasing transparency—which is a basic paradigm of egalitarian democracies—surveillance technologies and the cultures that accompany them have in fact cultivated radically new and postdemocratic formations of power and authority that are shrouded in fortified opacity."[7] These are the elements that the artists described below problematize through their creations. Some of them seek to reveal the materiality of state surveillance infrastructures, others demonstrate the objectifying effects of routine corporate surveillance systems, and still others take advantage of social media platforms to intentionally oversaturate viewers with personal images as a way of highlighting the irrationality of government programs targeting suspected terrorists. They each confront institutional surveillance by constructing *counter-archives* of visual material.

If transparency is the goal, then creating counter-archives is a way to transform surveillance programs into objects of scrutiny and critique. It is also a way to contest the legitimacy of institutional archives (of the National Security Agency, Google, etc.) by underscoring their partiality and incompleteness, which are archival limitations that suggest the presence of opacity beyond institutional parameters.[8] The artistic frame of transparency frays the link between archival truth and institutional action, and in so doing it betrays the irrationality of racialized surveillance—or, more accurately, it shows how racialized surveillance can be rational only under a generalized regime of crisis vision. To grasp the potential of this artistic frame, though, one must also reckon with the politics of archives more broadly in order to assess the extent to which archival practices shape and constrain movements toward opacity.

Politics of the Archive

Archives are technologies of power. Just as with the historical record, what is included and how the items are organized create truth claims in ways that are insulated from critique by nature of the implied neutrality of the technical apparatus—classification schemes, cabinets and shelves, algorithms, digital storage media, and so on.[9] Limitations to participation in archive construction or access reinforce exclusions that have political effects, for the legitimacy of cultural experience or knowledge is shaped by the degrees to which one can contribute to and mobilize archival materials.[10]

Furthermore, as Allan Sekula persuasively argues, archives perform a pedagogical function of normalizing social hierarchies and communicating one's place in those hierarchies; for instance, through exposure to circulated photographs of suspected criminals or honorific figures, one is trained to accept social hierarchies, recognize visual signifiers of value, and aspire for self-improvement to climb the social ladder.[11]

In his influential writings on institutions and the human sciences, Michel Foucault sets the stage for inquiry into the constitutive force of archives.[12] He notes how archives do not merely *reflect* changes in ways of seeing and being but function as instruments of administrative power to *produce* those changes.[13] The archive operates as a discursive system that determines what can be thought or said in any particular historical moment.[14] Jacques Derrida extends some of these observations to stress the importance of archives in articulating forms of political power: "There is no political power without control of the archive, if not memory. Effective democratization can always be measured by this essential criterion: the participation in and access to the archive, its constitution, and its interpretation."[15]

Because archival structures set the parameters for what can be included, the design of archives also embodies and advances political agendas that are often disguised by idealistic notions of the archive as a repository of materials for advancing the public good.[16] Indeed, notwithstanding contemporary views of archives as safeguarding "public memory," the earliest archives were those dedicated to the establishment of "royal memory" and sovereign power for administrative control of populations and territories.[17] What has been called the "imperial archive" produced instrumental and sometimes grossly inaccurate representations of colonial topographies, resources, and cultures, which were then imposed upon colonial subjects for purposes of resource extraction and population control.[18] Colonial archives, and their legacies, facilitated political division, oppression, and persecution, with the examples of apartheid in South Africa and genocide in Rwanda being just a few of the most notorious cases where arbitrary colonial classification and record systems set the foundation for racial violence.[19] The "totalitarian archives" of Nazi Germany and communist East Germany, among those in other countries, further illustrate the capacity of thorough, rationally produced and administered archives to subtend dehumanizing systems of oppression and killing.[20] Importantly, as Michael

Lynch argues, the decisions made in building an archive serve an interpretive function that channels future uses in particular directions, so there is no such thing as a "raw" archive.[21] Therefore, it is vital to confront the politics of those initial and ongoing decisions as well as the politics of archiving imperatives more broadly.

Even the concept of a "public archive," which is a form often romanticized as fostering equality and democracy,[22] was grounded from its inception in practices of surveillance and social control. For example, as richly detailed by Patrick Joyce, the advent of the free public library in mid-nineteenth-century Britain was designed to cultivate a liberal citizen who embraced a self-help ethos that depended on close monitoring of one's deficiencies and one's progress at correcting them in the quest for self-improvement.[23] In order to assist in this project, libraries collected data on the social characteristics of local populations, including their unique customs and dialects, to generate a public archive that could be used to diagnose social problems and direct cultural improvement projects, for instance, in partnership with educational institutions. The physical design of libraries began to change at this time as well, moving away from common tables where scholars could engage in discussion and resource sharing to individual stations in an open panoptic space, which afforded individuation of responsibility (for checking out books, paying fines, etc.) and observation by others, effectively transforming citizens into a "public police" to protect the archive from theft.[24] Because of the public archive's role in the formation of liberal subjects, one could view it as "a political expression of the nation state itself."[25]

Archival practices betray additional affinities with the surveillance of everyday life. The organizing principles of "archival reason," as theorized by sociologist Thomas Osborne,[26] include publicity (making information public), singularity (focusing on detail), and mundanity (concentrating on the everyday). Archival reason either guides surveillance activities or sets the conditions for them, particularly by providing a professional framework and impulse for the collection and cataloging of fine-grained, often mundane data in the interest of publics, even if those publics are sometimes narrowly delimited or exclusive. Importantly, this is a significant shift in what types of materials are assumed to be valuable, for "mundane" details reside not just in community or personal practices but in all institutional contexts as well. Osborne asserts:

So it is not just a question of a romantic focus upon the powerless. What is at stake here, in fact, is a distinctive way of making visible the question of power itself. If royal memory was a memory of the sovereign and great acts, then archival memory in its modern forms is a memory—even when it focuses on the great and the powerful themselves—of everyday detail; a style of memory that contains within itself the assumption that the everyday is a particularly revealing level on which to pose the question of memory.[27]

Archival reason, described in these terms, clearly underwrites contemporary surveillance practices, where the systematic amassing, classifying, and processing of mundane data are regarded as essential to the functioning of responsible modern subjects and organizations.

The law, frequently viewed as the legitimate response to surveillance abuses, also depends upon and reproduces archival logics. Abstractly, the law similarly adopts archival reason to concentrate attention on evidence, mundane detail, and precedent in its continuous reconstruction of a particular notion of justice, the liberal subject, and the public good. What we might think of as the legal archive would include more than simply legal doctrines and other trappings of legal thought but also—following Sekula's[28] insights about the social ramifications of archives—the role of the law in the ongoing constitution of the social. As Rosemary Coombe explains, "The law's greatest cultural impact may be felt where it is least evident . . . the law is working not only when it is encountered in its most authoritative spaces, but also when it is consciously and unconsciously apprehended. The moral economies created in the shadows of law, the threats of legal action made as well as those that are carried out, people's everyday fears and anxieties about the law, are all loci where the law is doing cultural work."[29] Beyond legal structures alone, then, the figure of the law operates through discourse and practice to shape subjectivities, with differential effects based on one's social position and racial identity.[30] This does not imply that the law is monolithic or totalizing, but rather that it signifies an assemblage of power relations whose contours and intensities vary radically depending on the sites of its materialization.

In that the law is perpetually in flux and negotiated through practice,[31] it provides a context for surveillance-based archiving and counter-archiving. For instance, government spying programs often push upon or cross legal thresholds in their capacious archiving of communications data, whereas artist-activist-scholars sometimes operate on the margins of legality (for example, trespassing or revealing state secrets) to compile and circulate counter-archives of those state programs and sites. The law offers rich zones of contestation, in part because it is so mutable and fragile, contrary to popular perceptions of it as being static and stable. Nonetheless, because of "law's primary allegiance to liberal political theory,"[32] it participates in the reproduction of racial capitalism and intersectional forms of oppression.[33] In these ways, crisis vision propagates through archival reason and the law, which are areas that many artists seek to destabilize through their counter-archiving projects that appeal to opacity.

Artistic Visualizations of Surveillance

In a time of information overload and constant crises, visualizations acquire prophetic overtones. As Orit Halpern explains, visualization is a way of bringing that which is absent into view for purposes of speculation and action.[34] The implied rationality of institutional surveillance and archiving practices, which strive to make the world knowable and governable, depends upon forms of visualization. This carries over into big-data discourses as the pursuit of total knowledge through technological efforts to map and represent unintuitive and unpredictable relations among disparate data.[35] That said, recent trends in data visualization prioritize aesthetics (colors, patterns, texture) over information clarity in their attempts to communicate complexity; they also stress the sublime, mystical overtones of "beautiful data," which perform simultaneously in both affective and logical registers.[36] The surveillance visualizations of government agencies and technology companies extend well beyond the video walls and closed-circuit television screens made vernacular by popular science-fiction films and television shows to include dynamic topographical schematics, interactive dashboards, network maps, sentiment-analysis diagrams, and more. There is performative force in the beauty of these objects, fueling their uptake and symbolically communicating omniscience even as their designers offer caveats and acknowledge limitations, mere whispers drowned out by the symphony of visual support.

Most critical surveillance art projects capitalize upon the visual force of surveillance representations while also attempting to destabilize institutional surveillance demands. They do so by making hidden surveillance programs perceptible through counter-archiving and visualization projects as well as by critiquing the violence of surveillance operations that reduce human complexity to manageable data elements. In other words, these artworks, like government or commercial visualizations, also navigate between aesthetics and clarity, but with different goals. They aspire not to total transparency of the entire surveillance enterprise but instead to provocative traces, glimpses, and clues that function metonymically to direct critical attention to the reductive and controlling logics of institutional surveillance. They also deconstruct institutional archives as dangerously inaccurate and flawed, and in so doing assert the simultaneous coexistence of vital opaque worlds that exceed archival reason. In this respect they approximate "diagrammatic thinking," a mode of engagement that sketches problem spaces and the conditions for imagining new social configurations.[37]

Although artists have different motivations and aspirations, it is important to interrogate the ways in which their critical surveillance projects enact archival reason. We can ask these questions: What are the assumptions behind the construction of counter-archives? How do such counter-archives perform, and what are their politics? As a starting point, these projects generate hidden transcripts of state and corporate surveillance practices and construct oppositional visualizations, suggesting a recalibration of power relations between individuals and institutions. As such, they appear to place great stock in the political efficacy of transparency. They also depend upon archival modalities that have historically been mobilized by the state to discipline subjects and codify racial hierarchies. At the same time, artistic counter-archives do not aspire to totalization. Instead, they agitate for change by juxtaposing transparency with opacity, by appropriating archival techniques to show transparency's inadequacy and violence. Thus, these art projects raise an additional question: what are the ramifications of responding to hidden systems of visualization with open ones, of constructing *aesthetic archives of disclosure* that poach upon institutional surveillance infrastructures to perform opacity?

Traces of the State

There is something elusive about state surveillance operations and the infrastructures upon which they depend. Beyond official conditions of secrecy, which limit exposure and awareness, contemporary surveillance resists investigation by means of its obscure materiality and bureaucratic banality. To visualize such surveillance requires more than pulling back the veil and showing it for what it is. Instead, it necessitates new ways of seeing.

Through investigative research and photographic methods, the work of geographer and artist Trevor Paglen illustrates the potential of artistic efforts to document the mundane materiality of technological infrastructures in ways that invite viewers to reflect on the hidden worlds of state surveillance. In photographing military drones, undersea cables, and secret military bases, just to name a few targets, Paglen transposes the tenets of archival reason into immersive surveillant landscapes. In museum exhibitions, for instance, he presents hazy panoramic images of massive white radomes[38] punctuating an otherwise idyllic English countryside in Cornwall (see figure 2.1), which is a site that serves as a satellite surveillance outpost for the UK's Government Communications Headquarters and the US National Security Agency.[39] Another image, this time a somber underwater landscape off the coast of Miami, depicts a blurry snake of fiber-optic cable hugging the sandy floor as it extends from the lower right and disappears into the murk at the center of the frame. This cable is one of many allegedly tapped by the NSA to gather global telecommunications data for its surveillance programs, which was a practice revealed by Edward Snowden in 2013.[40]

The motivation behind these photographs is to eradicate secrecy, which, according to Paglen, "nourishes the worst excesses of power."[41] It is clear from Paglen's projects that state secrecy is his primary concern and that the excesses which alarm him have to do not only with unchecked data collection but also with racialized violence against other human beings— as with drone strikes or rendition and torture of suspected terrorists—and the rise of a shadow military and intelligence complex. That said, while seeking transparency through the fabrication of a counter-archive, Paglen recognizes the insufficiency and perhaps even complicity of these efforts. He writes: "History shows that revelation and change can often work in tandem, but revelation, in and of itself, accomplishes little." Moreover, Paglen notes that "when covert actions and classified programs become public, their revelation is often used to legitimize their profoundly troubling purposes, to sculpt the state in their own image."[42] In other words, when confronted with unwelcome disclosures, such as with illegal NSA spying programs or CIA torture practices, the state moves to codify crisis vision in law by retroactively legalizing those proscribed activities and granting immunity to those who participated in them.[43]

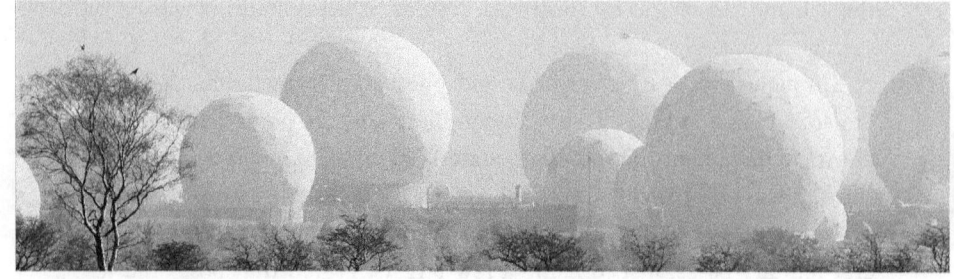

FIGURE 2.1. Trevor Paglen, *89 Landscapes* (2015). Courtesy of the artist.

What makes Paglen's work compelling is that the counter-archives he builds function simultaneously as evidence and as art. As forms of evidence, his photographs of specific sites may have little political or legal currency,[44] but the overall performance of constructing a counter-archive of state secrets signifies a direct challenge, communicating that one can infiltrate and document these hidden worlds, even if, it must be acknowledged, Paglen reproduces tropes of heroic masculinity (for example, as the intrepid adventurer putting himself in danger) to generate photographs for his archive. As art forms, Paglen's photographs resonate in entirely different ways. Although the motivation for their production might be transparency, as visual artifacts they create opacity. They resist decoding and assimilation in that it is often not immediately clear what his blurry images depict, how they were made, or what message is intended. In journalist Jonah Weiner's interpretation, "Blurriness serves both an aesthetic and an 'allegorical' function. It makes [Paglen's] images more arresting while providing a metaphor for the difficulty of uncovering the truth in an era when so much government activity is covert."[45] More subtly, Paglen explains that his works are "a way of organizing your attention" upon that which, like the sublime, moves you through its magnitude and incomprehensibility.[46] In his insightful analysis of Paglen's work, Matthew Potolsky posits that "the photographs make deep secrets shallow. There is little sense of just what purpose the dark sites or satellites serve, of who staffs them, or of what order of mysteries the great distances shelter. In place of revelations, the core expectation underlying a hermeneutics of secrecy, we find visual traces of secrets that are concrete and material—physically present rather than transcendent and ineffable—but still sublimely elusive."[47] By focusing perception on the materialities of state surveillance and violence, Paglen tries to make visible what the state is at pains to erase through techniques of archival control (for example, classified or redacted records, censored maps). In the process, his work sets the conditions for the transformation of subjectivities, for viewers to develop *a feel* for the systems of which they are a part and for which they share responsibility.[48]

Apart from Paglen's work, complementary projects by other artists add perspective on the dehumanizing enactments of crisis vision made possible by state archives. For example, Tomas van Houtryve's project *Blue Sky Days* presents an archive of photographs generated by the artist using a personal drone flying over US sites where the Federal Aviation Administration had granted permission for state drone use.[49] By making images of everyday events—such as weddings or children's birthday parties—from the perspective of a drone, van Houtryve lays a frame of violence over the prosaic, highlighting similarity among people and encouraging a sense of shared vulnerability. The counter-archive is not a "real" one of US drones or government-produced images; instead, it operates on the level of the imaginary to engender disquiet through forced juxtaposition of what is seen and what is unseen but known, namely, the "collateral damage" of US drone strikes on racialized bodies in other countries. In so doing, this public counter-archive draws attention to and stands in for the absent public archive of drone operations in non-US contexts.

Josh Begley's *Plain Sight: The Visual Vernacular of* NYPD *Surveillance* takes a different tack of appropriating and repackaging police images of Muslim neighborhoods, businesses, and places of worship.[50] These surveillance images were produced by the New York Police Department's Demographics Unit as part of its counter-terrorism operations following the attacks of 9/11.[51] As Begley explains, "Plain Sight is an attempt to catalog the banality and violence of the visual culture of the NYPD's secret spying unit. . . . Plain Sight re-presents that which has already been made public, and draws attention to the often mundane, innocuous, and indiscriminate nature of the information collected. Through this work, viewers are provided with different entry points through which they can see surveillance and examine this historical archive in a new light."[52] Using mostly images of buildings and storefronts, the artist forms a circular collage evoking a human eye, with pastel pinks and blues around the perimeter as the iris, and black-and-white tones in the center as the pupil (see figure 2.2). This molded presentation of NYPD's visual archive rejects static or neutral interpretations of the images and instead draws attention to a very specific

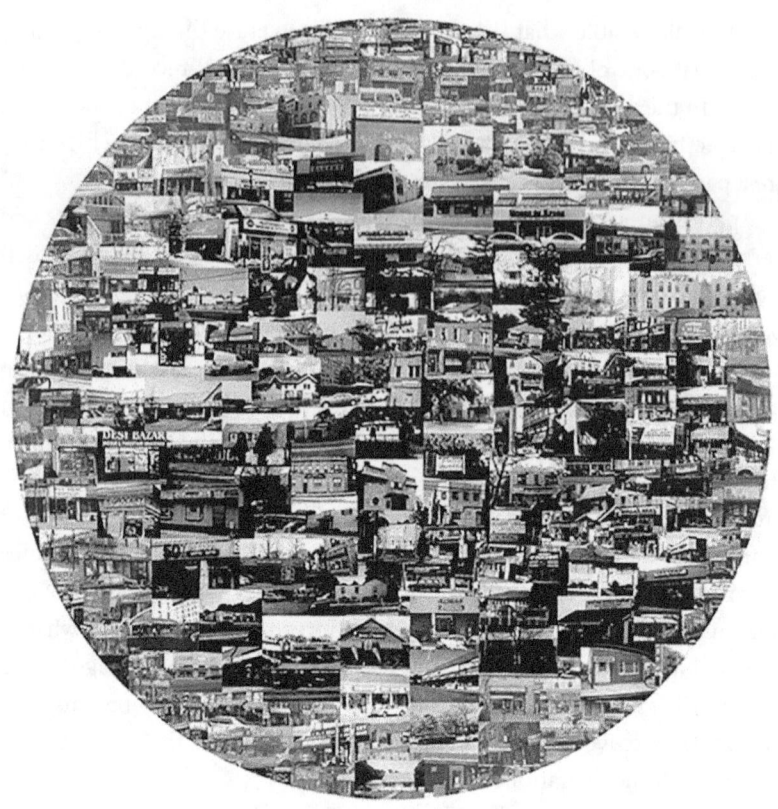

FIGURE 2.2. Josh Begley, *Plain Sight: The Visual Vernacular of* NYPD *Surveillance* (2014). Creative Commons.

act of looking. It emphasizes the illegal religious and racial profiling of certain populations in the absence of any evidence of wrongdoing. Whereas inclusion in the police archive was an act of symbolic violence, Begley's response offers a way of destabilizing the symbolic regime established by such police surveillance by subjecting it to scrutiny.[53]

Each of these artists' works trace state surveillance practices, whether through documentation (Paglen), simulation (van Houtryve), or compilation (Begley). The artists assemble counter-archives of photographic material to both visualize and contest secret state operations that often enact racialized violence. At the same time, these counter-archives do not aspire toward totalization. Rather, through blurry representations, suggested absent archives, and repackaged appropriations of visual evidence, they acknowledge the multiplicity of interpretive possibilities and in the process subvert the state's hold on symbolic authority. Thus, whereas the act of manufacturing counter-archives tacitly valorizes transparency, with included documents intended to serve as a resource for other forms of political engagement, the artists concurrently embrace opacity and reject realism. Their archives are objects to think with but not pathways to the truth. In this respect the logics of archiving are fissured within these works: archival reason prevails, with its focus on collecting, organizing, and publicizing mundane details, while at the same time representations of the truth are questioned. Where these efforts congeal most with previous articulations of archivization is in their implicit construction of normative liberal subjects. The artworks position viewers as agents responsible for their own political transformation, through the edification initiated by the artists, and the alteration of state practices, through individual or collective action.[54] The artists deconstruct archival logics and valorize the opaque, even as they partially recuperate liberal orders in their pursuit of change.

Ghosts in the Archive

Although much surveillance scholarship concentrates on the state and its governance regimes, corporate data systems now permeate and structure most aspects of everyday life in industrialized countries. The archives and algorithms of just about all industries (financial, health care, real estate, transportation, and so on) shape life chances in largely invisible—and often unequal—ways, dictating what resources and services one has access to based upon assessments of one's relative risk or value.[55] Industries obviously partner with government agencies as well, whether voluntarily or through legal mandates, to share data pertaining to possible national security threats or to act as surrogates for the state to do things like freeze bank accounts or prevent individuals from flying.[56] Government agencies also provide a lucrative market for security products and services, allowing for the easy flow of knowledge, personnel, and equipment across public and private sectors.[57] So, whereas clear distinctions cannot hold between the practices of public entities and private entities, artists and scholars have recognized that voracious data collection by private companies must be included in critiques of contemporary surveillance.

Data behemoths such as Google offer fruitful material for artistic probing of the corporate archive. For instance, artist Paolo Cirio's *Street Ghosts* project repurposes images from Google Street View (the application that delivers photographic representations of streetscapes) to draw attention to and problematize Google's visual archive of individuals in public space.[58] For this project, Cirio locates images of people in Google Street View and creates life-size representations of those blurred figures in the exact location in the urban landscape where the original photos were made. One work superimposes onto a rusted and graffitied wall an incongruous figure of a balding man in a long-sleeve pink shirt and light blue jeans (see figure 2.3). Overgrown weeds rise up around the man's lower legs, obscuring his feet, as he tilts slightly to the side with what appears to be a spade in one hand and a plant in the other. He seems to be gardening in the exact spot where the weeds now overtake his past efforts.[59]

This piece performs on several levels. It is a glimpse into the Google archive and a signification, through a singular figure, of the vast totality of personal images contained within it. By reproducing images of people in space, Cirio removes Google images from their corporate frame and imposes an artistic one that harkens back to, but does not recapture, the original. In the process, he calls attention to the violence of stripping data from context and challenges the unsanctioned production of personal images— images that become Google's property upon their creation. On another level, *Street Ghosts* fabricates a counter-archive that is etched into the built world. It comprises two-dimensional surface illustrations of what came before, communicating the incompleteness of all representation, including those of our many "data doubles" in institutions' digital archives.[60] Unlike many of those data doubles, Cirio's figures stage their own temporality and degradation, visibly eroding over time as analog instruments of memory and mortality.[61] They divulge their latent opacity and readily abandon their fleeting gesture toward the real, becoming palimpsests or backdrops for other urban articulations, other embodiments of meaning in space. Thus, contrary to Google's archive, even though this counter-archive points back to the moment of image creation, it is decidedly nonindexical. It offers intentionally ephemeral and ghostlike representations of representations, undermining the implied realism of the Google archive by demonstrating the necessary but arbitrary function of framing in establishing meaning or truth.

Other artists have used the urban landscape in a similar fashion to raise pointed questions about borders, walls, and other architectural manifestations of forced separation. For instance, Kai Wiedenhöfer's powerful

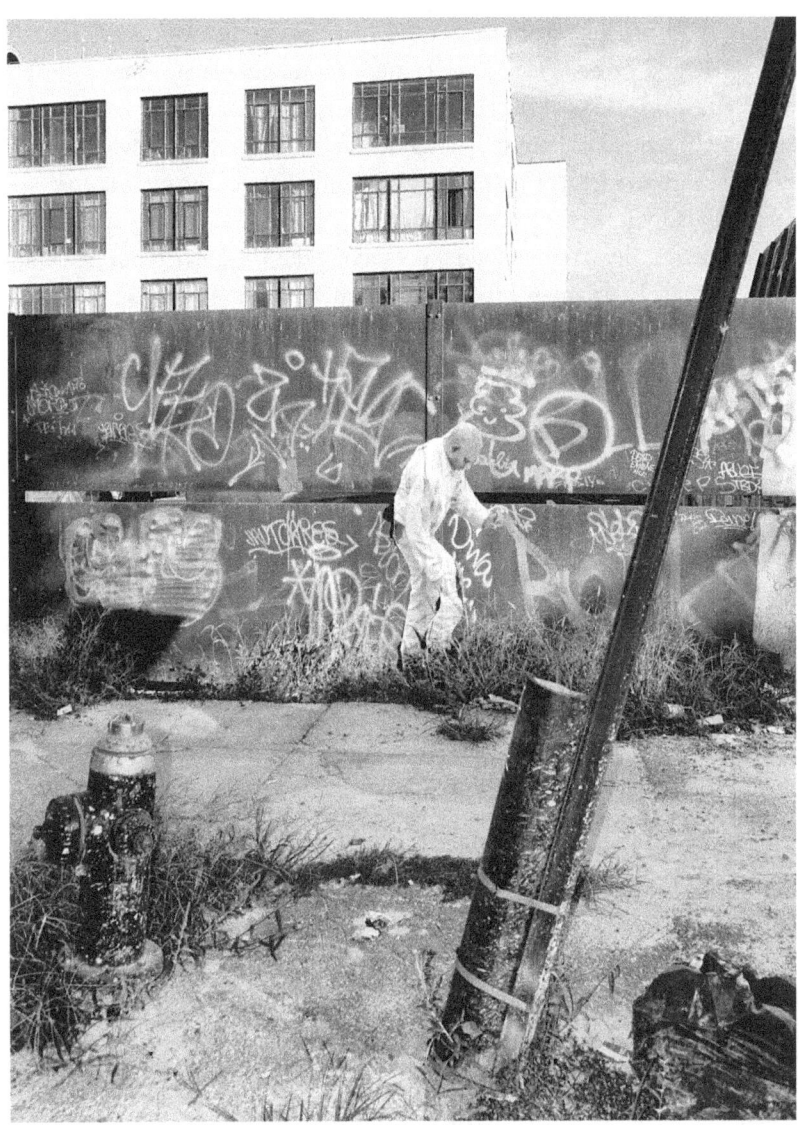

FIGURE 2.3. Paolo Cirio, *Street Ghosts* (2014). Courtesy of the artist.

WALLonWALL project reproduces photographs of border walls from around the world and exhibits them on separation walls in places such as Berlin and Belfast.[62] Dozens of these massive, 9 × 27 foot panoramic photographs stretch out, one after another, along the length of the walls, inviting viewers to absorb the images and reflect on similarities in the violence, strife, and inequality represented in the different scenes (see figure 2.4). Some of the barriers depicted include fences along the US-Mexico border, walls dividing Israeli settlements from Palestinian communities, separations between Sunni and Shiite neighborhoods in Baghdad, and fortifications between North and South Korea. In combination, Wiedenhöfer has created a well-curated archive of barrier images that he then strategically sites in public spaces to spark conversation about the destructive tendencies of walling and a reevaluation of walling practices. In his words, "A wall is always the last refuge. When you have a conflict between two parties, you build up a wall, you don't talk to each other anymore, and that's not a solution to any problem."[63]

Walls enforce separation, but they also invite surveillance to police that separation or regulate movement through or within it. They are apparatuses of crisis vision par excellence. They position others as different, as suspicious, as outsiders, and as potential threats to one's safety or well-being.[64] Even in places where one might imagine that established peace would lead to the removal of walls, they are nonetheless reproduced as if to hold fragile peace in place through reminders of fundamental differences that linger below the surface and could aggressively reassert themselves at any moment. Thus, Wiedenhöfer chose to display *WALLonWALL* along the Cupar Way "Peace Line" in West Belfast in 2019.[65] This is one of the many lengthy barriers that was erected to deter conflict by separating Catholic and Protestant neighborhoods in Northern Ireland. Counterintuitively, the number of these walls has grown since the Good Friday Agreement of 1998.[66] There are now close to 100 such structures, running a total of more than 21 miles in length; some are as high as 18 feet; and many contain security gates that are closed and locked every night.[67] Although Northern Ireland has plans to remove the peace lines by 2023, the uncertainty provoked by Brexit has made many local residents feel that the walls are necessary insurance against conflict on the horizon.[68] According to one former paramilitary member of the Ulster Defense Association[69] who now serves as a tour guide for the peace lines, "I'm sure you're probably fed up with hearing about Brexit. . . . But people are worried about a bad deal, the

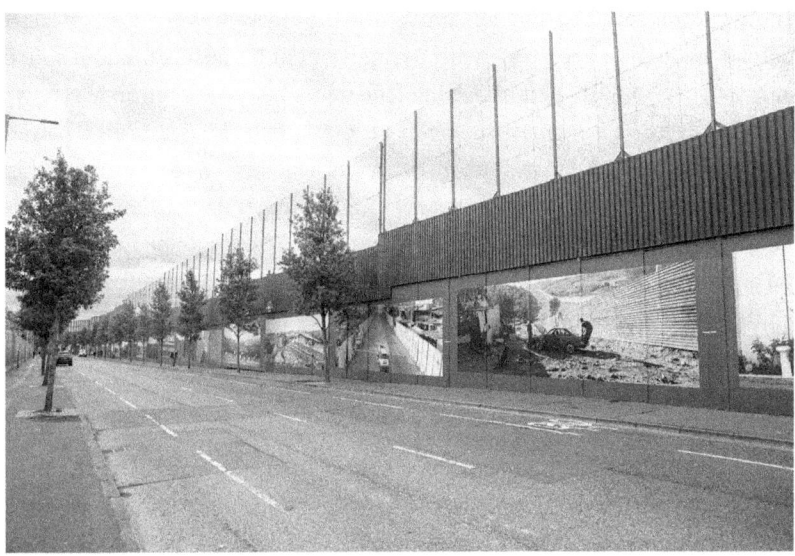

FIGURE 2.4. Kai Wiedenhöfer, *WALLonWALL*, Belfast (2019). Courtesy of the artist.

wrong deal or no deal. . . . [If things go poorly,] I think we're going to need these walls more than ever."[70]

Wiedenhöfer's project anticipates the lure of architectural separation in times of uncertainty and strives to symbolically interrupt those tendencies. By capturing the harsh desolation of fortified borders from around the world and affixing such images to barriers in public, Wiedenhöfer calls upon people to witness the global violence to which their walls contribute, to see themselves and their communities as connected to and overlapping with others. Placed upon walls, his photographs simultaneously represent and collapse difference. The images of other places and times haunt the embodied present. Then, at the conclusion of the exhibition, before becoming normalized themselves, the photographs are removed; they disappear to allow for new inscriptions on and in space.

A much different project by artist Andrew Hammerand produces an archive of photographs to critique the pervasive surveillance infrastructures that enable them. In a piece called *The New Town*, Hammerand accesses an unsecure webcam mounted on a cell-phone tower in a generic US Midwestern suburban community to build an image archive of the quotidian activities of residents. There are pixelated and fragmented images of what appear to be young teenagers in a park. A girl hugs someone from behind as another leans into a cartwheel; apparently the video stream did not refresh quickly enough to keep pace with her movement because a random splice of her upper body appears above her (see figure 2.5). Another image shows the silhouette of a woman sitting at an outdoor table as a brown-haired woman in a white T-shirt struts by with her head and shoulders appearing two strides before the rest of her, separated from her body by another digital glitch. In another frame one can vaguely make out two people meeting on a pathway through the grass and perhaps shaking hands or exchanging an item. For Hammerand the project provides a way to "reflect on the expansive use of surveillance technologies, the increasing loss of privacy, and the heightened sense of anxiety and vulnerability that are part of American life in the early 21st century."[71]

One could read these images as trafficking in menacing tropes of victims being watched without their awareness, spied upon by unknown others with unclear intent. The artist generates just such a situation, thereby attesting to the relative uncontrollability and unknowability of one's digital exposure. Particularly with the representation of young white girls, the piece invokes moral panics surrounding the presumed vulnerability of children or teenagers to the voyeuristic gaze of online predators.[72] Although digital surveillance does enable new forms of sexual harassment and does activate calls for patriarchal intervention, as feminist surveillance studies scholars have shown,[73] it also lends itself to masculinist forms of discrimination by abstraction—it evacuates embodiment and strips context much like the scientistic modes of visibility that I critiqued in the introduction.[74] From this perspective, *The New Town* splinters transparency through its presentation of fractured scenes and ambiguous action. The many visual defects violently segment bodies, making everyday life tainted and indecipherable. The screenshots cannot offer objective representations of people or events because context always exceeds the frame and the frame itself is flawed. Without being organized in archives and placed into discourse, meaning appears ambiguous and incomplete, which is a finding that highlights how the power of archives rests in their ability to reduce and deny opacity—to restrict the multiplicity of meaning inherent in representations. Moreover, *The New Town* draws attention to the vulnerabilities of corporate surveillance infrastructures, which can be hijacked to spy on others and insert collected images into different information ecosystems.

Placing these works in conversation with larger economies of surveillance draws out their crisis-vision overtones. Cirio's *Street Ghosts* poaches

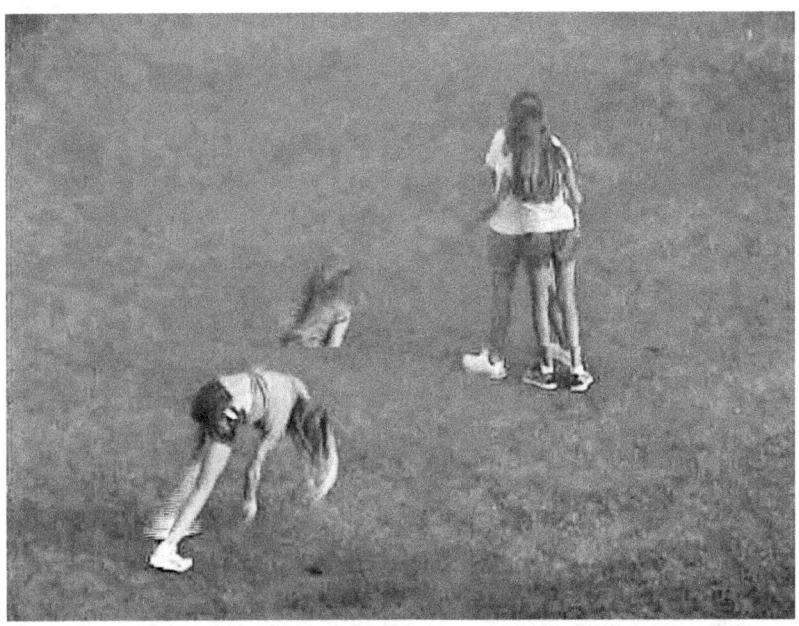

FIGURE 2.5. Andrew Hammerand, Untitled from the series *The New Town* (2014). Courtesy of the artist.

on an increasingly pervasive corporate layer of surveillance that generates profits through the production, categorization, and commercialization of data. Mapping systems such as Google Street View present themselves as objective catalogues of scenes and in the process mask their contribution to racial geographies of neighborhood classification along a spectrum from affluent to impoverished. With the normalization of Google Street View images, other spatial practices can similarly appear rational, such as algorithmic-based predictive policing or digital redlining of spaces coded as dangerous.[75] Wiedenhöfer's *WALLonWALL* produces knowledge through photographic documentation of interdictory spaces in disparate regions throughout the world. His intervention conjures into being an archive of political, ethnic, and religious divisions and makes it accessible to—and debatable by—the public. This work provides an entry point into critiques of racial dehumanization and abjection, which often manifest most profoundly along borderlands. Finally, Hammerand's *The New Town* focuses on white subjects and positions surveillance as an encroachment upon white society. If surreptitious monitoring of normative white subjects causes concern, it is undoubtedly because this troubles presumptions of white innocence and rights. It exposes white subjects to forms of unwanted visual scrutiny that have heretofore been reserved for racialized others, even if, as previously noted, surveillance-based violence remains unequally distributed.[76] By enfolding surveillance systems and security architectures into counter-archives, these works, in different ways, allow glimpses of such deeper racial politics.

Archival Oversaturation

In the contemporary conjuncture, most institutions are devoted to and constituted by archival logics. They endeavor to transform all elements of their domains of operation into data to be harnessed for decision making, regardless of whether they are in the public, private, or nonprofit sectors. Systems for the efficient production and management of data become essential within this context. Thus, tapping into the social media streams of individuals or capturing the "digital exhaust" of their online and offline activities (web searches, purchases, entertainment choices, travel locations) offers some of the most attractive ways to build valuable digital archives through automated or crowd-sourced data generation. As people are entrained to participate in systems of data production, they become compliant surveillance subjects whose labor generates value for others, often unbeknownst to them.[77] However, the very mechanisms that allow for and encourage participation by users in data creation also afford opportunities for artistic interventions that illustrate the insidious *illogic* of supposedly rational systems.

The work of artist Hasan Elahi plays upon this apparent contradiction. Following the attacks of 9/11, Elahi—who at the time was an assistant professor at San José State University—was wrongly placed on an FBI watch list and detained for interrogation in 2002 at Detroit Metropolitan Airport.[78] He was investigated and repeatedly questioned for months before finally having his name cleared, at which point he was advised to continue to inform the FBI of his travel activity.[79] His response was to inundate the FBI with an overabundance of photographic documentation about his daily whereabouts, purchases, toilets used, food eaten, and more. He created a public website (trackingtransience.net) to disseminate this photographic evidence as a performance and critique of state demands for transparency from victims of unwarranted suspicion and profiling. By 2014, Elahi had produced a counter-archive of more than seventy thousand images,[80] each of them another datum presumably conveying his innocence, pushed into FBI data streams as counterevidence to stifle and mock whatever spurious material led to his targeting in the first place.

Elahi's counter-archive oversaturates viewers, confounding attempts to make definitive interpretations about what is revealed or what really matters.[81] This strategy hinges on the premise that "more is less,"[82] that privacy can be maintained by drowning others in one's personal data without giving them a key for deciphering the many elements depicted or registering their relative importance.[83] More than that, copious disclosure masks selective nondisclosure. Elahi explains: "I still stand behind the idea that you protect your privacy by giving it up. . . . For now [in 2014], we're still in a transition between analog and digital, and for as long as we're in this state of flux, we'll develop a more sophisticated understanding of the consequences of living under constant surveillance. For now, at least, we still have control over what information we put forth publicly. Being mindful of how we do that feels like a good first step toward retaining control."[84] Therefore, oversaturation has a double meaning in the context of Elahi's work. It is an analytic device communicating, on one hand, that there is too much visual material to process and, on the other hand, that just as photographs lose their detail and take on an unnatural appearance with an increase in color intensity, so too do surveillance subjects lose definition with archival oversaturation. Subjects become opaque in the process as surveillance systems are overloaded and unable to render precise assessments of individual behavior. This, at least, is the primary conceit of Elahi's Tracking Transience website.

Elahi's massive counter-archive, while functioning as a critical art project in itself, has served as a resource for numerous spin-off projects as well. For instance, the work titled *Prism*, named after one of the NSA's internet spying programs, is a large, 10 × 24 foot poster of vertical, multicolored bars overlaid on a black-and-white background image of the roof of the NSA building (see figure 2.6).[85] The colored bars evoke those displayed on televisions during Emergency Broadcast System tests, which originated during the US Cold War period as part of the civil defense program to manage public communications in the event of nuclear attack.[86] Upon closer inspection, each of the bars is composed of thousands of photographs from Elahi's self-surveillance archive: meals, urinals, shopping centers, airports, and so on. This work tacitly asserts that within surveillance societies, national states of emergency metamorphose into scrutiny of the minute details of people's lives. Elahi compares the contemporary situation to that of people under the Stasi secret police in East Germany prior to the fall of the Soviet Union; the difference is that he is the one voluntarily sharing intimate details, rather than that information coming from a secret spy network of informants.[87] *Prism* thus acts as a critique of the totalitarian tendencies of modern states in their response to perceived insecurities. These tendencies may be grounded in fears with some empirical basis, but they are animated by the insatiable archival appetite of security institutions like the NSA, whose members want desperately to absorb and process *all* communications data throughout the world.[88]

If total knowledge is the goal of security agencies, Elahi challenges the depth and precision of conclusions drawn predominantly from surface representations. For example, another project of his, titled *Stay v1.0*, is a detailed print of many of the dozens of beds Elahi has slept in during his travels (see figure 2.7). Not a single bed is well made. The covers and sheets are bunched and twisted, with pillows askew and frequently stacked, all seen from the perspective of someone standing at the foot of the beds. As with all of Elahi's work, photographs of people, including of himself, are conspicuously absent, so beyond the fact of an unmade bed, viewers can ascertain very little about the artist from these pictures. We do not know if he slept well, if he slept alone, if or what he read or watched there, or if he stayed in the room all night. Each bed stands in for information that it cannot convey, and adding more photographs of similar beds does not increase depth of awareness; it only solidifies the pattern of partial, insignificant

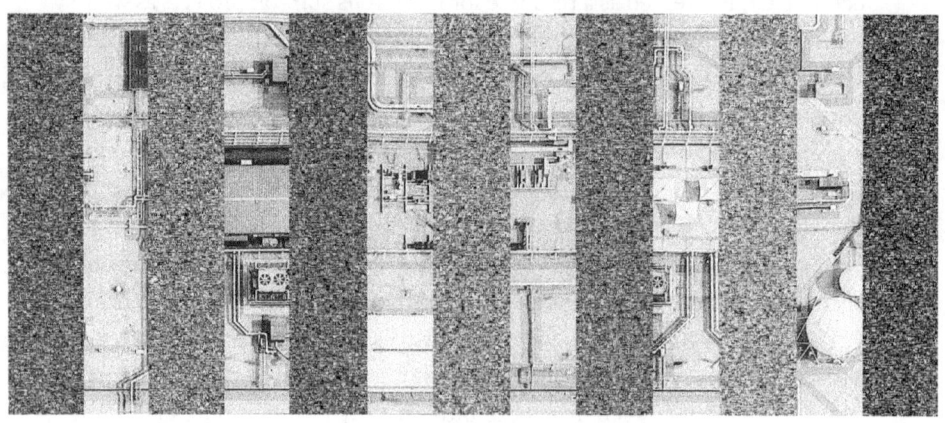

FIGURE 2.6. Hasan Elahi, *Prism* (2015). Courtesy of the artist.

revelation. As art scholar Sven Spieker relates, "Archives do not record experience so much as its absence; they mark the point where an experience is missing from its proper place, and what is returned to us in an archive may well be something we never possessed in the first place."[89] Elahi's work suggests, by extension, that law enforcement or security agency archives, in their expansiveness, produce a false sense of definitive knowledge of subjects when in fact they are best at reifying their protocols of classification and imposing them upon individuals.

Elahi draws upon and simultaneously deconstructs photography's historical aura of realism and authenticity. By nature of their verisimilitude and original copresence with that which they represent, photographs appear to have an indexical relationship to the physical world, but this indexical quality has always been a fabrication.[90] As a medium, photographs are necessarily shaped by the technical valences and constraints of photographic devices, as well as by the many other cultural factors that go into staging and processing photographic media.[91] The very language used to talk about photographs obscures this process of construction: the vernacular

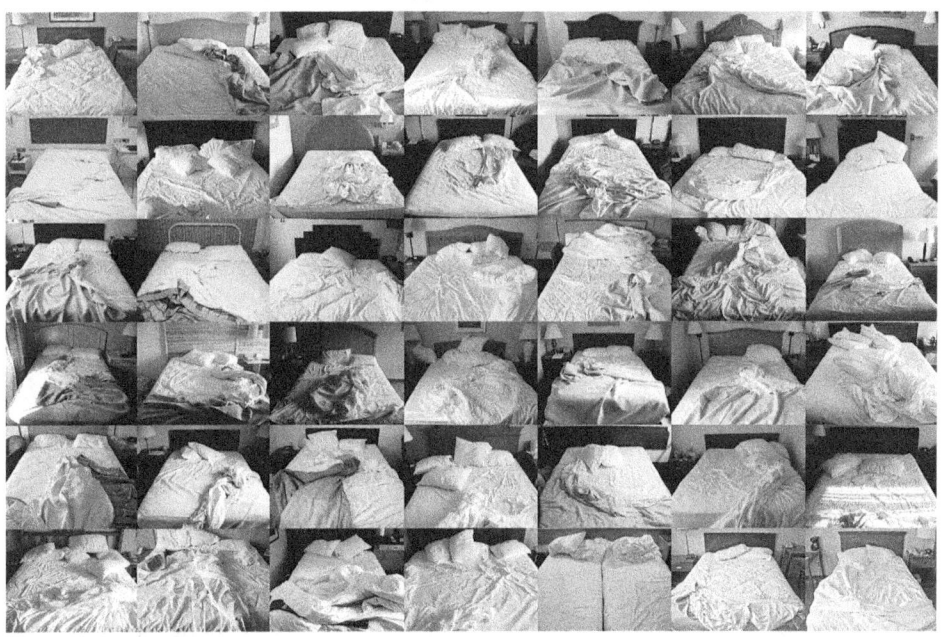

FIGURE 2.7. Hasan Elahi, *Stay v1.0* (2011). Courtesy of the artist.

privileges hunting metaphors of "shooting" photos or "capturing" scenes, when in fact all images are "made."[92] Additionally, photography is always embedded in discourses and institutional practices that work diligently to maintain the appearance of accuracy and singularity of meaning, thereby silencing interpretive multiplicity, especially with respect to law enforcement's use of photographs as evidence. John Tagg explains: "The function of photography as a means of surveillance, record, and evidence was the result of a more or less violent struggle . . . to hold in place certain discursive conditions. It depended on a machinery of capture that sought to curtail the productivity of photographic meanings, exhaust their legibility, and make the camera its own, as an instrument of a new disciplinary power."[93] Elahi pushes back on this disciplinary power by appropriating the trope of photographic evidence and claiming the right to self-document, multiplying representations of his interfacing with objects until meaning collapses under the symbolic weight of the archive.

At the same time, a variation of archival reason persists. Elahi contests the legitimacy of law enforcement archives by crafting a parallel archive to perform innocence. Although the primary audience has long ceased to be institutional agents, if it ever was, these works depend upon an oppositional framing that maintains the centrality of the hidden archives of the surveillance state. These state archives are the ones that matter, the ones that are consequential in determining the conditions of one's existence. The appeal to self-transparency asks viewers to hold these archives side by side—the visible one of quotidian scenes and the hidden one of incriminating evidence—and conclude that the artist is innocent and the state illegitimate. Still, to echo Rachel Hall's discussion of Elahi's work, the notion of protecting privacy by giving it up reinforces belief in an underlying right to privacy without accounting for "the degree to which the performance of voluntary transparency has become a symbol of distinction."[94] Building upon this, it is vital to note how crisis vision is normalized through everyday acts of voluntary exposure by those who believe they have "nothing to hide." The actions of normative white subjects who feel empowered to claim a right to privacy simultaneously produce a class of racialized others for whom privacy is foreclosed, which is a class that Elahi found himself placed in by the FBI.

There are several ways that elements of opacity also emerge from Elahi's creative work. Through image overload, viewers are confronted with the reality of archival absence, with a recognition that human experience, embodiment, and relations must exist outside depicted archival elements yet give rise to them. The opaque might be suppressed, particularly through its exclusion from archival classification, but it cannot be contained. The ghostly presence of uncodified life haunts and undermines archival-based surveillance systems. By directing attention to this vital absence, Elahi challenges the accuracy and legitimacy of the surveillance systems that shape human existence. In the process, his work suggests that efforts to activate opacity must extend beyond individual tactics (of avoidance, for instance) to include structures that could support ambiguity and uncertainty in the service of ethical possibility.

Conclusion

Crisis vision emerges from the cauldron of transparency, motivating heightened visibility and punishment of those seen as threatening social orders. In the context of this chapter, that could include targets of state violence in the War on Terror, outsiders crossing borders, or individuals made publicly visible—and therefore vulnerable—through the vast archives of corporations like Google. By challenging the supposed neutrality or accuracy of institutional transparency schemes, artists unsettle crisis-vision regimes and open a space for imagining different relations to archives founded on a recognition of the vitality of opacity.[95]

State and corporate archives facilitate some of the most violent articulations of crisis vision. By subordinating cultural repertoires, excluding nonnormative bodies, and imposing hierarchical classifications upon phenomena, they provide a seemingly objective basis for exercises of biopolitical or necropolitical control. Archival logics can be cruelly efficient supports for dehumanizing containment and extermination of populations, as seen with the totalitarian archives deployed by Nazis to perpetrate genocide,[96] but archives' relative inaccessibility both enables and obscures other abuses. For instance, forms of extralegal surveillance, interrogation, and detention of racialized others during the War on Terror hinged on conditions of secrecy and deeply flawed constructions of threat, most of which were later normalized and legalized, making appeals to the law impotent.[97] "Intensified surveillance and totalitarian tendencies are intimately linked," Anthony Giddens has perceptively observed, so one should not be surprised by these institutional developments or the role of the liberal archive in supporting them.[98]

As explored in this chapter, the production of artistic counter-archives excels at revealing the flaws and dangers of transparency. Far from being a rational ideal, transparency is a weapon regularly deployed against racialized populations to maintain the liberal order and eliminate perceived threats to it. By juxtaposing transparency with opacity, artists question not only the truth claims of institutional actors but the very grounds for those claims. Just as institutional surveillance systems can be grasped only in blurry glimpses and incomplete traces, so too are those systems afflicted by incompleteness and partiality, which is only aggravated by the impossible quest for totality. More data do not necessarily lead to greater truths, only to greater awareness of the breadth of the unknown.

Through the assembly of counter-archives, artists provocatively frame state and corporate surveillance systems as objects of critique. They problematize institutional archives and infrastructures to challenge existing institutional monopolies on symbolic authority. Key to this is not only circulating artist-generated images but also multiplying interpretive possibilities for all visual evidence. The art projects emphasize mediated traces and transience, alongside negotiated data representations, all in contradistinction to the presumed fixity of institutional surveillance archives. Thus, for most of the works discussed in this chapter, meaning is approached as being indeterminate and contingent, shaped by discursive regimes, technological protocols, and personal experience. In this context, counter-archive images do not seek to establish definitive representations of reality from the artists' perspectives so much as to draw attention to the interpretive dimensions of all visual materials, including those curated by institutional actors. They illustrate the opaque worlds that reside alongside and trouble archival certainty. They suggest a right to opacity, which, Clare Birchall asserts, is premised on "the demand not to be reduced to and understood as data as defined by the state . . . [and on a reconceptualization of] how we relate to and read others within a discourse that has already decided what is and what is not possible and knowable."[99] By gesturing toward the racial politics and inaccuracies of institutional archives, artworks erode faith in state-sponsored efforts at documentary realism and push for opacity as a recalibration of relations with others.

3. Complicity

In what ways can artistic endeavors alter people's perspectives of surveil-lance? What is the capacity of art to reveal systems of control and induce reflexivity in others, perhaps leading them to recognize their role in racialized surveillance systems and modify their behavior? As the previ-ous chapters have shown, critical surveillance artwork has blossomed in recent years, pushing inquiry of this sort through a number of different approaches.[1] The focus of this chapter is on artworks that emphasize view-ers' complicity or participation in the regimes in question, especially those works that seek to activate a sense of social connection and introspection to make recognition of collective responsibility possible.

In some respects, the so-called big-data revolution has set the stage for viewers to process visual imagery and abstract data along these lines. If *big data* connotes a universe of unintuitive but nonetheless meaningful con-nections across disparate domains,[2] then the current discursive field affords the *decentering* of subjects, encouraging them to see themselves as nodes in larger, consequential networks that elude their absolute comprehension. In such a space, viewers may more readily accept their relationships—and perhaps responsibility—to others whom they have never met. Critical surveillance art does not simply convey such messages to viewers through some form of transmission but rather strives to carefully construct the col-lision of people, representations, and media such that shifts in worldview are made possible.

Whereas John Berger's classic work *Ways of Seeing*[3] illustrates the his-torically contingent ideological underpinnings of viewers' conceptions of art, critical surveillance artworks interrogate *ways of being seen* in the pre-sent moment. They implicitly ask, "What kind of subject is the subject of surveillance?" Granted, as I have argued thus far, answers to this question depend fundamentally upon one's social position and the nature of the surveillance apparatus being deployed. Still, inquiry into ways of being seen requires attention to complex social relations often mediated by obscure technological systems and protocols. Such processes of mediation do not fit squarely within the conceptual frameworks of *discipline*, which overemphasizes containment and totalizing internalizations of rules and norms by subjects;[4] *control*, which hinges on the translation of individuals into discrete data elements for the profit of corporations but does not allow space for negotiation or contestation;[5] or *securitization*, which prioritizes the role of the state in applying reductive risk designations to populations and managing flows based on those measures.[6] Contemporary ways of being seen undoubtedly possess objectifying and controlling valences, but they may also afford new forms of connection and ethical responsibility among strangers. In this chapter I analyze a set of artworks that take the construction of such a complicit ethical subject as their objective.

The concept of *interpellation*—if pushed beyond its original emphasis on unconscious participation in ideological structures—can assist with this inquiry by directing attention to the ideological significance of relationships between watchers and the watched. In Louis Althusser's formulation, interpellation signifies the process by which ideology transforms individuals into subjects. As with a police officer's hail ("Hey, you!"), the target recognizes in that moment that they are a subject embedded in the power relations of social and political institutions and that they always have been.[7]

Situated in the context of crisis vision, interpellation performs a racializing function as well by differentially constituting white subjects as fully formed and dominant and nonwhite subjects as subhuman and subordinate. In reflecting on the production of such racial hierarchies, Ghassan Hage usefully delineates three forms of racialized interpellation:

> The first, non-interpellation, is a mode of racism linked with the experience of invisibility, where the racialized feel ignored and nonexistent. . . . The second mode of interpellation, and perhaps that most commonly associated with racism is negative interpellation. Here the racialized is definitely noticed and made visible. And the symbolic structure of society has a place for them, but it is a place defined by negative characteristics. . . . The third form of racialization, mis-interpellation, is a racism of a different order, for it is a drama in two acts: in the first instance the racialized person is interpellated as

belonging to a collectivity "like everybody else." . . . Yet, no sooner do they answer the call and claim their spot than the symbolic order brutally reminds them that they are not part of everyone: "No, I wasn't talking to you. Piss off. You are not part of us."[8]

Charles Mills describes such arrangements as a tacit yet definitional "racial contract" that undergirds the much-heralded "social contract" of the liberal state. Mills writes that within a society founded on white supremacy, "the nonwhite body is a moving bubble of wilderness in white political space, a node of discontinuity which is necessarily in permanent tension with it."[9] The interpellation of nonwhite bodies occurs as much with the officer's hail as with everyday forms of injustice and indignity, epitomized, for instance, with Frantz Fanon's famous recounting of his shock at a small child pointing him out and saying, "Look, a Negro!"[10] Nonwhite bodies are policed, and the racial order maintained, through a combination of ideological conditioning and physical violence,[11] through the everyday cues that position bodies along crisis vision's continuum of threat and the harsh correctives that punish individuals perceived as deviating from their assigned places.

Although the emphasis with traditional treatments of interpellation is on the role of discourse in constituting subjects—or, in Stuart Hall's words, addressing "how ideology becomes internalized, how we come to speak 'spontaneously'"[12]—discourse, broadly construed, also operates through nonverbal sign systems and visual imagery.[13] Thus, some scholars have mobilized interpellation to analyze how advertising images position subjects.[14] Others, such as W. J. T. Mitchell, write of the interpellative capacity of paintings, whereby "the image . . . takes the beholder into the game, enfolds the observer as object for the 'gaze' of the picture."[15] Finally, visual culture scholars such as Nicholas Mirzoeff have used interpellation in an expanded sense to stress the nonverbal "visual surveillance" implied in moments where one is positioned by being watched by others and by being enjoined to watch things like scenes of war.[16]

Therefore, along with ideological reinforcement by institutions, such as education or religion, visual imagery performs interpellative functions. For instance, even if someone might dismiss an advertisement for a product or disagree with a media message, they are still "hailed" as subjects who are targeted as part of a group; they are placed within the social system and in the process contribute to that system's maintenance.[17] This insight into interpellation productively emphasizes the role of social practice in the reproduction of ideology. In the words of John Fiske, "Ideology is not, then, a static set of ideas through which we view the world but a dynamic social practice, constantly in process, constantly reproducing itself in the ordinary workings of these apparatuses."[18] By attending to processes of interpellation, therefore, cultural critics can trace the workings of ideology in semiotic systems, social relations, and everyday practices. But in order to view interpellation as a technique for artists to transform commonsense understandings of surveillance, the concept must be recast so that its limitations can be interpreted as possibilities for political intervention.

Rather than being singular, there are frequently multiple interpellations operating simultaneously (for example, those positioning the subject as citizen, consumer, or criminal). The various discourses of which people are a part are constantly working, often in tension with one another, to constitute subjects both directly and indirectly, with or without an audible hail or dyadic confrontation between people.[19] Moreover, not all efforts at interpellation succeed, for one may reject the position ascribed or the authority of the agent or discourse in question. As Judith Butler explains, whereas discussions of interpellation typically yoke it to "the law" and perceive the law as having the force of conjuring subjects into existence, this effectively insulates the law from critique because an attack on it would destabilize the conditions for one's (social) being. Butler asks: "Under what conditions does a law monopolize the terms of existence in quite so thorough a way? Or is this a theological fantasy of the law? Perhaps there is a possibility of being elsewhere or otherwise, without denying our complicity in the law that we oppose. Such knowledge will only be answered through a different kind of turn, one that, enabled by the law, turns away from the law, resisting its lure of identity; an agency that outruns and counters the conditions of its existence."[20] Although the law, singular or multiple, may interpellate individuals, one need not view it as holding a monopoly on the constitution of subjects. Butler's notion of the "possibility of being elsewhere or otherwise" can also be understood as opacity. The opaque exceeds the law, affording conditions for recognizing one's ethical connection to others apart from institutional mediations of human existence.

If one views the contradictions and tensions with interpellative processes as both unavoidable and empirically grounded, this can direct attention to the mechanisms by which these elements hold together and potentially resolve. In his influential analysis of the Quebec sovereignty movement in the 1970s and 1980s, for example, Maurice Charland notes how pro-sovereignty documents instrumentally deployed a "constitutive rhetoric" that presumed, and thereby called into being, a subject who was supportive of the cause.[21] This was a mode of interpellation that capitalized upon the contradictions in subject positions (for example, competing national and ethnic identities) to reorient the subject and present new avenues for political action. For the purposes of interpreting critical surveillance artwork, then, we could question the extent to which artists invoke opacity by highlighting multiple modes of interpellation, destabilizing viewers, and suggesting possibilities for grasping complicity.

Philosophical conceptualizations of aesthetics complement such theories of opacity and interpellation. Jacques Rancière explains that aesthetics performs a distribution of the sensible, normalizing ideology through manipulation of the sensory realm (for instance, what one can see, hear, or say).[22] Rancière approaches aesthetics as an ordering function that enforces a restrictive "symbolic constitution of the social,"[23] thereby delimiting what thoughts and actions are conceivable at any given moment.[24] Nonetheless, Rancière expressed a belief that art movements could open up space for political change and catalyze forms of radical egalitarianism.[25] This view presents a potential contradiction because such an intervention would require not just the inclusion of excluded voices but also a shift in the aesthetic terrain, a recalibration of regimes of perceptibility and consciousness,[26] which, by Rancière's logic, would become the foundation for a new aesthetic (police) order. As with Butler's observation about the overdetermined force of the law, the elusive task of moving within and beyond such orders remains.

If ideology is reproduced through interpellation and aesthetics, then artworks could never truly function outside it, but they might nonetheless agitate from within or from the margins of the perceptible. They could trace the hegemonic operations of capital, truth, and value, or they could trouble the racial hierarchies that differentially position subjects within symbolic systems. They could unsettle conditioned ways of seeing the world or visibility imperatives of state and corporate institutions, as did the artists in the previous chapter on transparency. Whereas crisis vision reaffirms the ideological order (for example, through the imposition of racial categories or the assertion of police authority), artists, activists, and scholars can produce interventions that destabilize or refuse to accept as legitimate the grounds for that order.

Edward Snowden's 2013 revelations about the spying programs of the National Security Agency (NSA) offer an example of just such a moment of rupture to dominant visibility regimes, where suddenly the surveillance state was cast in a new light and individuals were momentarily granted space to recognize the ways that they were marked as suspicious and their data indiscriminately included in state surveillance programs. Not an artistic exercise in any obvious way, although documentaries and art projects followed,[27] the NSA revelations were certainly *aesthetic* in that they catalyzed the possibility for the redistribution of the sensible, for new forms of thought and action on the part of surveillance subjects.[28] This potential—which Clare Birchall aptly terms "the aesthetics of the secret"—was quickly neutered as the debate over state surveillance was folded into legal and technical discourses (for instance, about the meaning of "metadata" or about procedures for court-approved searches).[29] If critical art projects seek to materialize potentials for the redistribution of the sensible, then the lesson from the outcome of Snowden's revelations would be to hold resolution in abeyance for as long as possible and resist the impulse to quickly translate art projects into policy recommendations or legal demands. In other words, such artworks can achieve effects by performing opacity and maintaining a space for ethical reflection and connection with others.

"Participatory art," which is clearly part of a longer history of performance art, may offer one avenue toward achieving these goals. As summarized by art historian Claire Bishop, with participatory art, "The artist is conceived less as an individual producer of discrete objects than as a collaborator and producer of *situations*; the work of art as a finite, portable, commodifiable product is reconceived as an ongoing or long-term *project* with an unclear beginning and end; while the audience, previously conceived as a 'viewer' or 'beholder,' is now repositioned as a co-producer or *participant*."[30] By decentering both the artist and the artwork, participatory art uses firsthand experience as a mechanism for raising consciousness and altering social dynamics.[31] Some possible configurations might be performances that enlist viewers as participants or community-based projects that have explicit emancipatory goals, among other things. The focus on the transient or opaque (experiences, relations, energy) is what makes this mode of art so appropriate for the topic of surveillance, where the trope of invisible watchers with unknown purposes is fundamental to the anxiety that surveillance can produce. By using participatory art to highlight subjects' complicity with surveillance systems, artists can reveal the insidiousness of crisis vision, where unequal violence is frequently obscured by esoteric technical apparatuses. Such goals harmonize with the aspirations, if not the achievements, of participatory art, where "the desire to activate the audience in participatory art is at the same time a drive to emancipate it from a state of alienation induced by the dominant ideological order."[32]

Following these insights into participatory art, the concentration of this chapter is on critical art projects that fabricate or reveal conditions of opacity to render surveillance visible and cultivate a sense of responsibility on the part of viewers or participants. Some of the projects show the human costs of surveillance-facilitated racial violence and urge viewers to take action, others use tactics of defamiliarization to draw critical attention to everyday surveillance that has become mundane, and still others invite participation as a way of producing discomfort and reflexivity on the part of viewers. Inquiry into these art projects finds not their affordances for policy change but instead their various mechanisms for framing and enrolling subjects. They possess the potential to enact contradictions or tensions among forms of interpellation as a means of contesting the contemporary distribution of the sensible. Yet overall, the artistic frame of complicity reveals the resilience of crisis vision and its racializing modalities, which simultaneously depend upon and obscure differential interpellations of subjects.

Facing Drone Violence

As a response to civilian deaths caused by the US drone program, in 2014 an artist collective unveiled in Pakistan a project called *#NotABugSplat*.[33] This project involved the reproduction of a young girl's portrait on a massive vinyl poster measuring roughly 90 × 60 feet.[34] The girl, whose name is unknown, was an Afghan refugee who lost her parents and two siblings to a 2010 drone strike in a North Waziristan village in Pakistan. Though not legible close up, this blue-and-white pixelated image comes into focus from a distance, like a pointillist artwork, revealing a bushy-haired girl with a plaintive expression and wide eyes looking directly back at the viewer (see figure 3.1). She appears to be wearing a pale printed dress from which her hands emerge, holding an unidentifiable darker object, perhaps a piece of food, close to her chest. Because the artists could not secure access to the North Waziristan region, this print was briefly displayed in a field outside the city of Peshawar in Pakistan, some 150 miles from the site of the attack

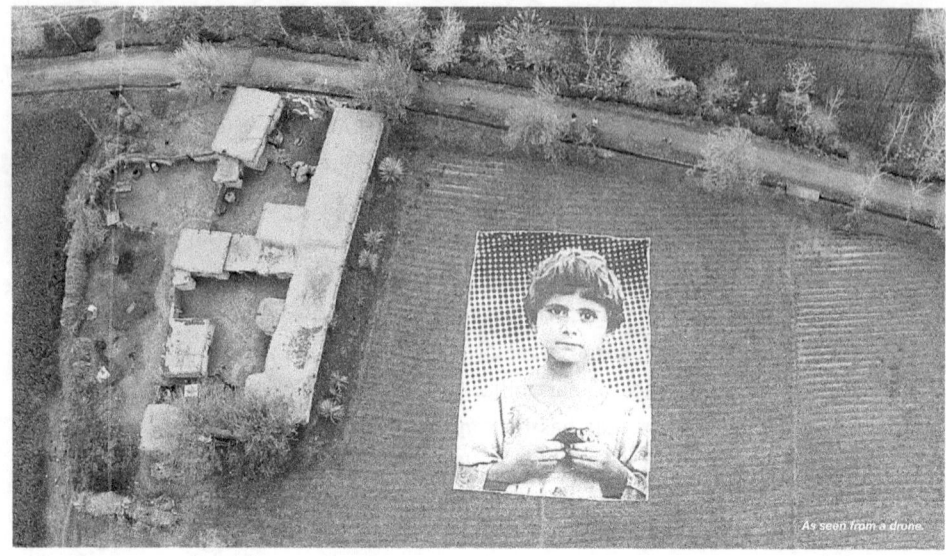

As seen from a drone.

FIGURE 3.1. *#NotABugSplat* (2014).

that killed the girl's family.[35] According to the artists, the villagers at the site of unveiling participated in the staging process and were "highly enthusiastic locals."[36]

The stated intended viewers of this artwork are drone pilots who might see the girl's face when flying their aircraft overhead. In the words of one of the artists, "We want to shame drone operators and make them realize the human cost of their actions."[37] Instead of perceiving the humans moving on the ground as akin to insects that could be crushed with little remorse, the artists want to rehumanize the people in these spaces and catalyze empathy—or even "shame"—on the part of pilots. Therefore, this project recognizes the deeply surveillant nature of drone warfare, where the monitoring and tracking of people, vehicles, and terrain constitute the bulk of the activities of drone pilots.[38] Drone operators watch to amass intelligence and direct interventions, sometimes violent ones,[39] so the artists seek to short-circuit that feedback loop.

Beyond the idealistic objectives of the artists, *#NotABugSplat* cannot extricate itself from the cultural context that motivates drone warfare in the first place. The War on Terror is sustained by masculinist tropes of rescuing helpless girls and women from fanatical religious men in backward and uncivilized places.[40] Articulations of this rescue complex, which have a long and sordid history,[41] infuse judgments of ethnic Others in Western settings too, as seen with the indignation about headscarves worn by Muslim women in countries such as France and the United States.[42] For instance, in her work on the surveillance of US Muslims, Saher Selod illustrates how gendered racialization informs cultural constructions of difference such that all Muslims can be treated as threats: "Muslim men are deemed to be a threat to national security because they have been cast as terrorists, or at the very least as having terrorist tendencies that could be 'activated' at any moment. Muslim women, particularly those who wear visible religious signifiers like the hijab, are seen as both imperiled and abused by Muslim men and in need of saving while they are simultaneously treated as a cultural aberration and threat to American core values."[43] This is a cultural context of crisis vision where racialized and gendered representations of threat animate and lend potency to interventions, including artistic interventions such as #NotABugSplat.

Thus, especially with respect to the salvation narrative, it is not incidental that the artists behind #NotABugSplat chose—or produced—an overexposed image of a young girl to stare back at pilots and represent the art project to the media and the world. Her face seems both light-complexioned and luminous, signifying innocence, purity, and vulnerability. She is integrated into existing visual economies that understand her sex, age, and simple rustic dress to connote someone in need of saving from the violence and violation of men. Her light skin color amplifies this drive, positioning her as someone close to whiteness who can be assimilated readily into a more "civilized society" and have a "promising future" if only she were granted the opportunities that she rightly deserves. Seen from this angle, it is not contradictory when the artists say, "It is only the loss of a child that can show the impact that drone strikes have on the residents of these regions."[44] The child depicted actually survived the attack that killed her family, but she suffers a social death in that she cannot be rescued from her cultural context. What #NotABugSplat adds to the standard heroic narrative is the addition of new categories of violent men that girls like this one need saving from: drone pilots, directly, and Western militaries and policy makers, indirectly. This addition reinforces more than challenges the imperial rescue complex, especially given that militaries blame civilian "collateral damage" from drones on suspected terrorists or on enemy combatants using civilians—and populated villages—as shields.[45] Therefore, the imperative to rescue innocent girls and women from abusive men remains.

Orientalism saturates the work in other ways as well. The pixelated, monochrome image stylistically references older black-and-white photographic media, thereby conjuring a sense of nostalgia for a distant, lost past. The child's image is static and fixed, arrested forever in a moment of simple innocence. The lack of modern adornment situates the girl, along with the other children in need of saving, in this innocent past, and the insertion of the image into contemporary media streams carries that sense of timelessness into the present and future.[46] Similarly, although the location used to display the image may have been selected for pragmatic reasons, there is an implied interchangeability, as if one region of Pakistan (or any neighboring country) could substitute for any other without a loss of meaning. The artists' claims about the villagers' eager participation in the project support this conclusion, as if the people at the site of the drone attack were the ones symbolically rising up against imperial powers, when in fact there have been few documented cases of drone attacks around Peshawar, where the artwork was displayed.[47] By invoking a sense of both timelessness and placelessness, #NotABugSplat reproduces some of the same Orientalizing rhetorics that were used to justify the War on Terror in the first place and to allow it to spread to countries such as Iraq. This does not mean that these rhetorics are ineffective—the attention this project has received suggests that they are quite successful—but their palatability alone should be reason for disquiet on the part of critical viewers.[48]

The artists produce a specific sort of subject through their framing mechanisms. By asserting that the goal is to make drone pilots confront the human cost of their actions, this ignores the ways in which pilots already grapple with these realities. Practically speaking, drone pilots do have close-up and sustained views of the damage they inflict, which can be profoundly visceral and psychologically disturbing for them, regardless of whom they hit.[49] Counter to mythologies that position them as generating disembodied representations for remote killing, drone systems are deeply material communication infrastructures.[50] This suggests that although the artists claim drone pilots to be the intended audience of this project, the real one is the larger public exposed to media reports of the work. Indeed, the artwork received significant press coverage (for example, CNN, Newsweek, Democracy Now!), in addition to being shared widely on social media. The larger viewing audience is compelled to watch a performance of drone pilots being assailed as culpable agents of racialized violence. In the process the art project interpellates the audience, calling it out as responsible for ending drone violence through image viewing and sharing: safe forms of political action in online spaces, in the vein of what Evgeny Morozov has termed "solutionism."[51] Of course, this does not preclude other forms of political action or activism, but as the hashtagged title for the piece illustrates, image circulation and consumption are the fundamental performative avenues offered to the audience.

Nesting in the Surveillance Landscape

Whereas repeated exposure to dedicated surveillance devices, such as public video cameras, can cause them to fade from active attention or recognition, uncanny and unexpected configurations of such devices can snap awareness back into place. This is the conceit of Czech artist Jakub Geltner's public art series titled *Nests*. For these installations, Geltner places a surfeit of video cameras and satellite dishes in unusual positions and sites, densely clustered along the walls of buildings, on rooftops, along walking paths, or even on rocky outcrops along seashores. The tactic is one of defamiliarization, or making strange, which follows from a mode of literary theory that finds the value of art in its ability to shift perception and understanding of everyday things.[52] Because Geltner's works appear in public places, their success at defamiliarizing is readily observed in the behavior of passersby who look up, point at, and take photographs of the arranged surveillance devices.

For some of his most powerful installations, Geltner places surveillance devices in natural settings and openly evokes the genre of landscape painting to situate the viewer and direct their attention. However, landscape is more than an artistic device; it functions as a medium that produces certain kinds of subjects that are granted a position of dominance over the terrain before them. As W. J. T. Mitchell eloquently explains, "Landscape as a cultural medium . . . has a double role with respect to something like ideology: it naturalizes a cultural and social construction, representing an artificial world as if it were simply given and inevitable, and it also makes that representation operational by interpellating its beholder in some more or less determinate relation to its givenness as sight and site."[53] Harmonious as the settings depicted in landscape paintings might seem, they have often been linked to racialized imperialist and capitalist projects that they both masked and made possible.[54] Landscape paintings tend to present a convenient fiction of relatively unpopulated scenes of naturalistic purity, scenes that willingly unfold for (normative white) viewers and invite them to perceive the world as a resource rightfully belonging to them.

Referencing a history of concerns about the disruptive force of "the machine in the garden,"[55] Geltner upsets these logics of landscape by placing unnatural technological artifacts in natural settings and having them look back at the viewer as if they are the rightful inhabitants who are disturbed by the viewer's presence and might turn on him at any moment. For example, the work titled *Nest 5* depicts a calm ocean view from the position of someone on the shore (see figure 3.2). Gentle waves lap at the sand, nudging a line of broken shells, rocks, and other detritus on the shoreline. The sea's clear water extends before the viewer as its colors gradually mutate to take on subtle variations in hue: browns, greens, and finally blues as the ocean meets a thin sliver of land on the left before transitioning to the cloudy sky above. Creating a stark contrast, the center of the frame is dominated by dark-brown rocks, stretching from the right, just past the shoreline. Green- and ochre-colored algae mottle some rocks, but the most conspicuous presence is what appears to be a flock of about two dozen white surveillance cameras perched on the outcrop. Situated like seagulls, the cameras in this vaguely surrealist work each look in different directions—some up, some down, some sideways, and at least one directly at the viewer. Apparently indifferent yet aware, the cameras convey uneasiness, as if they are shifting about and ready to take flight at any moment should they feel threatened.

By having cameras mimic the posture of birds, Geltner's installations create an ambiguous opacity and challenge assumptions about naturalness, perhaps destabilizing the centrality of humans as viewers and introducing doubt about humans' place of dominance in an evolutionary progression that might include machines. If landscape is a fluid "medium of exchange, a site of visual appropriation, [and] a focus for the formation of identity,"[56] then the human identities—and modes of perception—shaped by scenes like *Nest 5* are decidedly more fragile and vulnerable than those that came before. Visual appropriation may be occurring in the other direction, with the machines surveying viewers and assessing their threat or worth.

Another of Geltner's pieces, *Nest 6*, makes the predatory appraisal of the human viewer overt (see figure 3.3). Here, a tight cluster of cameras droops downward off a pole, almost like a prehistoric creature scanning the ground below for a worthwhile scrap of food. Beneath its gaze a concrete

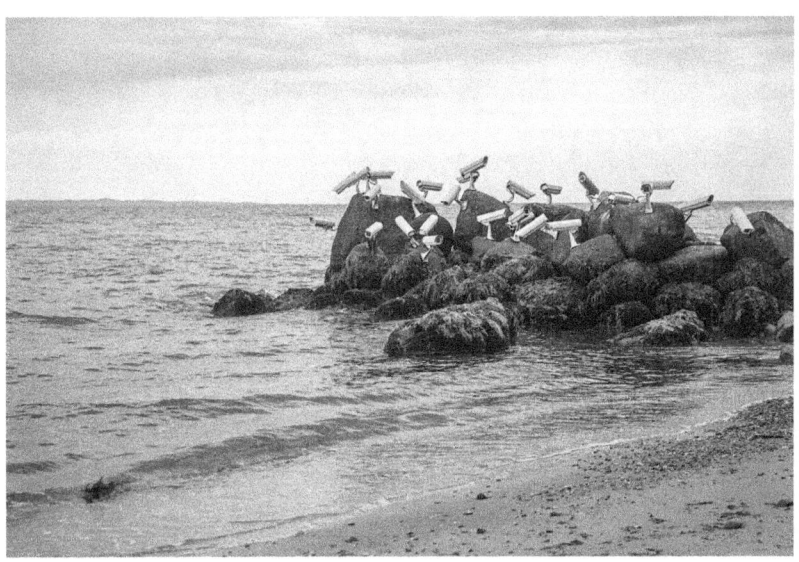

FIGURE 3.2. Jakub Geltner, *Nest 5* (2015). Courtesy of the artist.

walking path heads downward in a slight curve as it descends to the idyllic Bondi beach in Sydney, Australia. Pedestrians peer up and take photographs of the machinic animal above them, but the tableau of that mutual observation is an ominous one, seeming to reproduce a scene from a horror film. From our vantage point, the human in the frame is dangerously close to being viciously attacked and consumed. Because the cameras of the creature are fully functional and routed to an online webcam interface, this installation is participatory in multiple senses. First, those walking under its gaze cannot help but note its presence, which is designed to make them feel small, exposed, and possibly in danger. They respond by photographing the installation, looking back from a position of disadvantage both physically and figuratively: the people in the scene are dominated by the cameras looming over them and are also unable to track or regulate the circulation of images taken of them. Second, viewers of the webcam site become extensions of *Nest 6*, observing through its many eyes the people who pass beneath—who, it must be said, appear all the more defenseless in playing their expected role of tourists documenting their own exposure. Third, media stories and analyses such as this one assume the position of second- or third-order spectator, affirming the importance and persistence of audiences and spectators even within the genre of participatory art.[57]

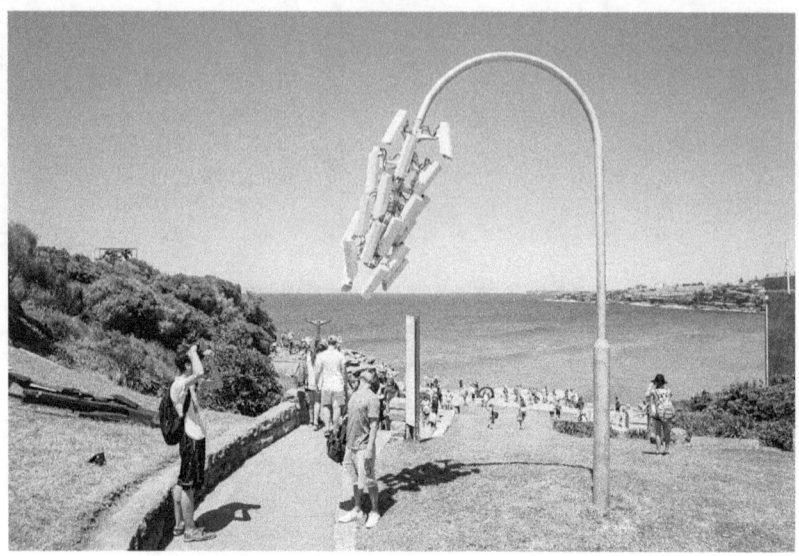

FIGURE 3.3. Jakub Geltner, *Nest 6* (2015). Courtesy of the artist.

The term *nest* cleverly symbolizes the tensions produced by these works. Nests are places of safety, shelter, and propagation. By placing surveillance devices in nest arrangements or suggesting that they possess attributes similar to (other) nesting creatures, Geltner naturalizes the potentially predatory behavior of surveillance as an expected, instinctual response to threats, such as humans who might seek to challenge the need for or appropriateness of surveillance. The hint of natural configurations for surveillance technologies defamiliarizes them for viewers, opening them up to renewed attention and inquiry. In the process, the nesting of technology and nature, machine and human, calls into question the primacy of the human, which is to say the primacy and dominance of white subjects who are relatively unacquainted with unreadable and unpredictable external threats to their being. After all, when nonhuman creatures in the landscape look back, the viewer is interpellated as a decentered subject, as one actor among many, and possibly as prey. The human viewer is marginalized and exposed, embodying a kind of vulnerability that under crisis vision is usually reserved for racialized subjects alone. Given that modes of perception develop alongside technological tools for apprehending the world,[58] the nesting arrangements highlighted—and made strange—by Geltner construct an opaque space for tracing the emergence of new ways of seeing and new subjectivities.

Troubling the Watcher Within

Most forms of technological surveillance evade scrutiny because their operations are hidden from view. This is true across the spectrum of surveillance possibilities, especially at the institutional level, ranging from national security programs to social media algorithms to workplace surveillance applications.[59] To the extent that people are aware of everyday surveillance, it is often normalized as mundane, as with frequent-shopper cards used by grocery stores, or as discrete, as with people assuming that data collected for one purpose will not be used for alternative purposes.[60] In the era of big data, especially, these are dangerous assumptions given that the emphasis is on penetrating discoveries that combinations of data may reveal, not on the initial purposes for data collection.[61]

The art installations by Belgian artist Dries Depoorter disturbingly and effectively probe the ethics of surveillance made possible through the combination of public data sources. For instance, his *Jaywalking* piece takes advantage of open video feeds from cameras at city intersections in different countries to "catch" pedestrians in the act of jaywalking across streets.[62] If pedestrians cross without the proper signal, Depoorter's algorithm will automatically flag that violation and take a screen capture, thus producing legal evidence; next, it will ask museumgoers whether they would like to report the infraction to the local police department with jurisdictional authority (see figure 3.4). Should viewers press the red button indicating their assent, the image will be emailed to the police department, which could then ostensibly cite the person guilty of the offense.

Although it is unlikely that images sent to police from this art installation will result in fines for the identified jaywalkers, this participatory art project reveals the promiscuous logics of data systems and interpellates subjects as complicit actors in those systems. The innocuous-looking camera on the street corner can easily be integrated within larger systems of control, perhaps—as shown here—completely unbeknownst to the people being watched or the very owner of the camera in question. If an artist could capitalize on such technological affordances, then so too could those with institutional authority or others with malicious intent. In this case the point is not simply that technological systems can be combined or data

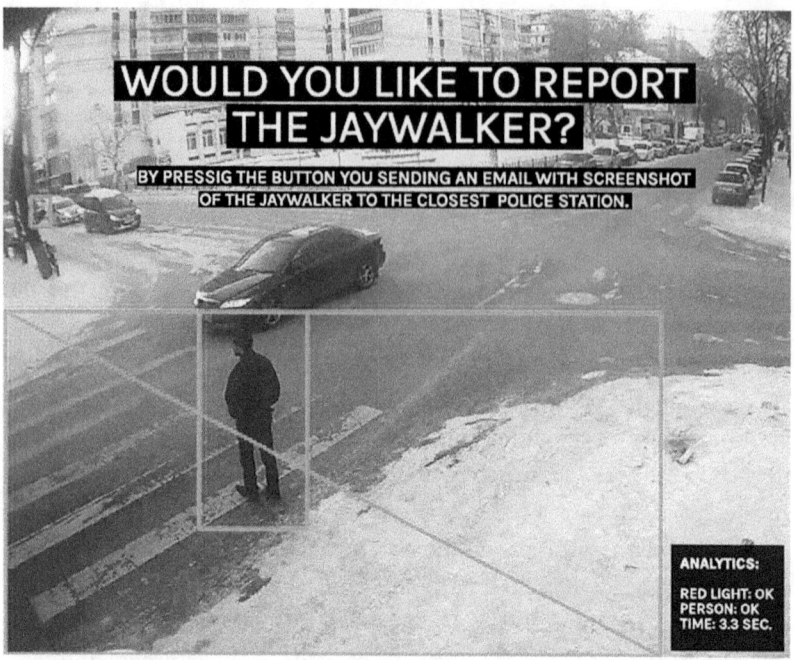

WOULD YOU LIKE TO REPORT
THE JAYWALKER?

BY PRESSIG THE BUTTON YOU SENDING AN EMAIL WITH SCREENSHOT
OF THE JAYWALKER TO THE CLOSEST POLICE STATION.

ANALYTICS:

RED LIGHT: OK
PERSON: OK
TIME: 3.3 SEC.

FIGURE 3.4. Dries Depoorter, *Jaywalking* (2015). Courtesy of the artist.

exchanged without checks, but rather that such systems and data can be appropriated by others and made to serve radically different institutional agendas than their originally intended ones. This is not a deviation; it is the driving logic. Technological protocols and contemporary economies facilitate and reward such data flows.[63]

Depoorter's *Jaywalking* piece also constructs viewers as subjects who are responsible for the outcome of the interaction and charges them to reflect on their ethical roles in the systems presented. Once a jaywalking match is found, the system hails viewers in this way: "Would you like to report the jaywalker? By pressig [sic] the button you [will be] sending an email with [a] screenshot of the jaywalker to the closest police station."[64] The decision rests with the person being hailed whether to act as a geographically removed "sheriff" to police the actions of others or to let them off the hook.[65] Regardless of the decision, the person is interpellated into an opaque ethical terrain where the role of passive viewer is foreclosed: one must decide to press the button or refrain from doing so. One must recognize that they are an agent. Thus, in generating discomfort for viewers by design, the artwork hints at the collective responsibility that people bear for the effects of the largely invisible surveillance systems permeating contemporary life. More subtly, this piece illustrates how abstract technological systems categorize people in nonnegotiable yet significant ways. For instance, the pedestrian crossing the street becomes a "jaywalker" only once the system algorithmically classifies him as such. The system interpellates the pedestrian as a lawbreaking subject even if the hail is silent and the person unaware, or aware only after the fact.[66]

Beyond art projects, public participation with actual disciplinary surveillance systems is not that far-fetched. Indeed, there have been a few well-publicized efforts to outsource to members of the public the labor-intensive monitoring of live video feeds. For instance, the state of Texas briefly ran the Virtual Border Watch program, which allowed anyone with access to a computer and an internet connection to monitor cameras along the US-Mexico border and report suspicious sightings to law enforcement.[67] In another context, community members of council estates in Shoreditch, London, were given access to closed-circuit television (CCTV) feeds from cameras in the neighborhood so that they could inform the police of any suspicious behavior they witnessed.[68] Rather than being a new idea, this is a recurring motif, dating back at least to similar failed experiments with piping closed-circuit video feeds into New York City public housing apartments in the mid-1970s.[69] Beyond the official rationales for these programs, it is easy to imagine that they cultivated fear and prejudice on the part of viewers.[70]

Depoorter's *Jaywalking* piece also brings to mind Philip Zimbardo's Stanford Prison Experiment in 1971 and artist Artur Żmijewski's re-creation of that experiment in his film *Repetition* in 2005.[71] In these cases, human subjects were called upon to intervene in the lives of others, as guards, or to subjugate themselves as the recipients of that intervention, as prisoners. Harassment, punishment, and deprival marked these relations, leading to trauma for the participants and criticisms of the researcher and the artist for their projects' ethical shortcomings.[72] Far from being exceptional, these staged events could be read instead as variations on a recurring diagram of power, where abusive behavior flourishes in spaces removed from clear protocols, authority structures, or public oversight. However, another complementary reading is that cues for behavior infuse these spaces, emanating both from architectures of incarceration and from spoken and unspoken direction from those staging the scenes. Thus, recent criticisms of the Stanford Prison Experiment call attention to the many methodological flaws of the study, including the fact that "precise instructions" were given to the guards about how to treat inmates at the containment site.[73] Similarly, Anthony Downey relates how for Żmijewski's *Repetition*, the artist interjected "forcibly, like a producer impatient for conflict to arise, in order to speed up the action or create circumstances where discord [would] thrive" while at the same time a surveillance-laden prison architecture upheld "carceral systems of abuse."[74]

In his writing on Zimbardo's and Żmijewski's work, Harding identifies similar problematics at play in the infamous War on Terror prison sites of Abu Ghraib and Guantánamo Bay. He argues that in these cases, it is likewise insufficient and probably inaccurate to simply conclude that the sites generated ethical vacuums where innate sadism asserted itself; rather, such sites are governed by "an unwritten but hardly ambiguous script" for behavior, and the actors within those spaces perform as expected: dehumanizing and abusing others while insulating authorities from accountability. In my terms, the soldiers in these spaces draw upon crisis vision to reassert white supremacy through the feminized and racialized debasement of nonwhite others. "While we need to ask how such arrangements might be avoided in the future," Harding continues, "they are hardly an anomaly, and it behooves us to ask now how they are woven into the very fabric of surveillance more generally."[75]

That said, there are fundamental differences between Depoorter's system and these other works, and these differences all center on the ethical relations made possible through opacity. First, with the *Jaywalking* installation, the actions of participants are semipublic, occurring in a space where others can observe and question one's actions. The situation of recursive watching—where others watch you watching others—could engender feelings of responsibility and conversations about choices made. In this way the piece invokes the seldom-referenced "public" criterion of Bentham's panopticon, where prison structures, guards, and inmates are subject to external observation from members of the public, who gain edification from that exposure while also deterring mistreatment of prisoners.[76]

Second, with Depoorter's work, viewers are encouraged to imagine the roles reversed, such that they were the ones being reported by unseen and unknown others. Viewers are implicitly asked to see themselves in the other and act accordingly. Thus, the *Jaywalking* piece has the capacity to produce empathy and compassion, or possibly compunction if one does press the button to report the stranger. It does this by setting the conditions for opacity, inviting self-reflexivity and an expanded notion of who is included in one's social sphere.

If *Jaywalking* is seen as an intervention, then Depoorter crafted a performative piece that generates discomfort in the service of ethical reflection. The participants are confronted with a decision they must make and will likely experience a lingering sense of doubt about whether the decision had consequences beyond their brief moment of interaction. The unavoidability of the choice positions viewers as agents in relationship with people they do not know and who are oblivious to the calculations that are being made about them. Though not explicitly stated, this relationship is structurally similar to the one being made by countless other systems and viewers, where decisions based on partial data and reductive criteria have profound consequences for life chances (for example, who gets a loan, who is granted asylum, who gets a job, who is targeted by the police). Just as those enrolled in Depoorter's system may be haunted by their actions or inactions, his work suggests that viewers should question both their complicity in and the justness of other surveillance systems.

Conclusion

The artistic frame of complicity introduces compelling possibilities for rethinking the relationships of people to larger systems of control. The objective of this chapter was to explore the ways in which some of these works draw upon opacity, illegibility, and participatory techniques to foster self-reflexivity and a sense of responsibility. By juxtaposing multiple, competing forms of interpellation, these artworks provide a different, if necessarily partial, perspective on the aesthetic orders that are coproduced by technological systems and institutional practices. They call into question the hidden logics of surveillance systems, which reduce people to decontextualized data elements to facilitate manipulation or, in the case of drone-based surveillance, elimination. By revealing some of these rationalities and pushing people to question their places within the systems, these art projects create a space for ideological critique.

If the goals are to challenge viewers and generate critical insights about surveillance, then the projects that nurture ambiguity seem best equipped to achieve these goals. For instance, the works by Jakub Geltner and Dries

Depoorter each fashion ambiguous situations that engender discomfort, reflection, and participation on the part of viewers. With Geltner's *Nests* installations, viewers must make sense of atypical arrangements and locations of video cameras that do not fit within standard explanatory models. Viewers appear to find the pieces oddly illegible and are kept ignorant about whether the cameras are real, if the footage is being watched, what the messages of the works might be, or perhaps even if the camera configurations are an artwork. With Depoorter's *Jaywalking* piece, viewers are forced to make a decision that might affect someone else's life, someone whom they see but who is completely unaware of them. The ambiguity rests in whether the action of pushing the red button will or will not generate a chain reaction for which the participant would be responsible. By contrast, *#NotABugSplat* is much more explicit with its messaging, which makes it easier for viewers to process, even if the content is more disturbing.

Another theme pertains to the decentering of subjects. In the spirit of participatory art, each of the pieces reviewed here enrolls viewers as participants who are part of larger networks that extend beyond the locally sited artwork and that exceed absolute comprehension. The artworks interpellate viewers into their surveillance schema, where roles are assigned and difficult to contest. Put differently, the works reproduce some of the protocols of mainstream surveillance systems but in a way that instills both awareness and discomfort. *#NotABugSplat* temporarily decenters the viewer by directing attention to the violent viewing practices of drone pilots; however, it quickly recuperates the viewer as an agent responsible for bringing about change or pressuring others to do so. This work is clearly effective at bringing renewed attention to drone violence, but unlike the pieces by Geltner or Depoorter, it mobilizes transparency rather than opacity: it relies on a stable construction of the normative liberal subject who is called upon to act based on the straightforward information relayed by the artists. Geltner takes a different tack by underscoring the agency and naturalistic community of surveillance apparatuses that might take an interest in humans but are certainly not controlled by them. With Depoorter's work, dissonance adds to this dynamic by lending the impression that viewers are in control of a particular instance of surveillance while also profoundly powerless within the larger matrix of surveillance systems that govern their lives.

These works connect to crisis vision in oblique yet revealing ways. They take as their object of scrutiny existing systems that were implemented to handle various crises of control—namely, systems designed to monitor populations for signs of deviance or threat and to intervene invisibly in the lives of those observed. The works call out collective complicity in surveillance apparatuses even if viewers are unaware, and perhaps even more so if they are unaware. One does not have to actively clamor for surveillance, exclusion, and punishment of bodies seen as threatening in order to be a part of a system that performs just those functions and establishes those violent relations. Individuals are interpellated into crisis vision as a dominant logic, even if they reject or are antagonistic to it. That said, surveillance systems perform a differential interpellation of subjects, meaning that determinations of crises are always infused with racialized and gendered judgment and that subjects are marked by those determinations. Finding ways to move beyond those social formations is crucial, so perception of one's own positionality within them offers a provocative starting point.

By fostering ambiguity and decentering the viewing subject, critical surveillance art can capitalize on the anxiety of viewers to motivate questions that might lead to greater awareness of surveillance systems, protocols, and power dynamics. Works that use participation to make viewers uncomfortable can guide moments of self-reflexivity about one's relationship—and obligation—to others within surveillance networks. The task seems to be to find ways of extending states of dis-ease beyond momentary encounters with artworks or installations, thereby setting the stage for the emergence of a new aesthetic landscape that harnesses the ethical possibilities of opacity.

4. Violence

Violence can never be understood solely in terms of its physicality—force, assault, or the infliction of pain—alone. Violence also includes assaults on the personhood, dignity, sense of worth or value of the victim. The social and cultural dimensions of violence are what gives violence its power and meaning.—NANCY SCHEPER-HUGHES AND PHILIPPE BOURGOIS, *Violence in War and Peace*

Visibility and violence are intimately connected, the former often acting as a condition for the latter. Those who are seen, who are present, who are deemed out of place or challenging authority frequently find themselves on the receiving end of aggressive corrections, whether on interpersonal or institutional levels. But violence, as Nancy Scheper-Hughes and Philippe Bourgois remind us, extends well beyond overt physical assault: it also propagates through economic and institutional mechanisms (structural violence) and seeps into the formation of subjectivities such that victims come to misrecognize their vulnerability as a *personal* failing or fault (symbolic violence).[1] Regimes of visibility provide the grammar, the unspoken rules and logics, of structural and symbolic violence. They enable the positioning of individuals within crisis-vision classificatory systems such that their abjection—or affluence—can be justified and managed through bureaucratic surveillance operations.[2] At the same time, visibility allows subjects to scrutinize and position themselves within social systems, reproducing tenacious cultural mythologies about warranted exclusion or inclusion, deficiency or entitlement.[3]

Critical surveillance art has also endeavored to visibilize and contest structural and symbolic violence in society. The strength of violence as an artistic frame is in revealing the objectifying and exploitative dimensions of crisis vision. Whether the focus is on the plight of refugees, prostitutes, precarious workers, or arrestees, most of these political art projects strive to uncover what is hidden from view, to shock privileged audiences into recognition of everyday abjection and the systems that support it. They seek to interrupt crisis vision by either humanizing targets of violence or pushing depictions of their dehumanization to the extreme. In the process, this frame facilitates critiques of media spectacle and bureaucratic surveillance, particularly those genres and systems that reproduce violent conditions and limit human agency, even when they are sometimes attempting the exact opposite.

However, a risk associated with this artistic frame is dehumanization itself, whether by objectifying abject bodies in the service of art, reproducing their nonrepresentation, or prioritizing universalist frameworks (such as human rights) that strip away difference or context in the service of progressive change. Dehumanization runs counter to opacity, forestalling its emergence within most of these works. Additionally, when artists or others adopt evidentiary techniques to document conditions of violence, as some of the projects do, this practice may reify discourses of realism and objectivity, which are the same discourses that animate racialized forms of institutional surveillance more broadly.

Adrift

Persistent refugee crises throughout the world epitomize structural violence. Whether fleeing ethnic genocide, political oppression, economic insecurity, or the effects of climate collapse, the circumstances of refugees are cruelly precarious. Refugees also frequently encounter dehumanizing treatment while they are in transit or when they arrive in host countries.[4] With vicious mobilizations of crisis vision, they are often portrayed as criminals or terrorists, thrust into detention centers, separated from their family members, or deported, becoming human jetsam on global currents.[5] If not ejected, refugees can face augmented surveillance in the form of compulsory biometric identification and data tracking or even remote electronic monitoring through ankle devices that pinpoint their whereabouts for law enforcement.[6] When refugees are forbidden to work in host countries, this expands their insecurity and dependency;[7] if they are permitted to work, however, this fuels tensions with resentful citizens who see them as unfairly taking scarce jobs and resources.[8] These are some of

the many ways that crisis vision engenders racialized forms of interpellation to scapegoat and demonize the abject, typically in the service of white
supremacy.

Clearly, the predicament of such outcasts, of people driven to relinquish
one home without legal claim to another, is both dire and upsetting. The
magnitude of refugee crises also defies comprehension, with approximately
25 million refugees worldwide and an additional 40 million people who are
forcibly displaced within their countries.[9] Although most people in Western countries may be vaguely aware of the problem, in large part because
of media attention to drowning deaths in the Mediterranean Sea or genocide in countries such as Myanmar, the crisis continually fades from view
as it becomes normalized and media outlets turn to other stories. Media
can inure publics to violence either through continual representational
presence or absence. Allen Feldman observes that "the quantitative and
qualitative dissemination of objectivity *increases* the social capacity to inflict pain upon the Other . . . [and] to render the Other's pain inadmissible
to public discourse and culture."[10] Relative invisibility perpetuates structural violence by obscuring the causes and conditions of global economic
inequality and persecution.[11] Therefore, artists dedicated to social justice
strive to find ways to force visibility of structural violence and cultivate
collective consciousness of it, agitating for what T. J. Demos calls an "aesthetics of migration" that reimagines citizenship as constituted by bodily
displacement.[12]

One such work, Marco Poloni's photography installation (and book)
Displacement Island, presents an austere photographic exploration of the
traces left by refugees and tourists on the idyllic Pelagian island Lampedusa.[13] This Mediterranean island, which is Italy's southernmost point,
is a mere seventy miles from Tunisia, making it a target destination for
North African migrants.[14] Because of the island's crystal-clear blue waters
and stunning beaches, it also lures tourists as a popular vacation spot.
Poloni's photographs play upon representations of presence and absence
as they suggest tense connections between these two groups. There are
discarded cigarette boxes with Arabic script, orange life vests being over-
taken by sand, nighttime photographs of the island's immigrant detention
center next to the airport, underwater images of snorkeling white tourists
suspended in motionless poses within encompassing blue frames, and aerial shots of fishing boats and pleasure craft dotting shallow blue waters,
with their smudged shadows following leisurely on the ocean floor below.

Throughout the work, Poloni also scatters images that play upon tropes of the region (the archer Odysseus), make unexpected allusions (orbiting space satellites or astronauts awaiting pickup as they float in the ocean), or reference racist narratives of invading migrants (black-and-white negatives of encroaching insects).

Rather than stage simple juxtapositions—of destitute refugees and affluent tourists—that could lead to facile interpretations of this work as being pedantically moralizing or judgmental, Poloni's presentation of symbolic excess pushes the piece into a wider and more personal context. He suggests that the romance of the region derives from its location at a crossroads, that narratives of invasion infuse both heroic and racist myths, that geopolitical instability and inequality drive migration, that planetary-scale awareness (for example, via satellites) makes claims of ignorance untenable, and that personal biographies intersect with these elements, for we learn that many of *Displacement Island*'s images come from Poloni's family album, presumably from time spent vacationing on Lampedusa.[15] The artwork operates not through juxtaposition, then, but through *constellation*. As Tom Holert explains in his discussion of this piece, "A constellation, in this sense, obeys a strategy of de-densification. Meaning and knowledge are no longer concentrated, in all their complexity, within a single, allegorical image, but unfolded: the condensed visual information is spatially dispersed."[16] The abundant use of white space between images attests to this orientation, where patterns and links are established but causality remains elusive (see figure 4.1). The meaning of the work comes from situating bodies within those distinct elements, the photographs, such that partial perspectives emerge and might be shared.

By consciously electing not to include images of refugees, Poloni eschews visual economies of surveillance wherein such images could contribute to the objectification of people in need.[17] Instead, *Displacement Island* speaks in the register of technoscientific evidence. As with police crime dramas, images of evidence are affixed to a white wall, but the relative importance, validity, and connections between them have yet to be ascertained.[18] The implied victims and the crimes must be read through these traces, but rather than seeking offenders per se, this work evokes humanity and pathos. The forlorn discards of transient migrants connote personal loss and perhaps death. Although representations of tourists and tourism generate dissonance within this constellation, as might be anticipated, the detention facilities hint at something worse: not the willfully

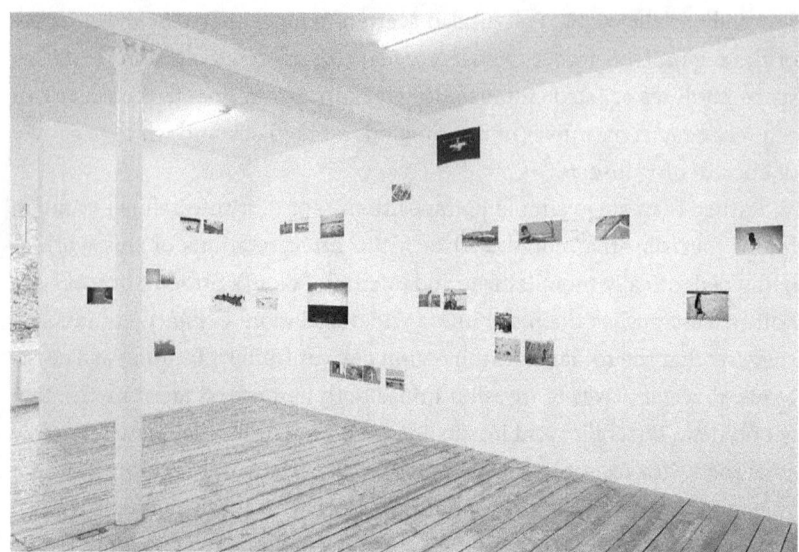

FIGURE 4.1. Marco Poloni, *Displacement Island* (installation view, 2016). Copyright Marco Poloni and Galerie Campagne Première Berlin. Photograph: Henning Moser.

ignorant revelry of the affluent but instead the cold intolerance of state policies and practices of detention and deportation. As Poloni recounts, while he was making this work, the island's only detention facility was located next to the airport, but an emergency decree in 2009 changed that by criminalizing undocumented outsiders, facilitating their rapid expulsion when found and prompting the erection of two new detention facilities in military zones—adjacent to a NATO base—on the island.[19] The state masks its actions on this island paradise while, in the process, erasing ready-made juxtapositions of tourist entry points and refugee holding zones. The reference to preexisting military territory on Lampedusa undercuts narratives of island purity, drawing attention to the fact that militarization has long safeguarded conditions of national and ethnic privilege in this region and beyond.

Hanne Nielsen and Birgit Johnsen's video art project *Drifting* tackles the European refugee crisis from a different direction. This multiscreen installation centers on a solitary figure floating aboard a crude raft in an empty expanse of sea. Taking its inspiration from a true story of a castaway found by a Norwegian gas tanker in the Skagerrak Strait near Norway in 2006,[20] this project mixes genre and narrative conventions, weaving together documentary footage with fictional reenactment while using multiple screens to layer different perspectives out of temporal sequence. The nonlinearity of the piece simulates the jumble and confusion introduced by the actual man, who initially failed to cooperate with Swedish authorities who questioned him, not disclosing his name, nationality, or the circumstances that brought him to his precarious position.[21] Thus, the figure reveals the centrality yet instability of legal systems dependent upon legible, unambiguous national identities. Without knowing who he was, it was unclear how to process him or where to send him; likewise, without knowing whether a crime was committed and where, state agents could not ascertain how to investigate or whom to prosecute. Although the man was eventually identified as a homeless Londoner who was tossed overboard from a British ship,[22] as a metaphor he underscores the profound importance of proving belonging or worthiness in a globalized world that is still defined by hardened national borders, especially for the most destitute.

Nielsen and Johnsen's artwork taps into pervasive cultural mythologies of the lone hero struggling against a hostile world. Whether through wide shots that show an actor at the mercy of the sea, all alone on a makeshift raft under an ominous sky (see figure 4.2), or through extreme close-ups of his ruggedly handsome face and intense eyes scanning the horizon (see figure 4.3), the piece conjures the romance of the individual apart from society, where masculine triumph can be found even in death. The prevalence of

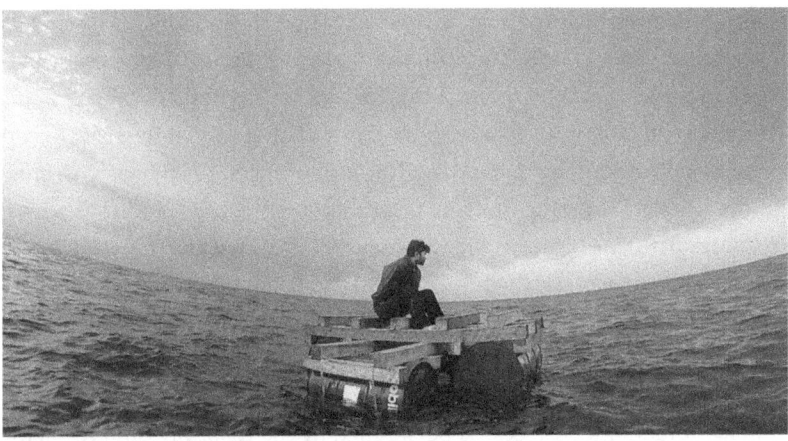

FIGURE 4.2. Hanne Nielsen and Birgit Johnsen, *Drifting* (2014). Courtesy of the artists.

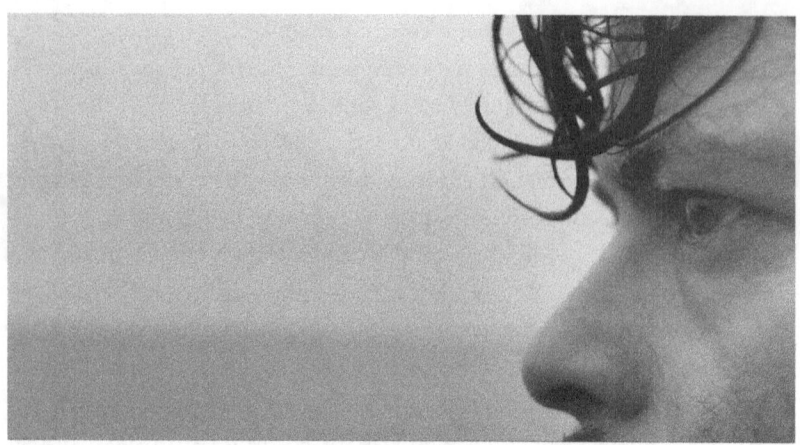

FIGURE 4.3. Hanne Nielsen and Birgit Johnsen, *Drifting* (2014). Courtesy of the artists.

such narratives in contemporary film and fiction makes them easily recognizable in works like *Drifting*. Once the drifting man is rescued, the piece folds into police crime genres, where state investigators struggle within bureaucracies to uncover the man's identity and the crimes perpetrated. Here, too, the outcast maintains heroic individualism by remaining enigmatic, by resisting interpellation into state systems that would delimit his potential: the potential of being anyone at all or no one.

Thus, whereas *Drifting* is a political work that problematizes the refugee crisis in Europe,[23] it does so by reproducing tropes of heroic, masculine individualism. Somewhat obliquely, the work invokes the story of mid-twentieth-century Norwegian adventurer Thor Heyerdahl, who, as Scott Magelssen recounts, sailed a primitive raft from Peru to Polynesia in an effort to prove that "the original inhabitants of Polynesia had been light-skinned, with blond, wavy hair, so similar to that of the Vikings they could be related to those most commanding of voyagers."[24] Likewise, *Drifting* proffers a form of daring individualism that is necessarily coded as white, in contradistinction to racialized portrayals of refugees. The strength of *Drifting*'s framing is that the refugee crisis can be distilled and inserted into a compelling story line, encouraging reflection on the overwhelming existential trauma of floating helplessly at sea. Instead of representations of dis-individuated masses clinging to rafts or crowded in detention facilities, *Drifting* humanizes refugees, as personified by the castaway (and the actor playing him), even if that person was not, in fact, a refugee. However, the limitations of this framing are a loss of scale and complexity, including the complexity of intersectional violence and inequality. By casting a light-complexioned man in the role of the protagonist, Nielsen and Johnsen may more easily engender empathy from white European audiences (the piece was exhibited at Sørlandets Kunstmuseum in Norway), but in the process they recenter whiteness. Moreover, they elide issues of routine sexual violence against women and children refugees and racism, where the backlash against refugees, more generally, is tied to manifestations of intolerance in host countries.[25]

Both *Displacement Island* and *Drifting* address the structural violence underlying the refugee crisis by personalizing it, whether through family vacation photographs or through depictions of a solitary figure with a hidden story. If, following Raymond Williams's observation that "the masses are always the others, whom we don't know, and can't know. . . . There are in fact no masses; there are only ways of seeing people as masses,"[26] these artworks resist the impulse to reify "the masses" as a category. In the process they attempt to humanize those who are most vulnerable, to render them familiar and proximate, not as strange, unknowable others to be pitied or ignored. The most powerful contribution of these artworks may be that they provide glimpses into the bureaucratic apparatuses charged with managing refugees, thereby directing attention to the often-concealed violence of processing and containment, of assessing the merits of one's claims based on biography while also treating people as part of a dehumanized group. *Displacement Island* and *Drifting* call out state (in)visibility regimes as complicit in the larger systems—or constellations—of structural violence.[27]

Recognizing that political art projects cannot do everything, it is important nonetheless to flag that the choices made by these artists limit their ability to confront human tragedy and state complicity under crisis vision. Representations of devastation, death, and loss are strangely absent in Poloni's photographic traces and Nielsen and Johnsen's mysterious castaway. Likewise, the former colonial projects of Italy (in North and East Africa) and Scandinavian nations (in West Africa) intertwine those states with the plight of populations facing displacement today, yet the bounded nature of these artworks makes those connections difficult to perceive. Ultimately, both pieces operate from a place of privilege, of creators and audiences processing the fact of the refugee crisis and what it means for them and their countries. Filtering the crisis through personal experience or heroic scenes may make it more palatable, but perhaps at the expense of those truly adrift, whose humanity is momentarily sketched but then erased once more when the artist and viewer reclaim the center, the position of visual dominance.

Working (on) Bodies

Art critics have noted a shift in creative emphasis over the past few decades away from tangible artifacts and toward performative contexts, the likes of which could be generated through collaboration with others.[28] In response to the erosion of social safety nets precipitated by the neoliberal economic policies of the 1990s and beyond, particularly but not exclusively in Western countries, many politically engaged artists have sought to critique the larger conditions of structural violence and find ways to enroll those individuals most marginalized and disadvantaged by such conditions.[29] For example, Santiago Sierra staged performances in which day laborers or refugees sat within boxes in a museum space for hours at a time,[30] Artur Żmijewski re-tattooed identification numbers onto the arms of Nazi concentration camp survivors,[31] and Francis Alÿs mobilized hundreds of volunteers to shovel a sand dune in Peru, moving its geographical location by several inches.[32]

Despite the social justice commitments of the artists conceptualizing such performances, critics have challenged the apparently exploitative and unethical arrangements and their potential to catalyze change. As Nina Möntmann writes, "The questionability of works in which social evils are not discussed but demonstrated, using living subjects treated as objects, is further heightened when most of the participants take part only because of their own deprivation, solely for the (small) fee being offered. Their own motivations and experiences play no role whatsoever; the participants merely perform, either actively or passively, in order to give an art audience the crassest possible sense of its own moral dilemmas by means of a form of shock treatment and the breaking of taboos."[33] Certainly, there might be possibilities for more empowering alternatives that foster opacity in the form of ethical connection and are directed by communities, such as projects enrolling nonartists in the creative design of public parks or children's centers.[34] These alternative works, to use Anthony Downey's term, seek an *ethics of engagement* that moves beyond provocation to reinscribe "the aesthetic as a form of sociopolitical praxis."[35] Setting these possibilities aside, critical surveillance art also brings to the fore questions about the relationship between visibility and violence in participatory art projects, between their fabrication of surveillance-infused contexts and larger systems of social inequality. What then are the implications of artists appropriating elements of crisis vision in the service of critique?

As with many of his other works, Santiago Sierra's *160 cm Line Tattooed on Four People* produces a situation intended to distress viewers (see figure 4.4). In this performance piece, which was staged and recorded for spectators, he located four heroin-addicted female prostitutes in Spain and offered them the price of a shot of heroin (roughly $67) to have a horizontal line tattooed across their backs.[36] The light-skinned women, who sit straddling wooden chairs and facing a white wall, strip off their shirts and lean forward to expose their bare backs. Two men in black coats extend a tape measure across their backs as another woman, the tattoo artist, marks the locations for the permanent line. Then the process commences. A couple of the women laugh and crane their necks to watch as their companions are tattooed, occasionally looking back at observers or the videographer, chatting animatedly with each other as if giddy about the absurdity of their situation. The woman who is last in line, conversely, appears to grimace as she surveys the tattooed mark on the person next to her, as if fearful of what will soon befall her. At the conclusion, the tattooist tapes white gauze to the women's backs before they pull their shirts on and get up to leave.[37]

This performance uses women's bodies as canvases to call attention to larger systems of structural violence. When receiving blowback for his mistreatment of people for his art, Sierra deflected by emphasizing the true target of his critique: "The tattoo is not the problem. The problem is the existence of social conditions that allow me to make this work. You could make this tattooed line a kilometer long, using thousands and thousands of willing people."[38] Yet the presence of social conditions that allow for artistic violence do not require it, any more than social inequalities more broadly compel the relatively well-off to demean and abuse the needy. The conceptual slippage apparently occurs in the translation of structural violence to directed bodily scarring, from using bodies as a means to an end while denying responsibility for violence perpetrated in the name of politically engaged art. In short, Sierra abdicates blame for precisely what makes this work so shocking: its intentional exploitation and permanent marking of others who willingly consent to be props for the artist. Instead, Sierra strives to implicate viewers, particularly "high-class" museumgoers

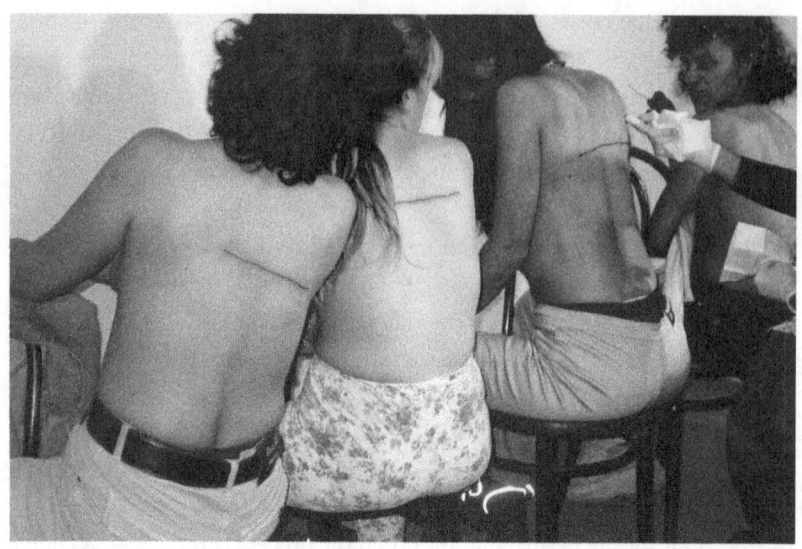

FIGURE 4.4. Santiago Sierra, *160 cm Line Tattooed on Four People* (2000). Courtesy of the artist.

who are enrolled in the performance by nature of being present and seeing an uncomfortable "portrait of themselves" as agents of dehumanization.[39]

Visibility is key to these dynamics. The prostitutes were both legible as such and accessible to the artist: "What I did was to find the womens [*sic*] in the, in the places where they offered their body and to ask her for the piece [the artwork]," Sierra relates, "They accepted. . . . It was not difficult." Through tattooed marks, one can watch the performance unfold and track its progress; moreover, the tattoos serve as lingering symbols of a shared experience that aims to scar—literally or figuratively—everyone involved. Videos and photographs document such violence and make it fluid, such that it continues to circulate across mediascapes and register upon other viewers, other bodies. Finally, the performance casts everyone as complicit witnesses, from the women watching one another, the tattooist watching them, the audiences watching the scene and one another, and the artist watching them all. It is telling that even as he directs the performance, Sierra maintains a space of privileged *invisibility* for himself within this assemblage of viewers, choosing not to reveal his face in interviews, for example, to ostensibly avoid fueling a cult of personality.[40] (Of course, one could posit that Sierra's calculated shyness has the opposite effect—it generates further mystery and allure about him as an auteur, even while blunting criticisms of his egocentrism.) Through this entire scene the visual lure of tattooed bodies obscures the structural and symbolic violence that would allow these women to respond to Sierra's subjectifying hail and see themselves as resources for art. They are victims of external forces, the unequal social conditions identified by the artist, and of internal ones that facilitate their cooperation.[41]

Many other art projects mobilize similar forms of "delegated performance,"[42] where artists hire nonprofessionals to engage in activities that produce situations, often in the service of social critique. For instance, for his piece *They Shoot Horses 2004*,[43] video artist Phil Collins recruited and paid nine teenagers from Ramallah in Palestine to dance to pop music for eight consecutive hours.[44] He divided the teens into two groups and filmed each group constantly as they performed with enthusiasm to many of the Western songs but eventually succumbed to fatigue, some of them sitting with backs against the pink background wall, leaning into each other, or resting their heads in each other's laps (see figure 4.5). The two video feeds were synchronized and displayed on adjacent museum walls at the Tate Museum in London, the Museum of Contemporary Art in Toronto, and elsewhere.

Collins's tactic is one of familiarization, where he seeks to illustrate the humanity and recognizable similarity of youths in Palestine to those in other parts of the world. By refusing simple narratives of Palestinian youths as either victims of crushing oppression or potential terrorists, Collins seeks to reorient the assumptions and focus of Western outsiders. He explains: "My question there is why is this [occupation and devastation] allowed to happen? People penned into what are effectively bantustans [racially separate areas], dying in ambulances waiting to cross checkpoints. Why, every day, when people die, in the large part children and teenagers, is there such a negligible public response? In the British press there exist entire seasons devoted to the subject of one death or a kidnap or a disappearance, reported salaciously as if they were picking over the bones."[45] Thus, Collins is not only challenging the fusion of crisis vision with cultural prejudice, which is something that allows one to see some lives as less worthy than others; he is also highlighting the violence done—and made possible—by media practices that augment the value of the local and singular over the distant and multiple. Likewise, his appropriation of reality television formats in this and other works is an attempt to unveil the

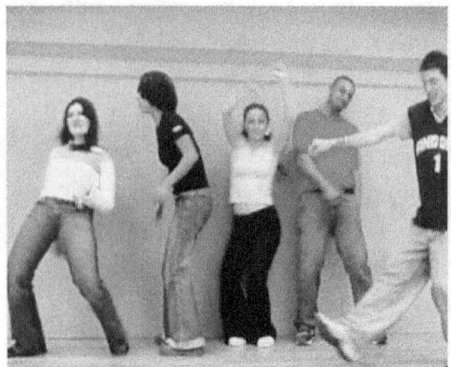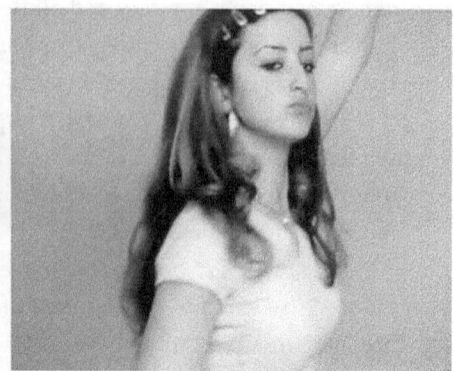
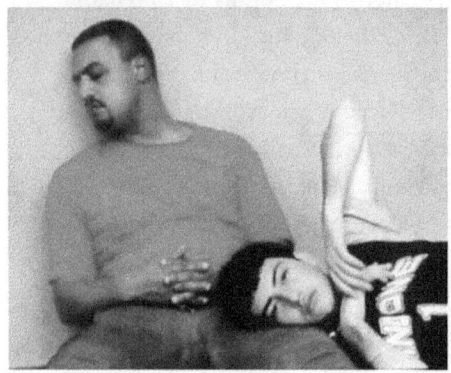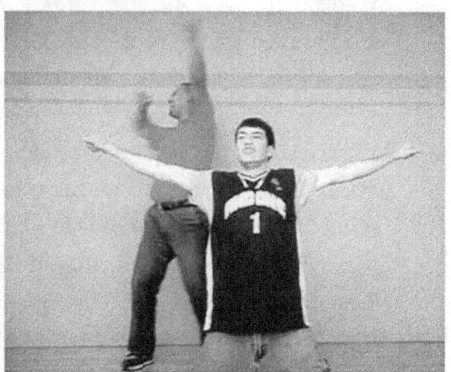

FIGURE 4.5. Phil Collins, *They Shoot Horses 2004* (2004). © Phil Collins, courtesy Kerlin Gallery, Dublin. Digital photograph: Photo © Tate.

destructive politics of popular media genres, which distract viewers from social problems, and reroute them for social justice ends.

Collins is clearly not exploiting his subjects to the same degree as Sierra, or producing obvious lasting effects, yet he is nonetheless compelling them to do what they otherwise would not, whether because of payment or the appeal of participating in an art project. In a time that predated widespread adoption of social media, these teenagers exposed themselves in potentially embarrassing or vulnerable ways to strangers throughout the world. The artist commodified their expressions of personal identity, their movement, dance, and gesture, converting them into labor that could be materialized and circulated to other markets, generating symbolic and financial value for him and art institutions along the way. However, what complicates this appraisal is the relative degree of freedom these youths have compared to the prostitutes in Sierra's work. They may be similarly enrolled in remunerative arrangements and approached as raw material to be molded by the artist, but the content of that artwork is open to negotiation and improvisation. *They Shoot Horses* does not demand debasement as a condition for participation, and as with other reality television or social media formats, it may foster limited forms of enfranchisement through visibility and the production of celebrity.[46]

Extending these themes, James Coupe's video and architecture installation *Watchtower (A Machine for Living)* brings the problematics of labor exploitation and participatory performances to the digital present.[47] In this work, Coupe interrogates the effects of widespread employment precarity and monopolistic digital platforms upon contemporary labor relations and identities. Themes of surveillance, visibility, and automated labor figure prominently in *Watchtower*. Whereas humans may have occupied observational towers and outposts in the past and—metaphorically—have been in central positions from which to monitor and assess the actions of others, today's distributed automated systems increasingly orchestrate and capitalize upon human activity. Coupe explains: "It's not just about being watched. It's about us performing, almost, for these systems, and establishing routines and metadata—those things that feed back into the system so they learn more about us."[48] All interactions on digital platforms generate data that the systems amass and learn from, the more intimate the data the better, which is one major reason social media platforms afford personal disclosure. Although labor automation is a risk, these labor practices also generate additional metadata that become profitable surplus value (for example, in the form of consumer profiles) without any need, as of yet, to compensate workers or prosumers for that surplus.[49] Platform companies such as Amazon or Uber create entire markets to maintain profitable precarious labor relations while hiding the human costs behind narratives of individual freedom and flexibility or by hiding human labor altogether. In Coupe's words, "Workers remain isolated, invisible and anonymous, like proletarianized ghosts in the machine."[50]

For *Watchtower*, Coupe erected a four-story wooden tower, modeled after watchtowers previously used to spot forest fires near the artist's home in Seattle (see figure 4.6). Instead of a human observer at the top, the watchtower room contains computer hardware managing labor tasks via Amazon's Mechanical Turk system, which is a digital platform that coordinates micro-tasks performed by humans for piecemeal fees, particularly tasks that computer algorithms currently have a difficult time executing accurately (e.g., identifying captcha images, filling out surveys). The anonymous, outsourced laborers in Coupe's project are asked to create videos documenting or relating a range of potentially personal information, such as their dreams, the food they eat, the view from their windows, them exercising or praying, and so on. The workers are paid to record one full minute every hour for the span of a typical workday. The computer system then pipes these feeds to a set of video displays affixed to the wooden watchtower (itself located in a building near Amazon's Seattle headquarters) such that at punctuated intervals the videos play, offering a window into the lives of these workers.

As with the art projects of Sierra and Collins, Coupe draws heavily upon delegated performances to breathe life into his *Watchtower* piece. There are a few important differences, however. First, Coupe fashions a *direct* correspondence between his actors' performances and the focus of his critique. Unlike Sierra, who targets problematic situations that would allow exploitative labor arrangements, Coupe criticizes those very labor arrangements as produced by and reflected in his work. Second, he makes visible what would otherwise be present but hidden, for his actors in all likelihood were already completing Mechanical Turk tasks for others. By contrast, Sierra's performers were not being tattooed for money before his invitation; neither were Collins's teenagers dancing under such contrived or demanding circumstances as those dictated by the artist. In making current labor practices visible, Coupe simulates Amazon's profiteering move of skimming surplus value off the top of micro-exchanges that occur on its platform, except that he generates aesthetic value that lends impact to his work. Third, whereas the content of Sierra's and Collins's delegated performances matters significantly for the artists' play with crisis vision (enacting dehumanization of the abject, for Sierra, and humanization of the Other, for Collins), for Coupe the content suggested by the actors is less important than the overall opaque *structure* of mediated labor processes. As a result, Coupe grants his workers substantial latitude in their disclosures and does not police noncompliance. They are made visible in ways that they otherwise might make themselves visible on social media. This does not suggest an absence of exploitation but rather an acknowledgment of the relative autonomy of his actors to represent themselves and tell their stories, knowing full well that those partial portraits may be repurposed. By making structure his primary focus, whether with the imposing wood

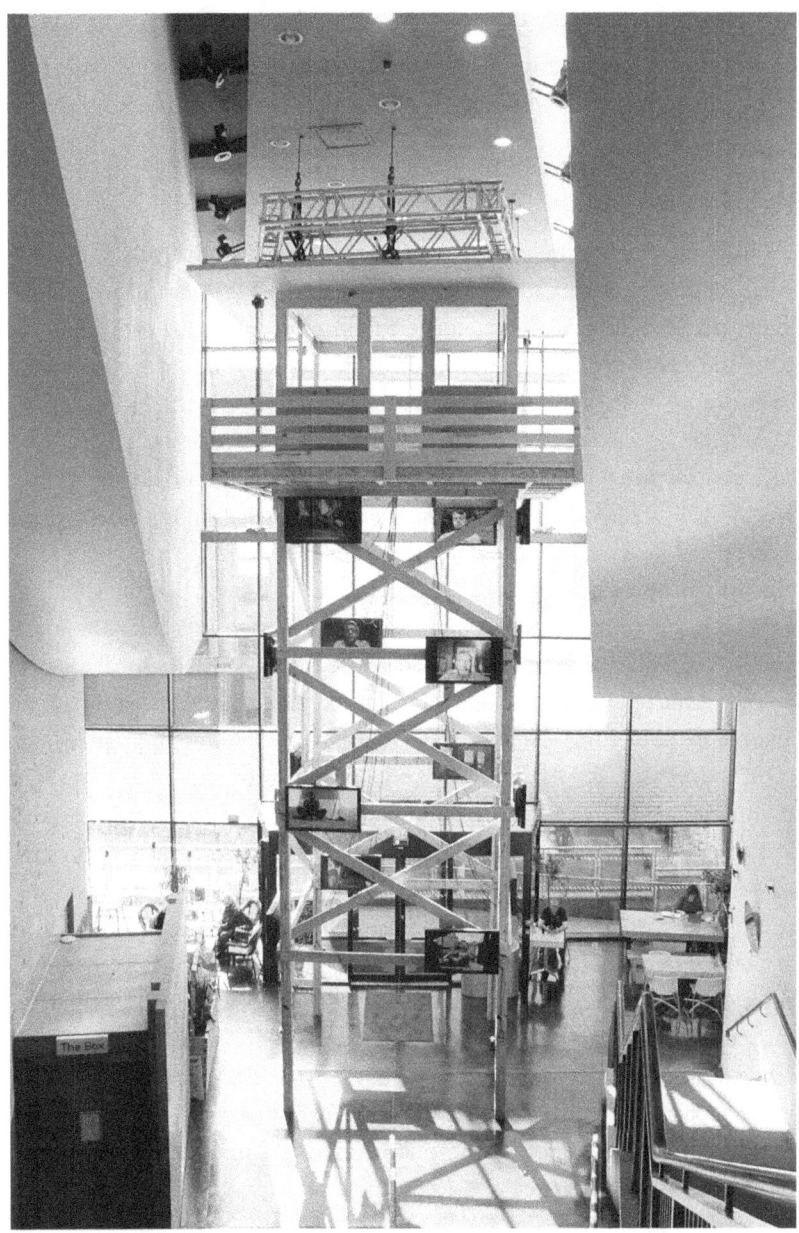

FIGURE 4.6. James Coupe, *Watchtower* (2017). Photograph: Louise Robson.
Courtesy of the artist.

watchtower or the pervasive digital infrastructures, Coupe harnesses exploitative arrangements for his work without augmenting them for his subjects, which makes his work distinct from Sierra's and Collins's projects.

Facing Cruelty

Visibility can be an unwelcome condition thrust upon individuals. Especially when produced as an explicit form of punishment or social shaming, visibility perpetrates symbolic violence by either constructing individuals as temporary outcasts from desirable social groups or involuntary members of undesirable ones. Visibility can serve as a catalyst for cruelty, which, as Marina Levina describes, is a material and affective manifestation of Othering, an "emotional force which acts upon the body . . . [and demonstrates] what power *feels* like."[51] The increasing prevalence of shaming mechanisms in criminal justice systems exemplifies the ejecting modality, where individuals convicted of crimes have been required to publicize their guilt in various humiliating ways.[52] For instance, people driving under the influence of alcohol have been forced to advertise that fact with bumper stickers on their vehicles, brightly colored bracelets on their arms, or their mugshots and names printed in local newspapers, each proclaiming their guilt (e.g., "D.U.I. CONVICT").[53] The second modality of involuntary inclusion seeks to interpellate individuals into dominant social or legal categories regardless of the fit or ramifications. This is the case, for example, with trans or gender-nonconforming individuals who are required to select "male" or "female" for government-issued documents or for security screening at airports, where the shame of being forced to perform state-imposed identities can be amplified by the sometimes very public nature of those performances.[54] In both of these modalities, whereas guilt connotes that one has made a mistake, shame suggests that the person is actually the mistake,[55] in large part because they do not fit or conform to expected social norms. Crisis vision animates both of these approaches, stigmatizing people as morality lessons or as flawed, and in the process it reaffirms a liberal social order predicated on cruelty and exclusion.[56]

In the US context, public shaming has deep roots as a form of official punishment. In the colonial period, small, tightly knit Protestant communities made shaming particularly effective because offenders were well known, could not easily escape their locales, and likely shared a culture of strict religious moralism.[57] This era was renowned for stocks and pillories, placing people in cruel contraptions on public display, branding, confessional letters, and other outward marks of guilt, such as the scarlet letter "A" signaling adultery in Nathaniel Hawthorne's classic novel.[58] The industrial period saw a reduction in these shame-based forms of punishment, at least for whites, perhaps because of the relative anonymity and mobility of individuals during this time. Forms of incarceration came to the fore instead as preferred modes of punishment, depriving people of liberty rather than reputation.[59] However, the past few decades have witnessed a return of shame-based punishments, as with the DUI sentences mentioned above, but also including sentences requiring individuals to wear in public large sandwich-board signs proclaiming their crime, such as "I stole mail. This is my punishment."[60] This has led some legal scholars to decry resurrected "public humiliation penalties" as dangerous anachronisms with unknown psychological effects.[61] Especially with the spread of social media and internet-based repositories, shaming tactics gain renewed traction—if not efficacy at deterrence—as people can be embarrassed in their networks, subject to mob attacks and doxing, and face long-term consequences for any accusation, real or fabricated.[62]

In his project *Obscurity*, artist Paolo Cirio engages this terrain of public shaming by addressing the violence inherent in the online publication and dissemination of police mugshots. In the United States, mugshot photographs are taken as part of the intake process for all arrestees, with those photographs legally considered as part of the public record, so most of those photographs can easily be found online on the websites of police departments, local media, or private companies. The circulation of these images, along with the person's name, age, charge, and arrest date, creates a persistent stigmatizing trace. Regardless of whether the charges are dropped or a person is convicted, the record remains, potentially damaging an individual's reputation and psychological well-being as well as their prospects for employment. Given that police display well-documented discriminatory practices, disproportionally arresting poor and racialized individuals,[63] it should not be surprising that the damaging effects of these records would accrue to the most marginalized members of society, adding another layer of what Oscar Gandy Jr. has termed "cumulative disadvantage."[64]

Cirio intervenes in this process by targeting third-party websites that compile mugshots and arrest data and make it easy to search for a person by name. These sites, such as MugShots.com and MugshotsOnline.com, skim data from the sites of reporting agencies and make money through linked advertisements to reputation-management services or, in some cases, by charging individuals to have their records expunged.[65] In these ways, Clare Birchall explains, the mugshot industry capitalizes on a larger economy (and rationality) of data sharing by "aping, cynically and darkly, the work undertaken by datapreneurs to transform open data into profitable forms."[66] Thus, the structural violence of economic inequality and institutional racism becomes a resource for sordid actors to exploit, such that they harness unwanted visibility as a form of "poverty capitalism,"[67] further debasing their targets and performing symbolic violence along the way. Cirio's *Obscurity* project draws attention to and disrupts these extortion tactics by spoofing the most popular mugshot websites, realistically mirroring their design but modifying the content. He has programmed an algorithm to blur the images and shuffle the data so that arrest information remains (preserving the ostensible public service of sharing arrest data) but individuals cannot be linked to specific arrests (see figure 4.7).[68] This culture-jamming project then deploys search engine optimization techniques to outrank the spoofed original sites in Google, thereby obfuscating not only the data represented but also the route for accessing them.

Cirio is clearly committed to privacy and the right to be forgotten, where giving people a fresh start is key for maintaining dignity and sociality, as well as for fostering rehabilitation if necessary.[69] His work performs a compromise position, illustrating how, through an enabling form of opacity, the public's right to know can harmonize with an individual's right to be forgotten. However, the equation breaks down in the proposed next steps. Cirio envisions radical democratic decision making on the internet as the antidote to the shaming tactics of mugshot companies; rather than let such companies decide what personal data should be revealed, he turns to the crowd: "My proposal is extreme, pushing boundaries with art, as eventually the democratic process becomes a popular jury open to everyone, where the people can judge to condemn or give mercy to those who have been arrested, by making public their information or removing it."[70] This proposal, a *Gladiator*-like scenario where the crowd can "condemn or give mercy," expresses a somewhat naive faith in the possibility of mature, principled democratic governance in online environments. Ample evidence points to an opposite tendency, toward bullying, trolling, slut shaming, mob rule, and doxing in online spaces.[71] *Obscurity* reveals, perhaps inadvertently,

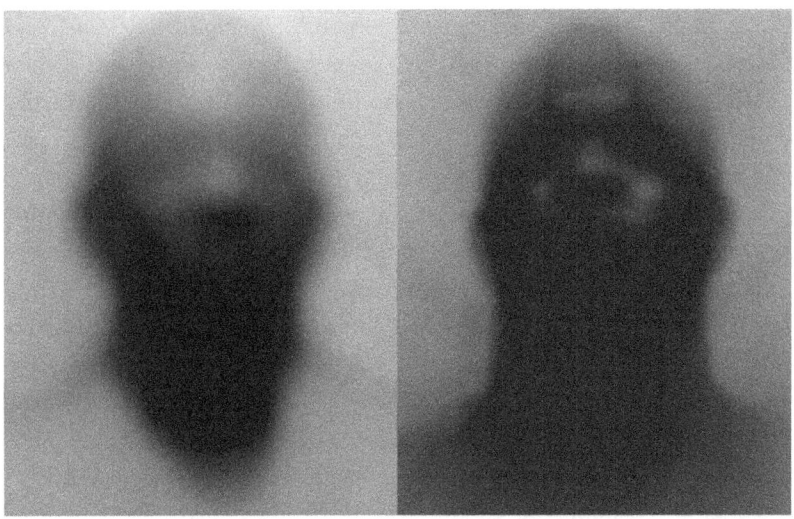

FIGURE 4.7. Paolo Cirio, *Obscurity* (2016). Courtesy of the artist.

the incommensurability between ideals of democratic governance and liberal personhood, on one hand, and crisis-vision cultures of racialized violence and cruelty, on the other. The problem is not solely technical or technocratic but cultural, where deep-seated racism and sexism infuse social practices online and off.

Public viewing of mugshots online feeds into base, voyeuristic impulses of audiences to discreetly view and judge others, at best, or circulate information to publicly shame, mock, or harass individuals, at worst. Instead of being anomalous, trafficking in online mugshots aligns surprisingly well with a broader culture of recent shame-based punishments, including those used by criminal justice systems and parents. For instance, some parents have forced their children to stand in public holding or wearing signs confessing their guilt for things like selling drugs or "twerking at a school dance," while other parents have hijacked their kids' social media accounts to say things like "I do not know how to keep [my mouth] shut. I am no longer allowed on Facebook or my phone. *Please ask why.*"[72]

Seen in this larger context, mugshot websites cannot be easily condemned as the product of disreputable actors seeking to profit from others' misfortune; they are part of a pervasive cultural logic insisting that shame-based practices are in society's best interests. Kumarini Silva has called this "love-cruelty," where declarations of love and affection become vehicles for cruelty in our time: "I see love as a necessary, even central, component of cruelty. Without love and its redemptive framings, we would recognize cruelty for what it is: a physical and/or emotional state of violence that produces a sense of precarity that is sustained by sociocultural and economic practices. Instead, we learn to rescue or redeem acts of cruelty by framing those transgressions and aggressions *as* love."[73] On the national level, love-cruelty manifested in the racist, anti-immigrant vitriol of President Trump and many of his supporters, providing a cover (love of nation) for cruel actions, such as separating immigrant children from their parents. On meso and micro levels, love-cruelty finds expression in the shaming tactics of the courts, parents, and online communities. In each case, crisis vision lends an assured morality to acts of love-cruelty. Actors assert dominance by mobilizing and amplifying conditions of structural and symbolic violence, demeaning vulnerable others while legitimizing their own actions behind discourses of love or care: acting, supposedly, in the interest of punished individuals or the greater public good.

Another artwork, Charlotte Haslund-Christensen's *Who's Next?*, confronts tacit rationalizations for cruelty by emphasizing the violence and partiality of legal classifications that valorize transparency. This project, whose title alludes to Martin Niemöller's famous poem about the failure of people to speak out against the roundup and extermination of groups in Nazi Germany,[74] appropriates the police mugshot genre to protest violence against LGBTQ+ people. The project endeavors to educate viewers about the persecution and criminalization of individuals in same-sex relationships throughout the world, where in at least seventy-six countries those relationships are outlawed explicitly and, in some countries, punishable by death. The artist used the basement of the Copenhagen Police Station as the staging area for producing mugshot photographs of forty-two self-identified LGBTQ+ individuals, one photograph made head-on and another in profile for each person (see figure 4.8). Unlike the smirks and smiles sometimes adopted by arrestees in police mugshots, the subjects in this project are serious and glum as they position themselves behind a black sign displaying the month, the year, and their identification number. The collection of photographs is then packaged as a commodity, placed in an elegant black box with a frontispiece of Niemöller's poem, the box's outside printed with "Who's Next?" on top and the author's name on the side. Proceeds from sales ($170 each) are then used to pay for a different intervention: the

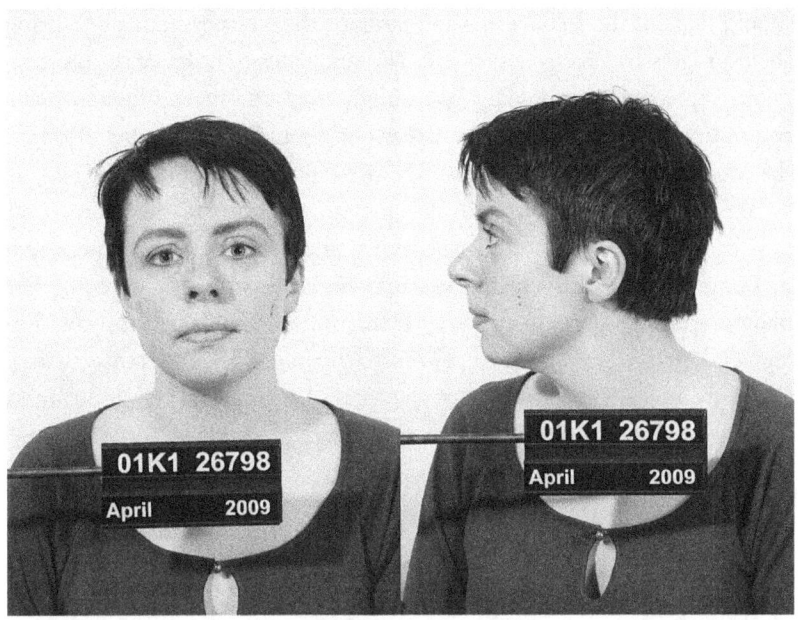

FIGURE 4.8. One of forty-two prints exhibited in original archival police sleeves from the project *Who's Next?* (2009) by artist Charlotte Haslund-Christensen. Courtesy of the artist.

smuggling of similar boxes into "regions where LGBTQ people are denied basic human rights."[75]

Haslund-Christensen's mugshot project performs through the creation of visual tension. The bulk of her subjects present as white, neatly dressed, and well coiffed, not the stereotypical images associated with racialized police mugshots, perhaps not even in a country like Denmark, which is often portrayed as being ethnically homogeneous. The tension comes from placing these subjects in a mugshot frame, complete with identification numbers. The effect reinforces Niemöller's sentiment that the authorities could be coming for anyone, even for those who do not fit expected criminal profiles, that even legal guilt is a mutable category contingent on place, time, and person. Additionally, the work communicates the corrosive invisibility of legally sanctioned and legally perpetrated violence against LGBTQ+ people in other regions throughout the world. The unstated implication is that although the law might be socially constructed, there is nonetheless a crisis-vision spectrum of civilized and less civilized countries, where people in ostensibly more civilized countries like Denmark should make it their concern—and perhaps their responsibility—to bring about progressive change elsewhere. The smuggling of boxes of the project's photographs into supposedly less enlightened countries illustrates this commitment; it suggests not only that one should intervene but also that the project will somehow be visually and culturally legible elsewhere, as an act of solidarity, perhaps, or an emblem of hope for the future. That said, by unreflexively assuming the civility and open-mindedness of people in Denmark, Haslund-Christensen may be unintentionally exposing her photographed subjects to attack or retaliation, as she has effectively catalogued them for ready targeting by those who might find them threatening. Certainly, in a US context, where hate crimes against LGBTQ+ individuals abound, the notion of a box of such photographs labeled "Who's Next?" could have terrifying consequences.[76]

As provocative as Cirio's and Haslund-Christensen's mugshot-based projects are, they both rely on implied cross-cultural comparisons that position the artists' Western European reference points as the aspirational ideal. With Cirio, the "right to be forgotten" legislation of the European Union could offer an important corrective to the shame produced by the public circulation of mugshot photographs and information in the United States. For Haslund-Christensen, countries more tolerant of LGBTQ+ individuals could serve as a model for those less tolerant. Both artists admirably advance projects that problematize and publicize the largely hidden violence of legal regimes that support stigmatization of the marginalized. By vilifying either third-party mugshot companies or countries that allow for the legal persecution of LGBTQ+ individuals, however, the artists deflect reflexivity about pervasive cultures of cruelty and intolerance that plague even the most idealized countries and their legal systems. Put differently, they sidestep direct confrontation with crisis vision's racializing and hierarchy-building effects in and between national contexts. As Mia Fischer reminds us in her work on state surveillance of transgender populations, "It does not suffice to focus on representational politics alone or even primarily if we are to account for the multifaceted operations of state power and its dispersal of violence . . . [, including how] the law's alleged impartiality and colorblindness continue to protect and advance white supremacy."[77] To advance opacity as ethical relations, crisis-vision politics must be reckoned with and defused in all cultural contexts, not shunted off to other groups or places.

Conclusion

This chapter has explored artistic efforts to problematize the structural and symbolic violence of crisis vision, making it accessible for contemplation and, perhaps, intervention. Whether in addressing the displacement of refugees, the objectifying labor of the precarious, or the cruel shaming of arrestees, queer, or gender-nonconforming individuals, each of the artworks discussed here embraces evidentiary modes to document acts or artifacts of violence. They frame evidence of the dehumanizing toll of economic and social inequalities upon bodies as powerful representations of ethical failings that should be readily discernible to viewers. In so doing, however, most of these works center viewing subjects while largely obscuring the nonneutral politics of evidence collection, presentation, and interpretation.

To the extent that artworks and photographs act discursively as forms of evidence, they depend upon an aura of realism, most prominently achieved through mechanical means and indexical allusions to concrete events.[78] All of this subtly masks the artists' mobilization of overt artifice (installation, staging, presentation) so that constructed truths can appear self-evident and pure, where even in Sierra's and Collins's spectacle-centered performances, the "fact" of dehumanizing sociopolitical conditions emerges as unadulterated and oddly decontextualized.[79] In the process, this artistic frame threatens to reify crisis-vision truth regimes that bolster the very conditions critiqued by the artists: those regimes that could posit some bodies as worthy and others as worthless, some as valuable and others expendable. "Art doesn't turn us into rebels by shoving repulsive facts into our faces, nor does it mobilize us because it has gone after us outside the museum," Néstor García Canclini cautions. Rather, "its critique, and not merely its indignation, might infect us if the art itself would let go of forms of language [and representation] that are complicit in maintaining the social order."[80]

Whereas the artistic frame of violence is ideally suited to uncover, and confront viewers with, the destructive, racializing effects of crisis vision, the frame also symbolically leans upon the promise of liberal systems of governance to live up to their mythology of equality, fairness, and justice when the evidence, as it were, illustrates how misguided those efforts can be.[81] For instance, the projects dealing with refugee crises and stigmatized identities notably refract those problems through the cultural and legal lenses of Western European countries, suggesting that if the espoused universal human rights of those states were consistently upheld, especially in less enlightened contexts, resolution would be achievable. By contrast, some of the projects on structural violence and labor exploitation are more cynical about these prospects and therefore concentrate instead on the dehumanizing and unequal effects of capitalist systems. Because discourses of liberal personhood and governance often provide a smokescreen for plunder and racism,[82] a focus on complicity—as modeled by the work of Sierra and Coupe—might be a more productive pressure point for artists, even if that approach risks offending audiences or exploiting their subjects. For example, delineating linkages among colonial legacies, racial prejudice, and structural and symbolic violence could begin to agitate viewers and undermine the presumed purity and superiority of Western states *and* political artists. The challenge for this artistic or activist frame, in particular, is to acknowledge the contributory violence of actors' orientations and approaches, even when individuals are driven by social justice concerns.

5. Disruption

Surveillance depends upon looking, whether literally or figuratively. Through various forms of measuring, calculating, and sizing up, surveillance strives to assert dominance over a field and the bodies within it.[1] It is about fixing subjects in place and rendering them compliant to the dictates or whims of others, regardless of the legitimacy of those who are assuming positions of dominance.[2] Through institutionalization (in the state, church, family, algorithm), surveillance evacuates possibilities for contesting the terms of assessment because those terms bracket context and protocol in advance, the ground upon which one could gain leverage for change.[3] In this respect, surveillance is a scientistic, patriarchal practice that generates *unmarked* knowledge and disowns its particularistic investments in the regimes it produces.[4]

Surveillance-based exercises of visual power infuse crisis vision, but they are never entirely stable or disembodied. Indeed, the threat of "eyeballing" the person in a position of assumed authority—and the predictable violent reactions to such insubordination—illustrates the ultimate fragility and interpersonal intimacy of these racialized control dynamics.[5] In this sense, insubordination directly undermines racial, class, gender, or other hierarchies that glue repressive systems in place; it is literally rejecting one's assigned status as subordinate to the other, which is why such challenges unleash some of the worst retaliatory abuse. The gaze of surveillance, especially in intimate, person-to-person encounters, seeks to arrest subjects in their places, freezing both them and the status quo. It is a performance of crisis vision that affirms the racial order of things by consolidating white supremacy and placing black and brown bodies under erasure with the threat of silence, punishment, or death.

Scholars working in the field of cultural studies offer a useful starting point for critical inquiry into visibility, racial violence, and art. In particular, Paul Gilroy has underscored the centrality of racial oppression and exclusion in the formation of national cultural histories, where notions of universal aesthetic taste have depended—from their inception—on the presumed inferiority of black creative expression and aesthetic capabilities.[6] In the process, not only has the work of black artists been disparaged, but assumptions about natural racial hierarchies have also been solidified through the decisions of cultural institutions and the judgments of art critics. From this vantage point, Gilroy encourages scholars to attend to shared communicative networks that expand across the African diaspora, even as differential experiences of trauma remain.[7] In a complementary vein, Stuart Hall also maintains the importance of situating black diaspora visual arts in their historical and political contexts such that one can trace "chains of causation and conditions of existence" and thereby avoid simplistic treatments of these works as homogeneous or apart from their objects of critique.[8] Engaged in this way, critical readings of art can discern, and assess, the capacity of creative works to open up semiotic fields and reveal latent indeterminacies that have been camouflaged by ideology. Kobena Mercer references this capacity in saying that "art is a kind of countercut that punctures openings into the smooth surfaces of hegemonic formations that want to close up or suture the signifying chain so that the world appears fixed and finalized."[9]

This chapter builds upon these insights to analyze contemporary artistic treatments of racialized surveillance and violence. In a moment marked by growing awareness of police violence against minoritized groups, artworks that challenge such relations hold potential for disrupting signifying chains and fabricating new cultural codes, new ways of orienting bodies to one another and to the state. Critical engagement with a selection of recent visual artworks and performance pieces suggests how relations of opacity might emerge from aesthetic disruptions of crisis vision.

Legacies of Racial Terror and Violence

If aesthetic practices and artworks are thoroughly enmeshed in the political and corporeal conditions they seek to trouble,[10] then what is the nature of those conditions, and how can one begin to transform them? In probing these questions, I draw upon Christina Sharpe's metaphor of "the wake." For Sharpe, *the wake* connotes multiple meanings: the turbulent social waters of the aftermath of slavery, extending beyond and reproducing in different forms the terror, containment, and abjection of those original slave ships; the mourning and protection of the dead, especially those pulled under by the many manifestations of racist violence, but also the celebration and remembrance of their lives; and the process of waking up, of achieving consciousness and conscious awareness of persistent conditions of antiblackness while embracing that which survives despite them. As Sharpe writes, "Racism, the engine that drives the ship of state's national and imperial projects . . . cuts through all of our lives and deaths inside and outside the nation, in the wake of its purposeful flow."[11] The metaphor of the wake provides a way of grappling with the fraught legacies of slavery, terror, and renunciations of black humanity as these legacies continue to live in and rupture the present.

Certainly, caught up in the wake are the daily victims of racialized police violence, whether filmed or not, as any encounter with law enforcement brings the threat of abuse and death, particularly for those inhabiting black or brown bodies.[12] Refugees seeking security, stability, and dignity are also increasingly rejected, policed, and contained in degrading, dehumanizing ways, as racial outcasts that nation-states paint as crime and terror risks.[13] The US hyper-incarceration of 2.3 million people,[14] with blacks five times more likely than whites to be jailed,[15] proves again, if such proof was needed, that the past is not past, that "the afterlife of slavery"[16] persists in the present. Economic and environmental insecurity intersects with these racial vectors, fueling housing and food insecurity, limiting educational opportunities, and increasing health threats and mortality rates for poor and marginalized groups who are on the front lines of both the COVID-19 pandemic and environmental catastrophes induced by climate change.[17] These are some of the many victims of crisis vision in the contemporary conjuncture. Their experiences are part of the wake of imperial projects, settler colonialism, slavery, and the history of capital that always was—and still is—bound to forms of racial subjection and oppression.

As previously discussed, dehumanizing violence lies at the heart of modern liberalism and its projects. Rather than seeing slavery and settler colonialism as exceptions along the road to universal freedom, fabricated racial hierarchies have undergirded modern liberalism, creating so-called uncivilized others against which white liberal subjects could be formed and assert their rights. This symbolic opposition between civilized and uncivilized, human and less than human, was deployed in the eighteenth and nine-teenth centuries to justify the expropriation of labor and resources in the name of progress. Lisa Lowe explains: "The uses of universalizing concepts of reason, civilization, and freedom effect colonial divisions of humanity, affirming liberty for modern man while subordinating the variously colo-nized and dispossessed peoples whose material labor and resources were the conditions of possibility for that liberty."[18] In the contemporary context, the ideal of a rights-bearing subject is encoded with residual traces of these originary exclusions, which normalize unequal treatment even, and per-haps especially, in encounters with the state and its agents.[19]

Whereas hopes for transformation, for the establishment of more eq-uitable and just sociopolitical configurations, often congeal within tropes of resistance, this may be a false start.[20] Resistance often presupposes, and appeals to, a legal and ethical order to which the abject may petition for entry. But if such an order is founded upon violent exclusions, whether acknowledged or denied, then such entreaties may unknowingly shore up those (racist, patriarchal, capitalist) ideological edifices by renewing their authority to arbitrate claims of worthiness or belonging. At the same time, ostensibly liberated groups cannot escape their symbolic and mate-rial connections to conditions of slavery. Hortense Spillers relates: "Before the 'body' there is the 'flesh,' that zero degree of social conceptualization that does not escape concealment under the brush of discourse, or the reflexes of iconography. . . . Even though the captive flesh/body has been 'liberated,' . . . dominant symbolic activity, the ruling episteme that releases the dynamics of naming and valuation, remains grounded in the originating metaphors of captivity and mutilation." The distinction between body and flesh in-troduces a conceptual challenge and a way of thinking differently about individuals' relationship to "dominant symbolic activity," as encoded in racist discourses, legal designations, or state institutions. The flesh pre-cedes and exceeds the body; violences may be perpetrated on the flesh, such that the imprint of capture, maiming, and containment might transfer generationally,[21] but it is apart from "the body" understood as a discursively constructed, ideologically embedded subject. Instead of privileging acts of resistance, there may be more analytic potency in attending to accomplish-ments of freedom within legal and ethical orders that would negate the body and reduce one to flesh.

Whereas Spillers deploys the concept of the flesh to trace the intersect-ing, iterating ramifications of slavery and patriarchy, Alexander Weheliye builds upon this theorization to locate moments of possibility and hope from the starting point of the flesh precisely *because* it operates outside the registers of "the body" and liberal personhood, or in what I understand to be spaces of opacity. Weheliye argues: "The flesh is not an abject zone of exclusion that culminates in death but an alternate instantiation of humanity that does not rest on the mirage of western Man as the mirror image of human life as such. . . . The flesh resists the legal idiom of personhood as property . . . [it is] simultaneously a tool of dehumanization and a relational vestibule to alternative ways of being."[22] Weheliye seeks to notice and credit as being important, even vital, the ways that humanity asserts itself under the most degrading and dehumanizing conditions (such as the slave ship, the plantation, the prison, the concentration camp).[23] He clarifies: "The particular assemblage of humanity under purview here . . . in contrast to bare life, insists on the importance of miniscule movements, glimmers of hope, scraps of food, the interrupted dreams of freedom found in those spaces deemed devoid of full human life."[24] As with Sharpe's work, there is a focus on what survives terror and violence, what is not eradicated under the weight of oppression. Hope rests not on the project or possibility of full integration into regimes of liberal personhood but instead on elements of humanity that emerge from opaque zones outside those regimes.

Hope in this sense is not an abstract yearning. It is a process of embodied labor and praxis: a reading, writing, and living of alternative futures in the face—or "mouth"—of what Audre Lorde would call the "racist, sexist, suicidal dragon" of capitalist nations like the United States. For Lorde, this involves tapping into the deep emotional reservoirs of the oppressed and channeling them into and through creative expression, such as poetry; as she writes, "Poetry is not only dream and vision; it is the skeleton architecture of our lives. It lays the foundations for a future of change, a bridge across our fears of what has never been before."[25] In a similar register, Sharpe refers to this praxis as one of "wake work," which concentrates not on assimilation or resolution but instead on "representing the paradoxes of blackness within and after the legacies of slavery's denial of Black humanity. . . . [Wake work is] a mode of inhabiting *and* rupturing this episteme with our known lived and un/imaginable lives."[26] Black creative expression—whether through poetry, music, visual art, or other media—serves as one avenue for this wake work, of inhabiting and rupturing without being restricted by logics of resistance.[27]

In the context of surveillance in particular, the process of securing humanity within conditions of crisis vision may hinge on disrupting the signifying regimes upon which surveillance relies. Simone Browne labels such creative disruptions *dark sousveillance*: "tactics employed to render one's self out of sight, and strategies used in the flight to freedom from slavery."[28] Such tactics might include forging slave passes, passing as white, sharing information about slave catchers (or the police or white nationalists in today's milieu), or otherwise circumventing or appropriating existing systems of antiblack surveillance. Similarly, Freda Fair relates how black women sex workers in Minneapolis in the late nineteenth and early twentieth centuries exploited the supposed scientific accuracy of the Bertillon criminal identification system by sharing aliases, such as "Mamie," to protect themselves from the police.[29] Because the history of surveillance is inextricably bound up with the history of racism and slavery, as Browne convincingly illustrates, antiblack racism saturates and is reproduced by surveillance apparatuses.[30] Thus, Amanda Glasbeek, Mariful Alam, and Katrin Roots claim that "the hypervisibility of black persons, made possible through the surveillance undertaken by white persons, indicates that racism is not something that occurs merely as a result of surveillance but, instead, that a racial ordering is part of the rationale for surveillance in the first place."[31] Creative disruption, through art or other means, offers a way of documenting legacies of racism that rupture the present, deconstructing the (techno)scientific basis for racist practices, and nourishing within opacity the resilient, generous humanity that points toward a different world.

Raising Up

Consider Hank Willis Thomas's 2013 sculpture *Raise Up*, which was displayed at the Goodman Gallery in Cape Town, South Africa, in 2014 as part of a solo exhibition titled *History Doesn't Laugh*. This sculpture presents ten bronze-cast, dark-skinned men facing away from the viewer with their arms extended over their heads (see figure 5.1). Only their heads, arms, and hands are visible, with the remainder of their bodies swallowed in a bright white shelf that serves as the base for this artwork. The figures are grouped together and adopt similar poses of accessibility to spectators, yet they betray unique qualities: they are different heights, some wear bracelets, some turn their hands slightly sideways, and some of their bald heads

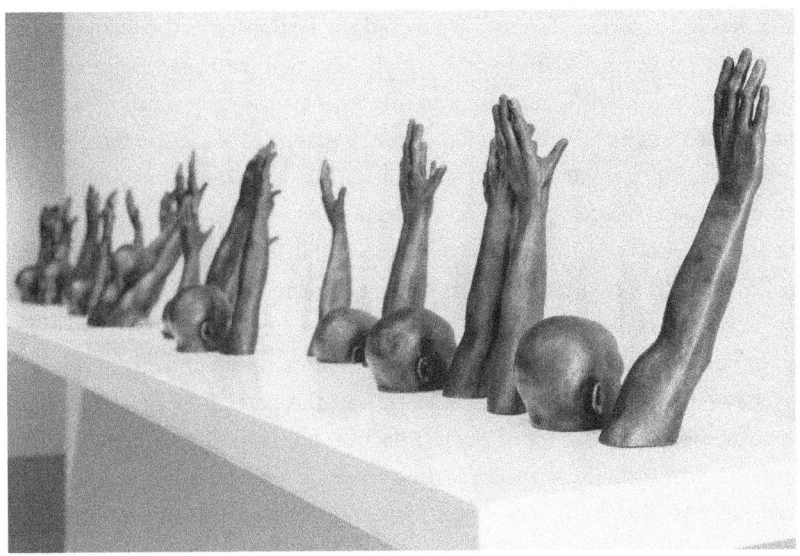

FIGURE 5.1. Hank Willis Thomas, *Raise Up* (2013). Courtesy of the artist.

are bisected by the white shelf while others extend further up, revealing their necks or muscular shoulders. This is a stark piece, devoid of context and much color variation, rendering a sterile tableau where the reflection of sculptured body parts on the glossy white mantle offers the only nuance of shading within the piece's white-brown extremes.

Although *Raise Up* was created for a South African exhibit and takes its inspiration from an apartheid-era photograph of naked black miners presenting themselves for invasive search,[32] it clearly resonates with crisis-vision economies of surveillance of and violence against black and brown bodies in the US context. Writing about the piece, Andrew Culp observes that "after the Michael Brown shooting of 2014, it would certainly be easy to imagine it paying homage to the activist [refrain] 'Hands Up, Don't Shoot!'"[33] Certainly, some of Thomas's other works, such as the *Branded* series, which depicts a Nike logo branded on the side of a black model's head, offer direct critique of the legacies of slavery in the United States, including various forms of ownership and control—even through market-based "self-branding"—that mark men of color today.[34] The title of the work, *Raise Up*, therefore signifies the ever-present even if unspoken police command, an injunction for voluntary, anticipatory submission with the full threat of death for any perceived lack of compliance. It is this line of interpretation that has led scholars such as Culp to call the sculpture an "embodiment of black social death."[35] However, to apply Sharpe's expanded notion of the wake as a collective waking up, the title may also suggest a call for action: to lift oneself, others, or society up from the manacles of racist oppression, to achieve a higher plane. Given the work's historical referent of the overthrown apartheid regime in South Africa, *Raise Up* simultaneously points to the potential of and need for rebellion and insurgency.[36]

Whereas the original photograph that informed *Raise Up* presents men in a state of complete nakedness, as dehumanized and docile objects for manipulation by the presumably white foremen, the sculpture consciously eschews such portrayals. It thus follows in the path of Saidiya Hartman, who in her book *Scenes of Subjection* notably refuses to reproduce yet another gratuitous description of the grotesque whipping of Aunt Hester—the passage that launches Frederick Douglass's autobiography—thereby allowing Hartman to break the cycle of normalizing representations of black suffering.[37] In the case of Thomas's artwork, the submergence of the figures in a sea of white also covers their naked bodies, preventing visual consumption of their anatomies while encouraging readings that extend beyond those of mere submission.

The overwhelming, almost blinding whiteness of the background for this work calls out for additional interpretation. On one hand, the oversaturation of whiteness may signify the defining, containing, and absorbing properties of white supremacy, which serve as the only basis for the emergence of liberal personhood. From this perspective, the reflection of heads and torsos on the white shelf is one where recognition is achieved only through distorted representations on the white body politic, always in relation to the foundational or dominant other.[38] The absence of white bodies in this relational schema harmonizes well with the racialized status quo that views whiteness as transparent, normal, and unthreatening, not in need of definition, radically unlike nonwhites, who seemingly demand enfleshment and visibility.[39] This is a core component of racialization, which Weheliye describes as operating "not as a biological or cultural descriptor but as a conglomerate of sociopolitical relations that discipline humanity into full humans, not-quite-humans, and nonhumans."[40] Thus, whereas full (white) humans may have presumed presence and status, nonwhite others struggle with achieving such absorption into the fictional, amorphous white norm while also seeking to escape from those symbolic constraints.

On the other hand, the hidden bodies in the *Raise Up* sculpture also speak to the hidden labor and violence of slavery and oppression upon which the modern liberal order was built. "The slave is the foundation of the national order," Hartman notes, but "the slave [simultaneously] occupies the position of the unthought."[41] The occluded bodies in the sculpture mimic the erasure of slavery and settler colonialism from the history of nation-states like the United States. These presumed present but undetectable bodies, like the subjugated bodies to which they refer, are relegated to the realm of the unthought and unacknowledged. As such, modern states are riven with contradictions at their core: much-heralded universalism is pitted against its repudiation in the form of slavery and racialized violence—the former made possible by the latter, and the latter done in the service of the former. At the same time, hints of liberation draw upon that fractured but whitewashed foundation. The arms and heads lifting up out of the sculpture create an outside to that white static totality, suggesting emergence, continuance, and solidarity in spite of the severe conditions and arresting gazes of crisis vision.

Facing Police Violence

Other artists problematize the relationship between surveillant vision and police violence more directly. For instance, Dread Scott's[42] powerful installation *Stop* takes as its content the social fact of men of color being stopped routinely by police for no reason other than their physical appearances or neighborhoods—or because of perceived mismatches between racial minorities and the spaces they inhabit, as witnessed with the disturbing preponderance of irrationally fearful white people calling the police when nonwhites rent Airbnb properties, tour college campuses, use public parks, and so on.[43] This video installation appeared at the Rush Arts Gallery in New York in 2012 as part of Scott's larger collaborative project, *Postcode Criminals*, which revealed similarities in the surveillance and profiling of minoritized individuals in the United States and the United Kingdom.[44]

Scott's installation juxtaposes two video walls facing each other, with life-size videos of three young, dark-skinned men from Brooklyn on one wall and three from Liverpool on the other (see figure 5.2). A wide space opens between the two video walls, allowing viewers to walk between them and be confronted, and surrounded, by the stares and statements of the men. The hairstyles and clothing of the men, while varied, harmonize well overall with the semiotic expectations for "urban" youth: dreadlocks, baseball caps, hoodies, shiny parkas, basketball sneakers, baggy clothes. Over the course of the 7:16 minute video, the men stand confidently, cross their arms or put their thumbs in their jeans' pockets, and mostly gaze directly at the camera as if asserting the right to look back at those who might stereotype them. There are long pauses of potentially uncomfortable silence as the men shift slightly but continue to look straight into the lens, into the eyes of viewers. Then, at intervals, the silences are punctuated by the men speaking in measured tones, saying how many times they have been stopped by the police: "I've been stopped sixty or more times," "I've been stopped by the cops a hundred-and-fifty times, probably a little bit more," "I've been stopped and searched more than a hundred times," "I've been stopped about twenty times," "Get stopped by the cops every day, but a hundred-and-fifty—that about sums it up," "I've been stopped seventy times," "I've been stopped by the police thirty times or more."

Stop achieves much of its impact from its clever audio pacing. Initially, there are pauses of eighteen seconds or more between the men's voices, but the temporal gaps gradually close so that eventually the men speak over one another. The piece audibly performs an experience of the compounding repetition of being stopped until it culminates in a kind of

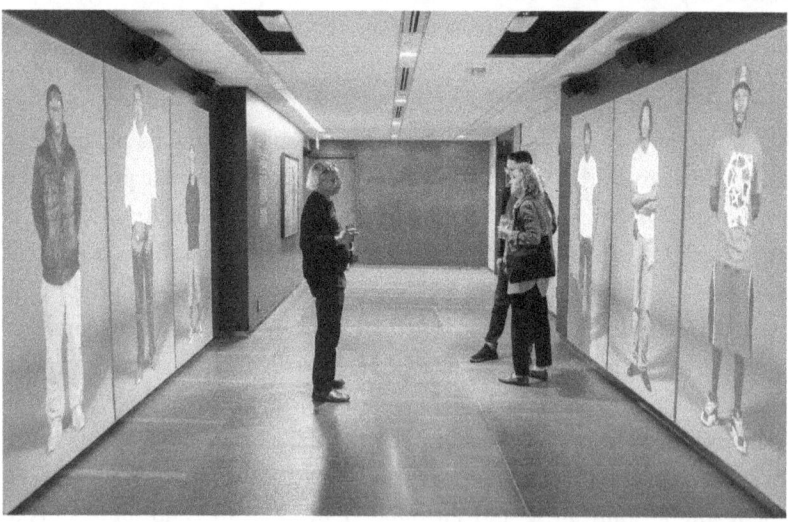

FIGURE 5.2. Dread Scott, *Stop* (2012). Courtesy of the artist.

background noise echoing the lived hum, for the men, of constant scrutiny and judgment by police and others. Then, near the end of the video, gaps begin to form in the enunciations, mirroring lived experiences of unwanted police attention, not subsiding so much as becoming normalized, expected, routine, and comprehensible. In these ways, *Stop* conveys a slice of the everyday reality for minority men in many cities across the Western world, but it cannot capture the indignity and violence of such encounters or the affective burden of these constant threats. Nonetheless, the piece establishes a relationship between viewers and these men, or many other men like them, exposing the viewer to the strong gazes of others, their matter-of-fact sharing of everyday subjection, and silences within which viewers might critically assess themselves when they face the Other.[45]

By collaborating with young men in Brooklyn and Liverpool, as well as with other artists as part of the *Postcode Criminals* project, Scott traces the intentional replication of zero-tolerance, crisis-vision policing strategies and their discriminatory effects across different national and cultural settings. Just as companies in the global security industry contract with cities to implement militarized security infrastructures and policies as "best practices" for crime control, mega events, or urban renewal,[46] so too do police agencies share tactics and technologies globally. One result of such sharing of zero-tolerance policing strategies in the 1990s, Scott explains, is "that youth in Liverpool and in New York were further criminalized and have been drawn into an unusual symmetry by police and governmental forces."[47] As a global phenomenon, targeted, discriminatory police surveillance spreads, reproducing as "normal" conditions of black suffering such that these conditions resist diagnosis as problematic. In Weheliye's words, "Because black suffering figures in the domain of the mundane, it refuses the idiom of exception."[48] Seen from the perspective of the wake, *Stop* underscores the embodied experience of living in the aftermath of slavery: being exposed to and normalizing racialized state violence. What *Stop* performs, then, is a tracing of these lines between racist policing practices across territories, semiotic constructions of black male threat, and the troubling normality of constant, expected surveillance that fuels the prison industry and threatens premature death. From the boundaries of this sketch, the voices of the men issue forth, asserting their presence and humanity.

Another of Scott's works, *Blue Wall of Violence*, is an installation designed to expose the racially corrupted perspectives of police who may be predisposed to view all black bodies as—always already—armed and dangerous (see figure 5.3). The piece, exhibited at Brooklyn's Museum of Contemporary African Diasporan Arts in 2008, contains a number of interrelated elements. There are six police target-practice posters, the kind displaying silhouetted black bodies with concentric white ellipses indicating the value of the shot. From each poster emerges a plastic molding of an extended black arm with a supposedly threatening object (a candy bar, a wallet, a squeegee) held in each hand. These held objects correspond to items held by unarmed individuals when shot by police who ostensibly misidentified the items as guns or other dangerous weapons. Above each poster is a black sign displaying in bold white letters the date of the actual shooting by police. Next, an austere wooden coffin rests on a table directly in front of the posters, a neat, blood-red tablecloth spilling downward beneath it. Finally, three police batons, poised on mechanized stands directly in front of the coffin, strike it loudly every ten seconds, sending discordant echoes throughout the room.

Although some of the symbolism of this work is straightforward, such as the red tablecloth conveying the blood of the victims or the black targets representing black bodies, the implications are more nuanced. *Blue Wall of Violence* can be seen as an unflinching critique of racialized state violence within the context of crisis vision. Whereas crisis vision has historically interpellated (white) viewers to a hegemonic and favorable view of police, this artwork draws attention to the fusion of police surveillance and threat assessments with sedimented racist cultural beliefs, leading to systematic and disproportionate deadly violence against black people.[49] This is a commentary on the institutionalized "professional vision" of police, which is inculcated through training for use of force such that police are primed to see and respond to threats and to ignore (and later erase) uncertainty.[50] Determinations of threat are obviously infused with racial bias but in ways that can be masked by the supposed objective nature of discrete training scenarios for police use of force, such that even police may be ignorant of the existence of such bias.[51] Then again, as has been empirically documented, police subscribe to a "blue wall of silence" (in reference to the color of their uniforms) that keeps them from reporting colleagues' infractions and even encourages them to assist one another in covering up instances of abuse.[52] Scott alludes directly to this self-protective police culture in calling his work *Blue Wall of Violence*; in so doing, he reroutes the signifying chain, stripping any sense of honor or admirable solidarity

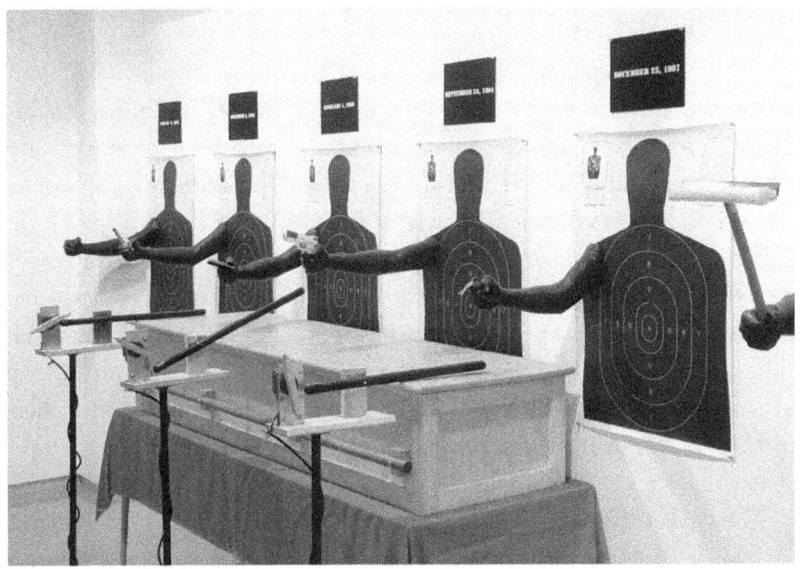

FIGURE 5.3. Dread Scott, *Blue Wall of Violence* (2008). Courtesy of the artist.

from the "wall of silence" and instead underscoring the ignoble acts festering within. He calls out institutionalized couplings of surveillance and violence but, as with Thomas's sculpture, refuses to reproduce images of victims' dead bodies for viewing consumption; by foregrounding shooting-target posters instead, he places the emphasis on the racist interpretive frames of police.

Perhaps not surprisingly, the disruption caused by this piece extended beyond the noisy baton hits in a single room of Brooklyn's Museum of Contemporary African Diasporan Arts. It was decried in the media as a "cop-bashing art exhibit,"[53] and the police union quickly called for city defunding of the museum, which did not occur.[54] Mirroring the resignifying moves of the supposedly offensive piece, Scott responded by attempting to shift the terms of the debate: "These works are against police brutality and murder. . . . What should be controversial is these killings, not this artwork."[55] Effective artistic interventions, according to performance studies scholar James Harding, should not remain relegated to safe, sanitized spaces but instead ramify out into the world, challenge established orders, and, when necessary, do damage.[56] If blowback alone is any measure, *Blue Wall of Violence* succeeded on these fronts.

Reclaiming Visibility

The seemingly constant onslaught of appalling stories of police killing of black men and women signifies, on one hand, the pervasiveness of anti-black violence and, on the other, potential catalysts for antiracist and anti-police-brutality interventions. Under the overwhelming weight of so many victims—Eric Garner, Michael Brown, Walter Scott, George Floyd, Breonna Taylor, and many, many more—black exclusion and death are revealed as normative outputs of crisis vision, as foundational components of the liberal state that police so vigilantly maintain. Yet forms of survival, solidarity, anger, and contestation emerge from this context as well. Many artists within the Black Lives Matter movement illustrate this with their symbolic creations that eschew confined, controlled museum environments to instead mobilize and engender collective power on the streets.

The goal of mediagenic disruption drives some of the most provocative art of the Black Lives Matter movement. These works include culture-jamming performances of injecting blood-red dye into a St. Louis fountain to protest the killing of Michael Brown in adjacent Ferguson, Missouri; placing an actor as a lifeless black body with a bloody, bullet-hole-riddled shirt in front of the iconic LOVE sculpture in Philadelphia and then capturing unperturbed nonblack tourists having their pictures taken amid the morbid tableau; or fabricating and marching with a massive papier-mâché figure of Michael Brown with his hands up to demand legal action against police like Darren Wilson, who killed Brown.[57] These performances recall Lorde's observation that democratic creative expression, in the sense of it being widely accessible, such as poetry, dance, or song, may hold greater promise for survival and transformation in part because it is difficult to restrict.[58]

To the extent that artworks invoke the cleansing power of visibility, however, they risk subtending crisis vision's symbolic order, which is an order that depends on and ignores unequal valuations of life, especially discounted valuations of nonwhite life. Take, for example, *The Mirror Casket Project*, created by artists De Andrea Nichols, Marcis Curtis, Damon Davis, Sophie Lipman, Mallory Nezam, Derek Laney, and Elizabeth Vega.[59] For this provocative performance, community members somberly carried a glass casket with a shattered lid down the streets of Ferguson, enacting a funeral procession to the site of Michael Brown's killing. The artists stress that their goal was to encourage empathy but also foster reflexivity on the part of viewers about their complicity in regimes of state and community violence.[60] In one notable exchange, as white police officers were reflected in the mirrored casket, a black activist explained to the police: "This is what you have wrought . . . We bring you this coffin to show you your reflection in the death and the suffering and anguish and pain and grief of our community. Look into the mirror. We are human too. You are not the only people who get to be human."[61]

The artists behind *The Mirror Casket Project* seek to mirror the truth back to onlookers, forcing recognition of the ways that viewers are "both solution and problem . . . both victim and aggressor."[62] Yet the execution of this performance smooths over that ambiguity by privileging scenes of police encountering their own reflections as they face, and symbolically oppose, protesters. The message becomes a call for police to recognize that they are racist aggressors who are destroying the community. Bracketing the hard-to-dispute empirical accuracy of that assessment, there are uneasy implications of this appeal to the redemptive or purgative function of mirroring. It is a call for recognition on equal grounds, a demand for police to see that nonwhite bodies "are human too" and deserving of equal protection, rights, and justice. In combination with protesters' signs demanding the prosecution of police, it is also—or ultimately—an appeal to the law to enfold the marginalized and abject into its loving, *protective* embrace. In friction with this logic is the possibility that the suggested form of legal universality was always predicated on racial exclusion. Jared Sexton, in his work on representations of racialized policing in film, explicates this problematic: "If the white subject—embedded in the institution of family-as-nation, metonym of the universal—has understood itself in the historic instance to be, both onscreen and off, under the enabling cover of the police and military, then the black ~~subject~~ (we must use the term under erasure) is not only prototype of that threat against which 'civilization' must defend, but also that animate figure that must aspire to the very form of existence from which it is constitutively barred."[63] If antiblackness underwrites the law, then appeals to the law, however necessary and pragmatic, will not short-circuit the prevailing racial contract of modern states.[64]

As it confronts and enlists audiences, *The Mirror Casket Project* may extend beyond the intentions of the artists to perform in other, unanticipated ways. For example, what might the project's messages be for the white police officer facing the angry crowd, the sympathetic antiracist ally consuming the mediated images from afar, or others? How could the social positioning of the unwitting actors unconsciously mediate their experiences as they face the casket's mirrors? Although one might seek to explore such questions empirically, more important here is acknowledging differential modes of subjectification and how they connect to crisis-vision regimes of violence. Such displays of caskets, bodies, and mediated depictions of violence, as with videos of police killing nonwhite others, threaten to become modes of *pornotroping*, which Weheliye, drawing upon Spillers, describes as "the enactment of black suffering for a shocked and titillated audience."[65] Through pornotroping, viewers are interpellated and positioned within the visual scene such that they may recognize their respective roles as nonwhite, for whom a similar form of death by police is a credible threat, or as white, for whom such an experience would be unlikely and exceptional.[66] In short, the mirror of the casket, as with the suggested photorealism of video recordings of police violence, distorts. It is less an objective representation of social conditions than a belief in the possibility and promise of forms of visibility that are not always already yoked to vectors of power.

In contrast, artistic projects that mobilize collectives to "look back" may productively depart from appeals to representational truths. A compelling example of such art manifested during the December 2014 Millions March in New York City. During this event, demonstrators, including family members of people killed by the police, marched from Greenwich Village to the NYC police headquarters to protest the lack of a grand jury indictment for police officer Daniel Pantaleo, who choked Eric Garner to death while arresting him earlier that year.[67] Protesters at the front of the procession carried eight large signs, which together formed a stunning black-and-white image of Eric Garner's eyes (see figure 5.4).[68]

This artwork, designed by the Parisian photographer and street artist JR, affords the heterogeneous crowd a shared, singular focus as it is unified in—and behind—a representation of human life under attack by state and police violence. The eyes stare resolutely into those of viewers and into the lenses of cameras; they produce a gaze that is both sad and hopeful, reaching out to the viewer for empathy and recognition of shared humanity. Still, the eyes do challenge. They place viewers under the gaze. More than simply demanding to be seen, they also look back. They call out police, policy makers, complicit bystanders, and indeed the country as a whole with its white supremacist roots. They destabilize by peering into the racist status quo and recognizing it as such, by not pretending that racial violence is exceptional or nonsystemic. This artwork draws upon its situated construction as part of a collective movement to contest the authority of

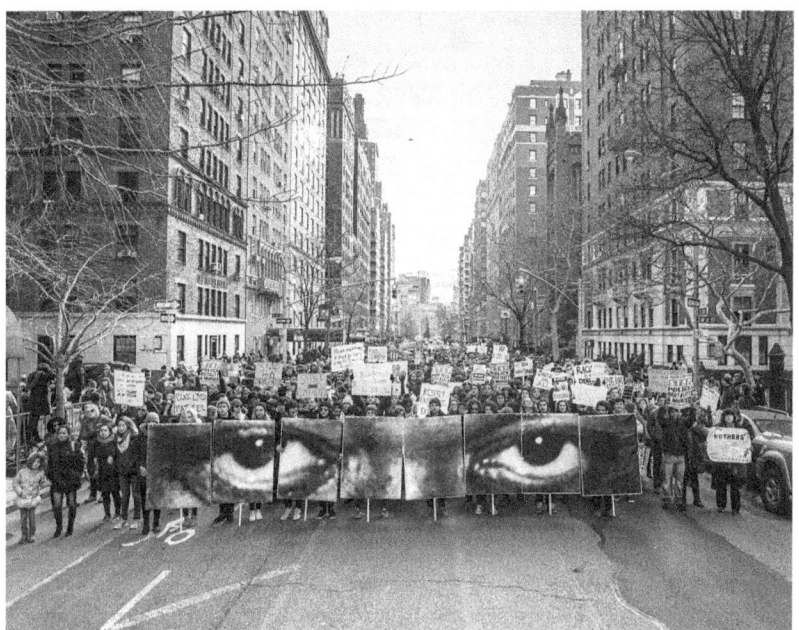

FIGURE 5.4. JR, *Eric Garner's Eyes* (2014). Courtesy of the artist.

crisis-vision regimes that would position black death as both normative and inconsequential or, worse, that would position it as fabrication. Rather than assert new visual truth claims or reify older ones, by looking back, this art project seeks to interrupt the status quo, to reject rationalizations of police violence and the racist system that grants them legitimacy.

What Remains

In *Scenes of Subjection*, Hartman writes of the vital role played by tenuous constructions of community within slave plantation cultures and beyond. Through shared dance, song, and stories, in fleeting spaces apart from the toil and terror of slave work, an essential semblance of community could be achieved: "The pleasure associated with surreptitious gatherings was due, in part, to the sense of empowerment derived from collective action and the precariousness and fragility of 'community.' . . . These practices were important because they were vehicles for creating and experiencing supportive, enjoyable, and nurturing connections. They were enactments of community, not expressions of an a priori unity."[69] Although Hartman is clear that one should not romanticize such notions of community, which were marked also by antagonism and disparity, they direct attention to the significance of relative opacity and resilient expressive cultural forms, such as dance, which can channel shared experience under the harshest conditions. In this respect, these enactments of community are forms of wake work that assert meaning and insist on survival within dehumanizing structures but apart from their logics.

The contemporary dance piece *What Remains* operates in this idiom, seeking to ground current modalities of antiblack surveillance within a historical context of slavery that continues to shape the present. Created by director and choreographer Will Rawls, poet Claudia Rankine, and visual designer John Lucas—and staged in multiple US venues from 2018 to 2019—*What Remains* interrogates the power and influence of "the void," a radically empty space of nonexistence that positions black life as invalid yet also offers some cover for survival and meaning making.[70] Rawls eloquently recounts: "The inspiration for this project is the rather dark desire to contour the space of erasure that is foisted upon people of color across cultural, legislative, and social fields in the U.S. . . . The void is a space of potential energy, one that is both deathly but also charged with liveness and willpower."[71]

Existing within "the already dead space" of the void, as Rankine characterizes it, is itself a major accomplishment for people of color in a white supremacist society. Crisis vision inflects this process as nonwhite bodies are continuously placed under conditions of hostile scrutiny and erasure, such that internalized self-surveillance and self-correction become necessary tools for survival. Rankine reflects: "That's one thing about being black in America . . . you have to curtail your movements, to live in such a way that what the white gaze projects upon blackness will not end your life. So you're always thinking, can I walk at night? Can I hold Skittles in my hand? Can I have my cellphone out? If it glitters, will somebody think it's a gun? At what point can I just be?"[72] From this view, whiteness serves as a pervasive background condition, a normative force field that modulates the lives and potentialities, the possibilities and impossibilities, of all bodies within its reach. Dance and other forms of creative expression can symbolize and enact lines of flight from such overdetermined conditions. According to Rawls, dance "really is the body insisting on its own presence, over and over and over, from second to second, minute to minute."[73]

What Remains traces an arc from the capture and enslavement of African people to the devastation of the Middle Passage, to escapes and attainments of freedom, and to persistent devaluations of black life in the present. Throughout this hour-long performance, four black dancers, three women and one man, dance, vocalize, and recite on the floor level of a small performance space mere feet from a mostly white audience.[74] Much of the piece occurs in darkened or shaded spaces, for the lighting establishes sharp monochromatic contrasts with only rare splashes of filtered dark-blue or warm golden spotlights. An ambient droning sound provides an aural undercurrent throughout the performance, suggesting a slave vessel's transit as heard from below deck; the sound is a constant throughout the dance, even as drumbeats and synthesizer instrumentation add other sonic layers later in the piece. At intervals, a disembodied female voice intones selected lines from Rankine's poetry:

Some years there exists a wanting to escape—
you, floating above your certain ache—
still the ache coexists.
Call that the immanent you—
You are you even before you
grow into understanding you
are not anyone, worthless,
not worth you.
Even as your own weight insists
you are here, fighting off
the weight of nonexistence.[75]

The performance begins with four figures draped in black robes, standing with their backs to a gray cinderblock wall. They stand straight, facing the audience as if on an auction block, presenting themselves for scrutiny but not without a hint of defiance as they stare directly ahead. Almost imperceptibly at first, the dancers walk forward with highly controlled, slow-motion steps. Their movement has the effect of gradually transforming a seemingly two-dimensional space into three dimensions, their presence and embodiment asserted through corporeal expression as they close the gap between performers and audience. Next, as if in recognition of their loss, the dancers repeatedly sing the word "you" and other minimalist vocalizations, creating chant-like harmonies that eventually crescendo into louder, overlapping tones interspersed with moans and cries. They throw their arms backward, perhaps pointing to their place of origin, some of their faces contorted in anguish as the theater lights dramatically extinguish, plunging the dancers and audience into profoundly shadowed darkness. In this darkened space, one can barely detect the dancers' shifting movements in front of a large projection of a silhouetted human head and torso. As deep undersea-hued blue lights fade in along with low organ-like tones, the three female figures move together across the stage, speeding up and slowing down, as they march and lunge with arms swaying back and forth (see figure 5.5). The male figure has been lost along the way.

As the piece develops, the remaining female dancers occasionally touch one another tentatively as they proceed: here holding a hand, there placing a supportive arm around another's shoulder. There are rare moments where their paths bring them into a warmer, golden-filtered spotlight— spaces of hope or perhaps happiness along their difficult journey. Before one can easily recognize it as such, the movement transforms into a collective, individuals who maintain their distinctness while moving as one. Together they run, duck, twist, and hide. They are separated and fall but not completely; their arms and outstretched legs support them just barely

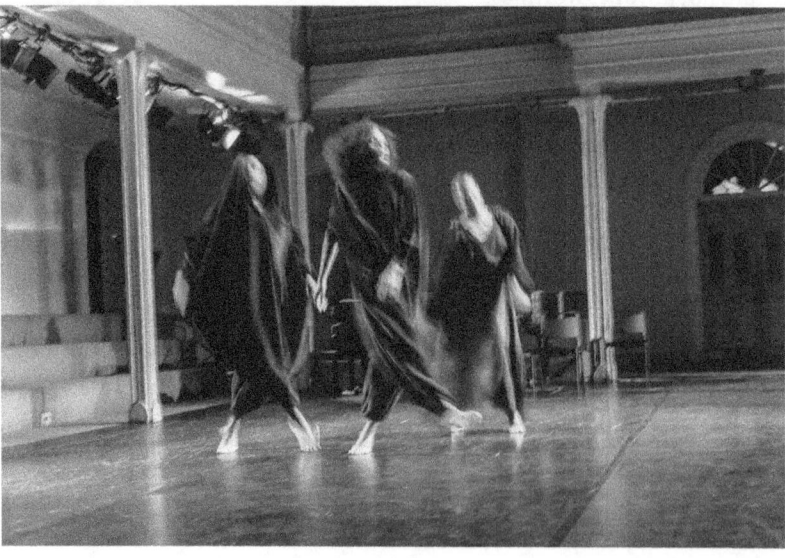

FIGURE 5.5. Will Rawls, Claudia Rankine, and John Lucas, *What Remains* (2017). Photograph by Rachel Papo for the *New York Times*.

off the ground (see figure 5.6). They violently bob and lurch into standing positions, carry each other, and huddle together before slowly moving apart. A voice speaks, "I thought I was dead." After this escape, the dancers shed their robes, at which point the male figure returns, emerging from the left, removing his own robes and walking briefly into the light before moving on.

Next, the four dancers stand in a spotlight facing one another. Tentatively and cautiously, as if both embarrassed and worried, they sing and laugh before belting out in harmony, "I don't want nobody fucking with me in these streets. . . . Ain't nobody got time for that shit." As the performance winds down, traces of the contemporary enter, with disco balls and drum loops, but the spoken words circle back to plaintive articulations of devalued life and of the struggle of pushing back on those truisms: "In so many words, I'm already dead," "I still count, she did say," "'If anything were to happen to me, I could live with that.' . . . . I think he means he could live with his own death, and I want to tell him that he doesn't have to, you know? Thou art nothing," "Our curious street fills with gaps created by the indirectness of experience. Thou art nothing." Eventually, the male

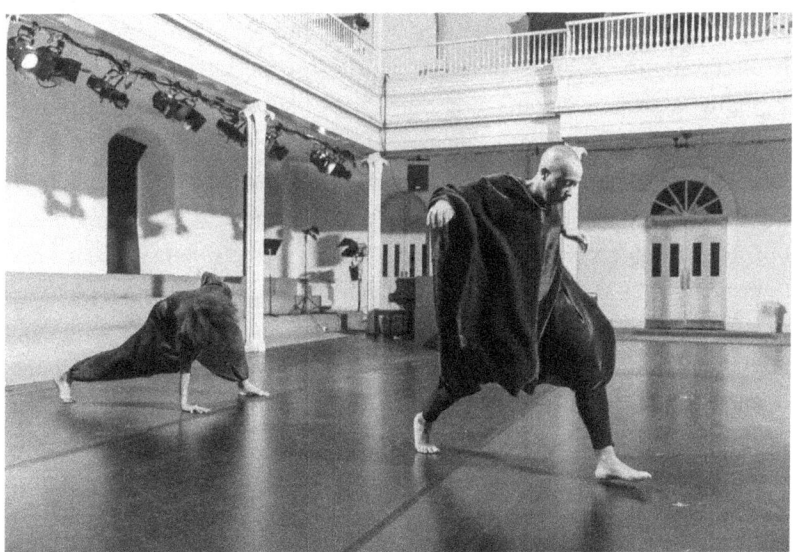

FIGURE 5.6. Will Rawls, Claudia Rankine, and John Lucas, *What Remains* (2017). Photograph by Rachel Papo for the *New York Times*.

figure departs while the three others dance again, flowing more freely than before. One by one they exit until only one remains, holding a pose with a palm facing the back wall, the past from whence they started. The remaining dancer turns off the digital soundtrack, picks up a disco ball, and leaves, drawing uncomfortable, tentative claps from the audience that is not certain whether the performance is over.

What does this complex, multilayered performance tell us about slavery's wake and what remains? Certainly, a sense of longing and loss remains. Tense, uncertain, and difficultly realized existence remains. Compromise remains, perhaps necessarily so, as conveyed by articulations of being able to live with one's own (social) death. Survival, song, dance, and poetry emerge from the darkness and push forward. Community is constituted and disbanded, hopefully to be reanimated again. Because the performance cannot be divorced from its relationship with an audience, because it is defined by that relationship, a constitutive relationship with white society remains, along with all that that connotes: that one is subject to the visibility, judgment, authority, and violence implicit in such relations. Therefore, links between surveillance and racism remain, leading to internalized surveillance and—following from Frantz Fanon[76]—the fabrication of corrosive split identities as a precondition for survival.

Opacity does dangerous work in such a context. It hides the dancers and their referents, offering a space for survival but also a cover for atrocity. It discomfits the shifting audience, violating expectations for compliant legibility and thereby contesting the racial order, which is a practice that has brought swift, retaliatory negation in nontheater settings (for example, from slavers, lynch mobs, police, vigilantes). At the same time, following the insights of Édouard Glissant,[77] the contouring and shading of the opaque deconstructs objective binaries, such as those between dark and light or survival and death. It productively obfuscates not only the performance but also linear temporalities that would position the past as remote and racial semiotic codes that would position darkness as a site of nonexistence. In this reading, opacity has the capacity to support a recognition of the persistent presence of slavery's wake while also interrupting pornotropic voyeurism of racialized violence. Crucially, while dance within and out of the shadows asserts being through movement, the creative potential rests not with opacity itself but instead with the collective coming together that occurs within it.[78] Thus, whereas the transient nature of live performances may catalyze relational adjustments, especially if viewers are decentered and forfeit control over the conditions of representation,[79] performances such as dance may also make visible, even if fleetingly, the constitutive elements of social lives in ways that may "leave a trace" and effect cultural change.[80]

Conclusion

This chapter has approached surveillance as entrenched in the tenacious, racializing logics of crisis vision. Surveillance may have discrete manifestations in classification systems or visualization technologies, but awareness of these instantiations can in fact distract one from recognizing the deeper discriminatory roots of such systems, as well as the continual physical and psychic damage perpetrated by them. Therefore, the artworks and performances analyzed here share a critical commitment to unearthing and problematizing these racist cultural underpinnings, to recognizing surveillance as both a symptom of racist social orders and a mechanism by which they reproduce themselves.

Sharpe's concept of *the wake* offers a way of thinking about the turbulent iteration of racial inequality and violence across time and space. There are no clean breaks within the powerful historical currents of slavery and oppression, only modulations and, hopefully, dissipation over time. Wake work insists upon remembrance that is supported by opacity but grounded in human relations and communities, remembrance that celebrates the lives of loved ones while mourning the devastating effects of systemic and arbitrary acts of racial violence. The ethical imperative of this work is to survive within and in spite of such noxious conditions but also to do what one can to disrupt them.

The art and performance pieces reviewed here each stage forms of creative disruption to crisis vision. They do this by troubling dominant signifying regimes that would position racialized surveillance/violence couplings as historical and exceptional rather than as foundational and routine. Thus, Thomas's *Raise Up* sculpture draws parallels between the violent subjectification of nonwhite bodies in apartheid-era South Africa and Western contexts today. By lodging that symbolic connection within a framework of oversaturated whiteness while suggesting (the need for) revolutionary acts of departure, Thomas underscores the lingering codependence of liberation efforts and persistent regimes of white supremacy. Scott's installations *Stop* and *Blue Wall of Violence* similarly trace patterns in the dehumanizing experiences and deadly effects of police surveillance and assault on people of color across national contexts. That Scott's works, based on empirical facts, have generated such public criticism reveals both the dominance and fragility of narratives of police virtuousness. Artwork produced and used by the Black Lives Matter movement disrupts through forms of culture jamming, such as representing and confronting white audiences with their own indifference, and through overt challenges to the police's monopoly on visibility. Finally, Rawls, Rankine, and Lucas's dance performance *What Remains* expresses in a grand narrative form the obstinate reproduction of slavery's social and human devastation across time. This piece's refusal to offer redemption, especially not in the form of piercing luminosity or white audiences' contentment, unsettles mainstream theater conventions and confounds easy conclusions about ways forward.

The primary tension with such works is between regimes of white liberal personhood premised on the exclusion and abjection of racialized minorities and the potential for alternative orders that depart from—or originate from opaque spaces beyond—those regimes. It is a dissonance inscribed in the very bodies of subjugated persons, which has led scholars such as Armond Towns to theorize the black body as a medium in its own right: "[Understanding] the Black body as a medium points not solely to white racial imaginations of us, but toward Black people's (but of course not only Black people's) creativity, toward the production of the new forms of humanness that lie at the crux of colonial projects that instrumentalized people and things."[81] I do not intend to suggest a resolution to this dissonance, for perhaps resolution itself would miss the point: the artistic frame of disruption, as presented here, achieves its creative vitality by holding these elements in tension and seeing what materializes. It inspires different ways of representing and grappling with the complexities of racial inequality and violence without reducing those complexities to ready-made solutions that could be measured against institutional practicalities (or "common sense") and found wanting. The power of these artworks rests in their ability to express the unspeakable, to manifest community, and to challenge authority, especially authorized forms of visibility and surveillance that support racial violence.

Crisis vision profoundly shapes how people perceive the problems of the world today. As it is materialized through practices, it carves out divisions among people and groups and encourages the scapegoating of others for rampant insecurities. It breeds new forms of authoritarianism and nationalism, leading to self-destructive isolationist stances, such as anti-immigration fervor in the United States and Brexit in the United Kingdom. It draws upon and solidifies structural racism and racial violence, rendering black and brown bodies as targets for dehumanizing police and state aggression. Finally, it interpellates subjects differentially, encouraging people to see themselves and others along a racialized continuum of threat and to accept those placements as accurate and true. As theorized in this book, crisis vision festers within the inherent contradictions of liberal humanism. Rights have never been apportioned equally and in fact have been secured for some through their denial to others. To the extent that racial subjugation serves as a *constitutive* feature of societies, not merely as a passing exception, then crisis-vision regimes can be seen as reproducing and regulating white supremacist racial orders.

Surveillance is essential to the operations of crisis vision. As a primary organizing principle of modernity, it infuses institutions and channels their activities toward the production of visibility, calculability, and control. Whether by state policing and security forces or by data behemoths such as Google and Amazon, surveillance activities are defined by power asymmetries, by relations of domination and extraction that are often obscured by the technical apparatuses being used.[1] The security agency embraces secrecy; the police restrict access to their visual evidence; the algorithm masks its politics in code. A key contention of this book has been that surveillance, far from being neutral, is an implement of racialization, an exercise of power that secures racial hierarchies. With roots in the visibility imperatives of the Enlightenment and the scientific revolution, surveillance as we know it today safeguards distributions of the sensible[2] that profess equality and democracy, on one hand, yet enforce inequality and exclusion, on the other. As James Harding succinctly comments, "Policing and surveillance technologies are simply manifestations of a society that despite its democratic pretenses is nonetheless regulated through the exercise of brute force, intimidation, and subtle forms of state-sanctioned domestic terror."[3]

In the current conjuncture, surveillance is both a weapon of and an outlet for crisis vision; it provides a way to activate racial divisions while grounding them in a seemingly rational and objective institutional foundation. In the years immediately following the attacks of 9/11, racialized surveillance took the form of airport screening, fortified borders, profiling of Muslims and Arabs, "If you see something, say something" campaigns, extraordinary rendition and torture, and targeted drone killings. More recent articulations have been grounded in conspiracy theories about threats posed to whites by racial and ethnic minorities, leading to intensified antiblack police violence, travel bans and immigration restrictions, social media doxing of progressive activists or politicians, and, under the Trump presidency, calls for (white) citizens to "monitor" polling places in minority neighborhoods or to organize armed militias to intimidate those protesting racial injustice.

This hardly inclusive list demonstrates how differential forms of interpellation occur based on how one is being hailed by crisis vision. Racialized bodies straddle a tense invisible/hypervisible relation, where, to invoke Ralph Ellison's *Invisible Man*, social invisibility within a white supremacist society may be expected and normalized.[4] Charles Mills further explains: "Ralph Ellison's famous trope of invisibility . . . relies on the notion of a peculiar class of bodies that appear only to disappear . . . [such that] black presence becomes absence, so that one is seen as the unseen."[5] Importantly, I would add, perceived deviations from that category of the unseen can render black and brown bodies hypervisible, as a challenge to the racial order.[6] Thus, interpellation can play upon a sense of what W. E. B. Du Bois described as a "double-consciousness . . . of always looking at one's self through the eyes of others" so that one is aware of how one is expected to be (un)seen as a minority.[7] Rankine's articulation of apprehension, recounted in the last chapter, captures this sentiment precisely, where the challenge for minoritized individuals is "to live in such a way that what the white gaze projects upon blackness will not end your life."[8] However, normative white subjects are positioned either as unjustly threatened, whether by racialized others or state scrutiny, or as responsible for mitigating that threat by acting as unofficial proxies for the state.[9] The fact that there is significant slippage among these assigned categories—for instance, with diverse coalitions of proponents for racial justice—illustrates some of the ways that dominant modes of interpellation can fail or be destabilized by competing calls upon subjects. These are the types of slippages that artworks can effectively stage as forms of intervention.

Artistic Inquiry and Intervention

As we have seen, artworks can be especially generative at revealing the contemporary problematics of crisis vision. At the outset, they can help us locate crisis vision temporally by tracking the proliferation of critical surveillance art starting in the early 2000s and accelerating rapidly after Snowden's revelations of mass state surveillance in 2013. Although there were important precursors, such as artist Julia Scher's installations exploring gender and security in the 1980s, which are themes that she continues to investigate today,[10] the recent coalescence of art projects points to a formation of a problem space around issues of technological surveillance, ambiguity, and instability throughout societies.[11] Technological advancements with big data, algorithmic processing, pervasive smart systems, and artificial intelligence run alongside social attunement to widespread racial injustice and violence, global pandemics, destructive climate change, and xenophobic state policies and practices. In my book *Surveillance in the Time of Insecurity* (2010), I described these nascent conditions as being driven by neoliberal logics percolating throughout societies, making increasingly privatized surveillance and security solutions seem viable and necessary.[12] At the present moment, however, crisis and conflict have come to the fore of collective consciousness. Trust in state institutions—law enforcement, public health, and environmental protection—is disintegrating, and media-spheres (especially online) are riven with conspiracy theories and hyper-polarization of audiences in algorithmically policed filter bubbles.[13] In this milieu it is impossible for concerns with surveillance to be *simply* about technology, security, or privacy alone; rather, such concerns are saturated with overwhelming apprehension about crises that reside on the border of one's comprehension but well beyond one's control.

Just as earlier art movements revealed how subjects or viewers were composed by their times,[14] critical surveillance art performs ways of seeing and being seen under conditions of crisis vision. Across the book's chapters, I mapped these relationships thematically onto artistic frames: avoidance, transparency, complicity, violence, and disruption. The frame of "avoidance" highlights a sense of white privilege under attack. Whereas populist rejections of masking during the COVID-19 pandemic reasserted aggression as a response to perceived encroachments on white freedom, artistic masking projects operated on the other end of the political spectrum to claim freedom from—or control over—surveillance. In both cases the performances tacitly affirmed crisis vision's continuum of threat by centering whiteness as the locus of privilege, as the subject position from which any infringements could be seen as a violation of inherent rights.

The frame of "transparency" illustrates how crisis vision depends on institutional archives that obscure their own biased operations as they segment populations and manufacture consequential truths about them. The archives of national security agencies, law enforcement, or companies like Google each exert significant yet concealed influence on social and political domains. Through the fabrication of alternative and explicitly partial archives, artists expose the fragility of the epistemological edifices supporting crisis vision.

Focusing on audiences directly, the frame of "complicity" sketches some of the fraught connections among subjects under crisis vision. By playing upon relationships among viewers, artworks in this register make the background dissonance and discomfort of crisis vision audible. They bring to awareness ever-present conditions of ambiguity and vulnerability, which are conditions that are aggravated by processes of technological mediation and automation. Attending to complicity can foster recognition of shared responsibility for the discriminatory or violent outcomes of crisis vision.

Moving to a direct confrontation of the destructive ramifications of crisis vision, the frame of "violence" troubles how vulnerable groups are constructed and treated globally. Crisis vision informs both policies and cultural narratives that normalize structural and symbolic violence against racialized minorities, refugees, precarious laborers, arrestees, LGBTQ+ individuals, and others. At the same time, and symptomatic of crisis-vision logics more broadly, this artistic frame leans upon regimes of liberal personhood and idealistic articulations of universal human rights in ways that often occlude racial difference and neglect issues of complicity.

Finally, the frame of "disruption" tackles this very weakness by exploring how surveillance-based applications of crisis vision are always racialized. From this perspective, revitalized liberal orders cannot be the response to racialized violence because those orders are premised on racial domination through conquest and possession. This artistic frame forces recognition of how crisis vision constructs and positions subjects differentially, such that fundamental change may be impossible without the fabrication of an entirely new system of relations.

Although art can provide a glimpse of the nuances and complexities of crisis vision and can further collective understanding of its problematics, I have approached art as being much more than just diagnostic or mimetic. Instead, I have interpreted artworks as being constitutive of the problem spaces they frame and as agential in intervening in those spaces. Just as with this book, artworks about surveillance do not stand apart from what they critique; rather, they participate in what I have described as the cultural production of surveillance. They contribute to a larger discourse about the problems of, and solutions to, surveillance. Therefore, whether they recenter or destabilize racial hierarchies matters; whether they privilege individualized or collective solutions matters; whether they confront or deny complicity matters. These positions are crucial because through them the artworks contribute to the formation of subjects and relations, responsibilities and possibilities. They provide an ideological hail to viewers and participants that can serve as a potentially influential counter to crisis vision.

Envisioning Opacity

Opacity offers an aesthetic intervention in the destructive patterns and dynamics of crisis vision. Following from Édouard Glissant, the valorization of transparency, which I have described as a core function of surveillance, necessarily reduces subjects in order to make them legible and governable. It diminishes and restricts possibilities for alternative subjectivities or social relations. Transparency folds bodies and epistemologies into a universal frame such that even a recognition of "difference," which might otherwise be seen as a progressive development, ultimately reifies a hierarchical system within which one could be recognized and assessed: "In order to understand and thus accept you, I have to measure your solidity with the ideal scale providing me with grounds to make comparisons and, perhaps, judgments. I have to reduce."[15] This hierarchical system, as I have asserted in conversation with black studies scholarship, is one of racial subordination and exclusion, one where participation implicates subjects in the maintenance of a system of white supremacy.

The concept of opacity evades the gravitational pull of transparency, including its reformist but problematic discourses of inclusion, to stress ethical relations within conditions of irreducibility. Opacity focuses not on depths or essences but instead on points of contact and interchange. Glissant writes: "Opacities can coexist and converge, weaving fabrics. To understand these truly one must focus on *the texture of the weave* and not the nature of its components."[16] Thus, opacity should not be understood as privacy or obscurity but instead as an embrace of ethical responsibility, of living with others without positioning them, sizing them up, controlling them. It places value on the texture of the weave, the interfaces among rather than the truths below. The difficulty of speaking of opacity or pinning down its definition is precisely the point. That impulse toward encapsulation, while completely understandable and rational, emerges from a scientistic worldview that would place primary value on clarity, not acceptance of messy conceptual—and embodied—entanglements. Approaching the opaque demands an *unraveling* and an *untelling* of the metanarratives of scientific mastery and the liberal project.

Although it may seem counterintuitive, articulations of opacity emerge from and are enabled by crisis vision. Because crisis vision encourages the dehumanization of racialized Others, marking them as unknowable and unassimilable, it also admits of the persistence of life beyond the rationalities of liberal society. Thus, as my analysis of artwork in the last chapter found, conditions of social exclusion can foster unrestrained and unaccountable state violence against minoritized groups, but the premise of radical difference that covers for that violence fabricates a space apart, an irreducibility that itself is interpreted as a threat to the racial order. By inquiring into these spaces, as artists such as Hank Willis Thomas, Will Rawls, Claudia Rankine, and John Lucas do, one can detect traces of the opaque and possibilities for coexistence and collective coming together. This is neither to romanticize exclusion nor to argue that crisis vision is a necessary orientation for the conjuring of opacity. Instead, it is a recognition of what Weheliye calls "freedom in zones of indistinction,"[17] where even under the worst conditions, the possibilities for meaningful collective life remain and assert themselves against that which would negate their existence.

Throughout this book I have argued that the artworks that make the greatest incision into the social are those that confront and destabilize crisis vision and its socially corrosive racial hierarchies. The artworks that challenge viewers to question their places within inherently unjust social orders are those that also tilt toward relations of collective opacity. For instance, Kai Wiedenhöfer's WALLonWALL project confronts viewers with the materiality and prevalence of border walls that maintain political, ethnic, and religious divisions. This photographic display resignifies existing border walls in communities by showing how they are part of a larger project of egregious bordering practices around the world. Viewers are called out, both individually and collectively, as complicit parties in the violence of bordering. The provocation is toward conversation and collective reassessment of borders both locally and beyond. Likewise, Dries Depoorter's Jaywalking project, though not didactically about racial inequities, challenges participants to see themselves as part of surveillance apparatuses with unknown, unaccountable, but likely discriminatory outcomes for targets. By injecting accountability into that schema, where participants must make a choice (to report infractions or not) in the presence of others, Depoorter produces a competing relationship of complicity to add friction to the notion of stable subjects who are not responsible for the plight of others. In a different vein, Dread Scott's installation Stop also forces a recognition in viewers of the humanity and inhumane treatment of people of color who are routinely stopped and searched by police. The video walls of nonwhite men facing viewers and insisting on being seen and heard as fellow human beings generates a space of collectivity and collective responsibility. In each of these examples the artworks fabricate a zone of opacity that emphasizes ethical connections among strangers, a starting point for disrupting or rerouting crisis vision.

While not engaging with complicity head-on, the artworks that question the archival foundations of state and corporate surveillance systems are able to stage what Karen Louise Grova Søilen would call "atmospheres of surveillance" that can "subtly and suggestively penetrate everyday life down to our feelings, moods, and the movements of our bodies."[18] Paglen's photographs of security installations, Cirio's reproduction of Google Street View images, and Elahi's photographs of self-disclosure generate conditions of uneasy ambiguity to underscore both the partiality and uncertainty of institutional transparency schemes. These works unmoor crisis vision from its scientific or bureaucratic basis. In my terms, they point to liberating opacity that could manifest on a structural level: they invite reassessment of archival relations that could support the irreducibility of subjects.

Finally, the critical surveillance art projects that do not activate opacity, or that have trouble doing so, nonetheless reveal the difficulties of change under a crisis-vision regime. A common approach is one that positions a liberal subject as being under assault from surveillance systems that would encroach upon their privacy. Most of the masking and makeup works covered in the chapter on avoidance would fall into this category. A related approach recognizes unjust and unequal forms of surveillance—for instance, of refugees in Europe, arrestees in the United States, or drone victims in Pakistan—but responds by embracing universal frameworks (such as human rights) as antidotes to those articulations of crisis vision. The projects that would fall into this category include Hanne Nielsen and Birgit Johnsen's *Drifting*, Paolo Cirio's *Obscurity*, and *#NotABugSplat*. Both the individualist and universalist lenses, though easily achieving traction and resonance with progressive audiences, recuperate a framework of liberal personhood, thereby failing to interrogate the role of that framework in the problems they identify.

The flight to opacity is a flight away from surveillance.[19] It is not about watching the watchers, dyadic resistance, or a retreat into privacy. Instead, it is about securing spaces for collective existence without being categorized and sorted, without being atomized and diminished. It is a project more radical than reform or accommodation within social hierarchies because it questions the very basis for those hierarchies. It questions promises of inclusion and rights when they are consistently foreclosed. It is not a destination but instead a commitment to being in the weave, with others, without boundaries.

NOTES

INTRODUCTION

1. Monahan, "Surveillance and Terrorism."

2. Roberta Smith, "Watch Out: You're in Ai Weiwei's Surveillance Zone," *New York Times*, June 8, 2017, accessed January 5, 2019, www.nytimes.com/2017/06/08/arts /design/watch-out-youre-in-ai-weiweis-surveillance-zone.html.

3. A portion of the *Hansel & Gretel* installation does allow visitors to scan for their own faces in the automatically generated photo archive. This does not reveal underlying code so much as demonstrate biometric capability, or lack thereof, as the failure rate is high. Smith, "Watch Out."

4. For example, Levin, Frohne, and Weibel, *Ctrl [Space]*.

5. Greenwald, *No Place to Hide*; Lyon, *Surveillance after Snowden*.

6. Grinberg, "Tracking Movements"; Monahan, "Built to Lie"; Parks and Kaplan, *Life in the Age of Drone Warfare*.

7. Benjamin, *Race after Technology*; Eubanks, *Automating Inequality*; Noble, *Algorithms of Oppression*.

8. Harcourt, *Exposed*; Lewis, *Under Surveillance*; Monahan, "Built to Lie"; Woods, "Asking More of Siri and Alexa."

9. Kreiss and Mcgregor, "'Arbiters of What Our Voters See'"; Marwick, "Why Do People Share Fake News?"

10. Lyon, *Surveillance Society*; Monahan and Murakami Wood, *Surveillance Studies*.

11. For a comprehensive overview of the origins and development of the transdisciplinary field of surveillance studies, see Monahan and Murakami Wood, "Introduction." For a few recent works that tackle issues of domination and oppression directly, see Beauchamp, *Going Stealth*; Browne, *Dark Matters*; Hall, *Transparent Traveler*; Harding, *Performance, Transparency, and the Cultures of Surveillance*; Kapadia, *Insurgent Aesthetics*; and Monahan, "Regulating Belonging."

12. Brighenti, "Visibility"; Fyfe and Law, "Introduction"; Mirzoeff, *Right to Look*.

13. Rancière, *Politics of Aesthetics*.

14. Mirzoeff employs the term *visuality* to signal Rancière's "distribution of the sensible." In this book I use the term *visibility* instead: (1) to underscore the relationship between

how one is seen and treated, and (2) to tackle more directly the social construction and constraints of visual apparatuses (surveillance systems, archives, infrastructures) that enfold artists and activists (and scholars) in complicit arrangements with that which they critique. Mirzoeff, *Right to Look*.

15. As will be discussed in later chapters, the frame of "the distribution of the sensible," while provocative, is overdetermined and does not adequately explain the process by which new or different social or cultural formations could emerge. Victor Turner, in a different register, reminds us that symbols also have the capacity to point toward or generate different (idealized) social orders, not merely reinforce current ones: "Symbols may well reflect not structure, but anti-structure, and not only reflect it but contribute to creating it." Turner, *Dramas, Fields, and Metaphors*, 270.

16. Merchant, *Death of Nature*, 169–72.

17. Shapin, *Social History of Truth*.

18. Terrall, "Gendered Spaces, Gendered Audiences."

19. Haraway, *Simians, Cyborgs, and Women*, 188–89.

20. On a parallel track, feminist science studies scholarship has likewise problematized the ways that medical imaging devices reduce bodies to visible representations of data, such that performances of scientific transparency often efface context, embodiment, and experience. As Paula Treichler, Lisa Cartwright, and Constance Penley caution, "Visibility is itself a claim that must be carefully examined: in acknowledging what is seen, and newly seen, we need to be equally vigilant about what is not seen, or no longer seen." Medical imaging technologies, as with other tools of visibility, draw upon and operate within cultural and media contexts to produce instrumental, but necessarily partial, meaning and value. Treichler, Cartwright, and Penley, "Introduction," 3. See also Cartwright, *Screening the Body*; Dumit, *Picturing Personhood*; Joyce, *Magnetic Appeal*; Saunders, CT *Suite*; and Van Dijck, *Transparent Body*.

21. Daston and Galison, "Image of Objectivity."

22. Scott, *Seeing Like a State*.

23. Scott, *Seeing Like a State*.

24. Cowen, *Deadly Life of Logistics*.

25. Frank Wilderson asserts that "the position of the Black is . . . a paradigmatic impossibility in the Western Hemisphere, indeed, in the world . . . [because] a Black is the very antithesis of a Human subject." Wilderson, *Red, White & Black*, 9. See also Sexton, *Amalgamation Schemes*; Spillers, "Mama's Baby, Papa's Maybe"; Hartman, *Scenes of Subjection*; and Weheliye, *Habeas Viscus*.

On a related note, there is ample debate and hand-wringing by authors and editors about whether to capitalize the word *black* or keep it lowercase. The dominant convention at the moment is to raise "Black" to uppercase while keeping "white" as lowercase, which grammatically flags the presence and importance of nonwhite groups. However, I worry that this convention risks normalizing whiteness, once again, as the absence of race, as that which does not need capitalization because it is assumed. I am also uncomfortable by the implied collapse of racial difference into a single proper-noun signifier, be it "Black," "Brown," or something else. Although my decision not to capitalize *black* is provisional, and I may have changed my mind by the time this book is in print, I find myself further persuaded by the eloquent treatment of this topic by La Marr Jurelle Bruce:

> I do not typically capitalize *black* because I do not regard it as a *proper* noun. Grammatically, the proper noun corresponds to a formal name or title assigned to an individual, closed, fixed entity. I use a lowercase *b* because I want to emphasize an *improper* blackness: a blackness that is a "critique of the proper"; a blackness that is collectivist rather than individualistic; a blackness that is "never closed and always under contestation"; a blackness that is ever-unfurling rather than rigidly fixed; a blackness that is neither capitalized nor propertized via the protocols of Western grammar; a blackness that centers those who are typically regarded as lesser and *lower cases*, as it were; a blackness that amplifies those who are treated as "minor figures," in Western modernity. I appreciate that some use the big *B* to confer respect, signal gravitas, and indicate specificity. However, the impropriety of lowercase blackness suits me, and this mad black project, just fine. Besides, my minor *b* is replete with respect, gravitas, and specificity-in-collectivity, too; its smallness does not limit the infinite care it contains. (Bruce, *How to Go Mad without Losing Your Mind*, 6)

26. Spillers, "Mama's Baby, Papa's Maybe."

27. Musser, *Sensual Excess*, 7.

28. I am referencing here the police killing of George Floyd in 2020, Eric Garner in 2014, and Daniel Prude in 2020, respectively.

29. Browne, *Dark Matters*, 9.

30. Browne, *Dark Matters*; Cole, *Suspect Identities*; Mirzoeff, *Right to Look*.

31. Whereas the emphasis here is on scientific and state institutions, feminist scholars have also illustrated the destructive ramifications of a normalized male gaze, which differentially positions women as passive objects to be scrutinized (or self-scrutinized) and controlled. See, for example, Dubrofsky and Magnet, *Feminist Surveillance Studies*; hooks, "Oppositional Gaze"; Monahan, "Dreams of Control at a Distance"; and Mulvey, "Visual Pleasure and Narrative Cinema."

32. For example, Andrea Mubi Brighenti uses the term *surveillance art* to describe aesthetic works that engage with "topics, concerns and procedures" relevant to the study of surveillance in society. Brighenti, "Artveillance," 175. For Elise Morrison, surveillance art includes a range of art and performance projects "in which surveillance technologies are central to their production, design, content, aesthetics, and/or reception." Morrison, *Discipline and Desire*, 7.

33. Berger, *Ways of Seeing*; Crary, *Suspensions of Perception*; Crary, *Techniques of the Observer*.

34. Crary, *Suspensions of Perception*.

35. Canclini, *Art beyond Itself*, xiii.

36. I borrow the term *visual economy* from Deborah Poole and adapt it throughout this book to frame crisis-vision economies of surveillance. For Poole, the term is better suited than other terms, such as *visual culture*, for "thinking about visual images as part of a comprehensive organization of people, ideas, and objects." Whereas *visual culture* might better reference "shared meanings and community," *visual economy*

stresses "social relationships, inequality, and power." Poole, *Vision, Race, and Modernity*, 8.

37. Kapadia, *Insurgent Aesthetics*, 39.

38. This orientation harmonizes with J. Macgregor Wise's development of the concept of the "surveillant imaginary" to analyze the performative effects of surveillance themes in popular films: "The surveillant imaginary is a regime of representation, an attempt at a coherent and seamless narrative about how the world is. . . . The tension in film is between the ways it papers over the contradictions and antagonisms of the social and the ways it can reveal those antagonisms." Wise, *Surveillance and Film*, 6. See also Fang, *Arresting Cinema*; Lefait, *Surveillance on Screen*; Pallitto, *Bargaining with the Machine*; and Zimmer, *Surveillance Cinema*.

39. Morrison, *Discipline and Desire*, 11.

40. Brighenti, "Visibility," 328.

41. Bishop, *Artificial Hells*.

42. See China Medel for an account of how artworks might catalyze "ethical spectatorship" on the part of viewers by activating feeling and the corporeal components of seeing. Medel, "Transactional Seeing and Becoming Flesh."

43. Monahan, "Reckoning with Covid, Racial Violence, and the Perilous Pursuit of Transparency."

44. Andrejevic, *Infoglut*.

45. Monahan, "Regulating Belonging."

46. Hall, *Transparent Traveler*.

47. Hall, *Transparent Traveler*, 7.

48. Hall, *Transparent Traveler*.

49. In keeping with my previous critical scholarship in surveillance studies, I see this book as contributing to feminist and antiracist surveillance studies. As Rachel Hall writes, "Feminist scholars of surveillance . . . shift critical surveillance studies away from matters of privacy, security, and efficiency to a consideration of the political problem of combating new forms of discrimination that are practiced in relation to categories of privilege, access, and risk." Hall, *Transparent Traveler*, 19. See also Beauchamp, *Going Stealth*; Benjamin, *Race after Technology*; Browne, *Dark Matters*; Dubrofsky and Magnet, *Feminist Surveillance Studies*; Fischer, *Terrorizing Gender*; Koskela, "'You Shouldn't Wear That Body'"; Magnet, *When Biometrics Fail*; Monahan, "Surveillance and Inequality"; Monahan, "Dreams of Control at a Distance"; Monahan, "Regulating Belonging"; and van der Meulen and Heynen, *Expanding the Gaze*.

50. The concept of opacity should not be conflated with privacy, for the two operate in completely different registers and in many ways are at odds. Whereas opacity emphasizes collectives and the irreducibility of subjects, privacy emphasizes individuals and their representative data elements. Whereas opacity underscores violent exclusions, erasures, and incommensurabilities at the heart of liberal social orders, privacy invokes discourses of universality and shared fundamental rights within those orders. The different orientations of these concepts can also be mapped onto modes of activist or artistic resistance to surveillance, in which those seeking ways of rejecting categori-

zation schemes may be working toward opacity, whereas those striving to "obfuscate" data are more likely embracing privacy.

51. Glissant, *Poetics of Relation*, 114, 190.

52. This is consonant with what Rachel Hall describes as critical "antirealist" approaches to surveillance studies, which assume "that surveillance data is impoverished by comparison to the rich, inexhaustible, and unpredictable quality of lived experience, which includes the interior life of the imagination, creativity, memory, and desire." Hall, *Transparent Traveler*, 15.

53. Glissant, *Poetics of Relation*, 113.

54. Birchall, *Radical Secrecy*; Birchall, *Shareveillance*.

55. Beauchamp, *Going Stealth*; Blas, "Informatic Opacity"; Hall, *Transparent Traveler*.

56. Blas, "Informatic Opacity," 199.

57. Musser, *Sensual Excess*, 9–10.

58. Ruha Benjamin writes: "Glitches are generally considered a fleeting interruption of an otherwise benign system, not an enduring and constitutive feature of social life. But what if we understand glitches instead to be a slippery place . . . between fleeting and durable, micro-interactions and macro-structures, individual hate and institutional indifference? Perhaps in that case glitches are not spurious, but rather a kind of signal of how the system operates. Not an aberration but a form of evidence, illuminating underlying flaws in a corrupted system." Benjamin, *Race after Technology*, 80. In my discussion of opacity, glitches reveal the dehumanizing logic of crisis vision, which is a logic that undergirds its violence but also indicates its weakness.

59. As queer studies scholar Nicholas de Villiers posits, "Opaque and transparent— taken to their limits—don't work as opposites, since for something to be fully transparent it would be invisible, and for something to be completely opaque would mean complete blockage of vision altogether, another invisibility. So *opacity* is visible only outside of the purity of the opposition opaque/transparent itself." De Villiers, *Opacity and the Closet*, 22.

60. Eagleton, *Ideology of the Aesthetic*, 9.

61. Portions of Stephen Graham's work stand as early exceptions to this scholarly trend of deploying art merely as a resource for advancing social science arguments (Graham, *Cities under Siege*; Graham, *Vertical*). Andrea Brighenti also performed some foundational conceptual mapping of surveillance art projects ("Artveillance"). The field of surveillance studies is now growing rapidly, with more sustained and nuanced treatments of art. See, for example, the impressive critical work of James Harding, *Performance, Transparency, and the Cultures of Surveillance*; Elise Morrison, *Discipline and Desire*; Ronak Kapadia, *Insurgent Aesthetics*; Katherine Barnard-Wills and David Barnard-Wills, "Invisible Surveillance in Visual Art"; Simone Browne, *Dark Matters*; Susan Cahill, "Visual Art, Corporeal Economies, and the 'New Normal' of Surveillant Policing in the War on Terror"; Claudio Celis, "Critical Surveillance Art in the Age of Machine Vision and Algorithmic Governmentality"; Karen Louise Grova Søilen, "Safe Is a Wonderful Feeling"; and Agostinho et al., "Uncertain Archives: Approaching the Unknowns, Errors, and Vulnerabilities of Big Data through Cultural Theories of the Archive."

62. In this regard I share with Mark Andrejevic an approach to critique that does not stop with an investigation of symbols and their use but instead (also) analyzes the "social systems that generated [such symbols] and which they helped reproduce." Andrejevic, "Whither-Ing Critique," 222.

63. The primary performance studies books have been Elise Morrison's *Discipline and Desire* and James Harding's *Performance, Transparency, and the Cultures of Surveillance.* There are important differences between *Crisis Vision* and these other books. Whereas Morrison places faith in the potential of creative interventions and Harding agitates for artistically inspired activism, my theorization of opacity embraces art that uncovers slippages or glitches in surveillance regimes and that shows routes toward survival and escape. Rather than valorize acts of resistance, which might suggest a social order that could be reformed and recuperated, I place value on works that strive for opacity and destabilize liberal orders in the service of antiracism and ethical coexistence. At the same time, I also add to this scholarly domain by explicitly analyzing how artworks contribute to the cultural production of surveillance in ways that can unwittingly solidify liberal orders founded on white privilege and racial exclusion. See Harding, *Performance, Transparency, and the Cultures of Surveillance*; and Morrison, *Discipline and Desire.*

64. Piper, *Out of Order, Out of Sight*, 1:248.

65. Feeling operates as a form of knowledge, as an alternative epistemology that can mold a sense of shared opacity. With respect to technological surveillance in particular, Randolph Lewis writes: "*Feeling surveillance* is a complex experience with real implications for individual emotional lives as well as our collective political lives. . . . Instead of rendering ourselves frozen with fear, apathetic, or hyper-alert in response to the scrutiny of the powerful, we could think about the alternatives, the other ways of being in our bodies in this country right now." Lewis, *Under Surveillance*, 51.

CHAPTER ONE. **Avoidance**

Portions of chapter 1 were published as "The Right to Hide? Anti-surveillance Camouflage and the Aestheticization of Resistance," *Communication and Critical/Cultural Studies* vol. 12, no. 2 (2015).

1. Ashley Parker, Robert Klemko, and Mark Guarino, "Trump Blames 'Far-Left Politicians' for Violence in Wake of Police Shooting on Visit to Wisconsin," *Washington Post*, September 1, 2020, accessed September 17, 2020, www.washingtonpost.com/politics/trump-blames-far-left-politicians-for-violence-in-wake-of-police-shooting-on-visit-to-wisconsin/2020/09/01/5e65f89a-ec66-11ea-99a1-71343d03bc29_story.html; Gregory Krieg and Eric Bradner, "Trump Wants Americans to Believe Biden Is a Radical Leftist. It's a Tough Sell," CNN, July 9, 2020, accessed September 17, 2020, www.cnn.com/2020/07/09/politics/trump-biden-radical-left-attacks/index.html; Trump, "Remarks by President Trump in Press Briefing."

2. Maria Godoy and Daniel Wood, "What Do Coronavirus Racial Disparities Look Like State by State?," NPR, May 30, 2020, accessed July 14, 2020, www.npr.org/sections

/health-shots/2020/05/30/865413079/what-do-coronavirus-racial-disparities-look-like
-state-by-state; Rho, Brown, and Fremstad, *A Basic Demographic Profile of Workers in Frontline Industries*; Justin George, "For Many 'Essential Workers,' Public Transit Is a Fearful Ride They Must Take," *Washington Post*, April 11, 2020, accessed August 5, 2020, www.washingtonpost.com/local/trafficandcommuting/for-many-essential
-workers-public-transit-is-a-fearful-ride-they-must-take/2020/04/11/8dec874a-79ad
-11ea-a130-df573469f094_story.html; Center on Budget and Policy Priorities, "Tracking the Covid-19 Recession's Effects on Food, Housing, and Employment Hardships."

3. Nicole Gallucci, "8 Karens and Kens Who Threw Huge Tantrums instead of Putting on Masks," *Mashable*, June 29, 2020, accessed September 17, 2020, https://
mashable.com/article/karen-no-mask-videos-tantrums-coronavirus; Tiffany, "How 'Karen' Became a Coronavirus Villain."

4. Hall, *Transparent Traveler*, 13.

5. Aamer Madhani and Darlene Superville, "President Trump Says He Looks Like Lone Ranger in a Mask and Likes It: 'I'm All for Masks. I Think Masks Are Good,'" *Chicago Tribune*, July 1, 2020, accessed September 17, 2020, www.chicagotribune.com
/coronavirus/ct-nw-trump-coronavirus-mask-20200701-icf63vlvmfd37i3u4rclyyg3rm
-story.html.

6. *Countersurveillance* is defined as "intentional, tactical uses or disruptions of surveillance technologies to challenge power asymmetries." Monahan, *Surveillance in the Time of Insecurity*, 129.

7. Following Hanna Rose Shell, I approach camouflage as "a way of seeing, being, moving, and working in the world. It is a form of cultivated subjectivity. As such, it is an individuated form of self-awareness that is also part of a network of institutional practices." Therefore, I read these resistance efforts as part of larger cultural processes and critically interrogate their symbolic and performative functions. Shell, *Hide and Seek*, 19.

8. Mirzoeff, *Right to Look*, 6; Scott, *Seeing Like a State*.

9. Mirzoeff, *Right to Look*.

10. Mirzoeff, *Right to Look*; Agamben, *Homo Sacer*; Mbembe, "Necropolitics."
I am choosing to acknowledge human insecurity here without seeking to recuperate a rights-based approach to solutions. Whereas "human security," with its emphasis on freedom from fear or want, gained popularity as an attractive alternative to "national security" in the 1990s and has been embraced as a human rights and feminist approach to addressing the insecure status of the most vulnerable throughout the world (especially women and children), postcolonial scholars and others have questioned the ways that such human rights and humanitarian frames have been deployed in the service of imperial projects and perhaps cannot be separated from them. Puar, *Terrorist Assemblages*; Monahan, *Surveillance in the Time of Insecurity*; Suárez-Krabbe, "Other Side of the Story."

11. Mirzoeff, *Right to Look*; Monahan, "Regulating Belonging."

12. Graham, *Cities under Siege*; Foucault, *"Society Must Be Defended."*

13. Wall, "Unmanning the Police Manhunt"; Wall and Monahan, "Surveillance and Violence from Afar."

14. Gates, *Our Biometric Future*; Magnet, *When Biometrics Fail*.

15. Gilliom, *Overseers of the Poor*; Magnet and Rodgers, "Stripping for the State"; Monahan, "Surveillance and Inequality"; Wacquant, *Punishing the Poor*.

16. Monahan, *Surveillance in the Time of Insecurity*. Surveillance subjects are produced—or interpellated—through encounters with agents of authority, be they human or technological. As Tobias Matzner explains, "Somebody who is stopped at a border, denied a visa, or excluded from boarding a plane based on Big Data becomes a subject for the respective authorities in the very moment these verdicts happen." Matzner, "Beyond Data as Representation," 207. I build here upon my previous work on the discriminatory and uneven nature of these forms of surveillance-based interpellation. For related explorations of racialized interpellation, see Browne, "Digital Epidermalization"; and Fanon, *Black Skin, White Masks*.

17. Marx, *Undercover*.

18. Gandy, *Panoptic Sort*; Graham and Wood, "Digitizing Surveillance"; Lyon, *Surveillance Society*.

19. Ball, "Organization, Surveillance and the Body"; Koskela, "Video Surveillance, Gender, and the Safety of Public Urban Space"; Monahan, "Dreams of Control at a Distance"; Steeves, "Online Surveillance in Canadian Schools"; Wright, Glasbeek, and van der Meulen, "Securing the Home."

20. Dubrofsky and Magnet, *Feminist Surveillance Studies*.

21. Mason and Magnet, "Surveillance Studies and Violence against Women."

22. Harvey, "cv Dazzle."

23. Harvey, "How to Hide from Machines."

24. Meyer, "Avoid Facial Detection Algorithms . . . with a T-Shirt."

25. Harvey, "cv Dazzle."

26. Harvey, "How to Hide from Machines."

27. Compare Fernandez and Huey, "Is Resistance Futile? Thoughts on Resisting Surveillance."

28. Andrejevic, *Infoglut*; Murakami Wood and Ball, "Brandscapes of Control?"

29. Harvey, "How to Hide from Machines."

30. Andrejevic, *Infoglut*.

31. Marwick, *Status Update*; Duffy, *(Not) Getting Paid to Do What You Love*.

32. Fisher, "Tattooing the Body, Marking Culture," 102.

33. Barnard-Wills, *Surveillance and Identity*; Beauchamp, "Artful Concealment and Strategic Visibility"; Lyon, *Identifying Citizens*; Moore and Currah, "Legally Sexed"; van der Ploeg, "Illegal Body."

34. An interesting paradox emerges from these examples: hiding becomes a form of expression, and uniqueness is asserted by obscuring identity markers. This can be juxtaposed to other treatments of surveillance and media, such as reality television or films such as *The Hunger Games*, where *performance of nonperformance* signals "authenticity." Dubrofsky, "Surveillance on Reality Television and Facebook"; Dubrofsky and Ryalls, "Hunger Games." cv Dazzle, by contrast, overtly performs its own performance in an attempt to create a space for the cultivation of authentic subjects. It is worth probing the extent to which this is a largely white and privileged form of expression.

As Rachel Hall asserts, in the pursuit of state security the contemporary "aesthetics of transparency" holds the white body as the transparent ideal, whereas the perceived opaqueness of nonwhite bodies is viewed as threatening and in need of further investigation. Hall, "Of Ziploc Bags and Black Holes."

35. Morrison, *Discipline and Desire*, 202.

36. Browne, "Digital Epidermalization," 133–34.

37. Meyer, "Avoid Facial Detection Algorithms . . . with a T-Shirt."

38. Magnet, *When Biometrics Fail*.

39. Ca'Macana, "Old Tradition of Disguise"; Lévi-Strauss, *Structural Anthropology*.

40. Castells, *Power of Identity*; Matt Dellinger, "A Civil War Political Movement Reawakens—Complete with Capes," *New York Times*, September 15, 2020, accessed September 17, 2020, www.nytimes.com/2020/09/15/style/wide-awakes-civil-war -activists.html; Juris, *Networking Futures*; Thomas Nail, "The Politics of the Mask," *Huffington Post*, November 12, 2013, accessed May 25, 2014, www.huffingtonpost .com/thomas-nail/the-politics-of-the-mask_b_4262001.html; Shaw, "When Fashion Speaks."

41. Leslie Katz, "Anti-surveillance Mask Lets You Pass as Someone Else," CNET, May 8, 2014, accessed May 25, 2014, www.cnet.com/news/urme-anti-surveillance -mask-lets-you-pass-as-someone-else; Selvaggio, "URME Surveillance: Indiegogo Campaign."

42. Katz, "Anti-surveillance Mask Lets You Pass."

43. Selvaggio, "URME Surveillance: Indiegogo Campaign."

44. Selvaggio, "URME Surveillance: Indiegogo Campaign."

45. Michael Zimmer, "Mark Zuckerberg's Theory of Privacy," *Washington Post*, February 3, 2014, accessed May 29, 2014, www.washingtonpost.com/lifestyle/style/mark -zuckerbergs-theory-of-privacy/2014/02/03/2c1d780a-8cea-11e3-95dd-36ff657a4dae _story.html.

46. Selvaggio, "URME Surveillance: Performing Privilege," 182.

47. Bell, "Inner City and the 'Hoodie'"; Tuttle and Schneider, "Stopped-and-Frisked"; Nguyen, "Hoodie as Sign, Screen, Expectation, and Force"; Wall and Linnemann, "Staring Down the State."

48. Quoted in Katz, "Anti-surveillance Mask Lets You Pass."

49. Goffman, *Presentation of Self in Everyday Life*.

50. Haggerty and Ericson, "Surveillant Assemblage"; Barnard-Wills and Barnard-Wills, "Invisible Surveillance in Visual Art"; Lyon, *Surveillance as Social Sorting*; Nissenbaum, *Privacy in Context*.

51. Bowker and Star, *Sorting Things Out*; Monahan, "Surveillance as Cultural Practice"; Pfaffenberger, "Technological Dramas"; Winner, *Whale and the Reactor*.

52. Morrison, *Discipline and Desire*, 210.

53. Butler, *Gender Trouble*; Butler, *Bodies That Matter*.

54. Hall, Monahan, and Reeves, "Surveillance and Performance," 157. See also Butler, *Bodies That Matter*; Butler, *Gender Trouble*.

55. The artist's original Twitter post explained the project's primary rationale: "Made this service that prints your face on an N95 mask, so you can protect people

from viral epidemics while still being able to unlock your phone." Baskin, "Made This Service."

56. Baskin, "Facial ID Respirator Masks."

57. Chen, "How Coronavirus Turned the 'Dystopian Joke' of FaceID Masks into a Reality."

58. Chen, "How Coronavirus Turned the 'Dystopian Joke' of FaceID Masks into a Reality."

59. Blas, "Facial Weaponization Suite."

60. Blas, "Facial Weaponization Suite"; Bering, "There's Something Queer about That Face"; Rule et al., "Accuracy and Awareness in the Perception and Categorization of Male Sexual Orientation."

61. Queer Technologies, "Queer Technologies."

62. Cole, *Suspect Identities*; Fisher, *Gender and the Science of Difference*; Harding, *"Racial" Economy of Science*; Terry, *An American Obsession*.

63. Graham, *Cities under Siege*.

64. Derrida, *Limited Inc*, 113.

65. Sheehan, "Noisebridge Anti/Surveillance Fashion Show."

66. Sheehan, "Noisebridge Anti/Surveillance Fashion Show."

67. Berlant, *Cruel Optimism*, 195.

68. Sheehan, "Noisebridge Anti/Surveillance Fashion Show."

69. With these designs, the discourse of individual responsibility mirrors the dominant discourse surrounding rape. Women are problematically framed as complicit in their own abuse if they do not take steps to minimize their exposure to potential objectification or violence, where now those steps might include the adoption of surveillance shields such as "crotch dazzlers."

70. Koskela, "'You Shouldn't Wear That Body.'"

71. Noisebridge, "Anti Surveillance Fashion Show."

72. Rancière, *Dissensus*, 134–36.

73. Juris, *Networking Futures*, 140–41.

74. Monahan, "Counter-Surveillance as Political Intervention?"; Surveillance Camera Players, *We Know You Are Watching*; Morrison, *Discipline and Desire*; Harding, *Performance, Transparency, and the Cultures of Surveillance*.

75. As John McGrath noted early on in his work on surveillance and performance, "While surveillance is routinely justified in terms of crime prevention and routinely criticized as an invasion of privacy, an accommodation between these two universalizing viewpoints will do nothing to affect the experience of the black man under surveillance in the streets of New York or London. Protection of privacy is not relevant to the ways in which the camera targets him. The terms in which surveillance is routinely critiqued obscure his experiences, and those of many others, in the name of a 'privacy' fantasized as a universal right." McGrath, *Loving Big Brother*, 23. See also Gilliom, *Overseers of the Poor*; Eubanks, "Technologies of Citizenship."

76. Murakami Wood et al., *A Report on the Surveillance Society*; Patton, "Protecting Privacy in Public?"

77. Coll, "Power, Knowledge, and the Subjects of Privacy," 1.

78. Mattelart, *Globalization of Surveillance*. See Wall and Linnemann for a complementary analysis of police crackdowns on citizens' filming of their activities, which Wall and Linnemann read as a "diagnostic moment" for interrogating the ways in which the social order is fabricated through police elimination of perceived threats to security. Wall and Linnemann, "Staring Down the State." Furthermore, as Reeves and Packer argue, inquiry into the intersections of police and media should also attend to the ways in which the police control and restrict access to the logistical capacities of media: "Police maintain superiority not simply through a monopoly on the use of violence, but by creating a monopoly on the use of logistical media as well." Reeves and Packer, "Police Media," 378.

79. Rancière, *Dissensus*, 36–37.

80. Wall and Linnemann, "Staring Down the State"; Huey, Walby, and Doyle, "Cop Watching in the Downtown Eastside"; Simon, "Suspicious Encounters."

81. Goodman, "Yes Men Hoax on BBC Reminds World of Dow Chemical's Refusal to Take Responsibility for Bhopal Disaster."

82. Prior, "Anonymous vs. Steubenville."

83. As an important caveat, in keeping with this chapter's critical approach to countersurveillance artworks, forms of resistance should not be romanticized but instead subjected to additional scrutiny and problematization. For example, Huey, Walby, and Doyle's empirical study on Cop Watch in Toronto found that contrary to the claims of Cop Watch members, on the whole the community in question did not feel that this group represented them or their interests. Huey, Walby, and Doyle, "Cop Watching in the Downtown Eastside." Likewise, each of these interventions also runs the risk of creating new harms, such as when the hacktivist collective Anonymous publicized the rape victim's name in the 2012 Steubenville, Ohio, rape case, leading to further harassment of and threats to the victim and her family. As Heather Woods cautions, "Digital activists [must] weigh carefully the benefits of visibility alongside possible limitations of that goal. In particular, feminist activists must guard against losing control of a campaign's message and be especially cautious of overexposing potentially sensitive individuals related to the cause." Woods, "Anonymous, Steubenville, and the Politics of Visibility," 1096.

84. Steve Mann's work, though resonating with many scholars, represents some of the most simplistic and problematic materializations of this impulse. Mann, "'Reflectionism' and 'Diffusionism'"; Mann, Nolan, and Wellman, "Sousveillance." For a detailed critique of sousveillance, see Monahan, "Counter-Surveillance as Political Intervention?"; Monahan and Murakami Wood, "Resistance and Opposition"; and Monahan, "Reckoning with Covid, Racial Violence, and the Perilous Pursuit of Transparency."

85. Koskela, "Hijacking Surveillance?"

86. Some of Trevor Paglen's excellent work has operated in this vein to identify CIA agents involved in extraordinary rendition, "black sites" where torture likely took place, and drone flights. Paglen and Solnit, *Invisible*; Tim Gaynor, "Artists Take Aim at Hidden World of Modern US Surveillance," *Al Jazeera America*, September 26, 2014, accessed October 2, 2014, http://america.aljazeera.com/articles/2014/9/26/covert-operationsscottsdalemuseumcontemporaryart.html.

87. Glissant, *Poetics of Relation*, 189–90.

88. Glissant also astutely perceives the tenacity of hierarchical sociocultural systems, including those that may seem receptive to or tolerant of the opaque: "If one is in too much of a hurry to join the concert, there is a risk of mistaking as autonomous participation something that is only some disguised leftover of former alienations. Opacities must be preserved; an appetite for opportune obscurity in translation must be created; and falsely convenient vehicular sabirs must be relentlessly refuted." Glissant, *Poetics of Relation*, 120.

89. Million Hoodies Movement for Justice, Action Network website, www. actionnetwork.org/groups/million-hoodies-movement-for-justice, accessed January 18, 2022.

CHAPTER TWO. **Transparency**

A version of chapter 2 appeared as "Visualizing the Surveillance Archive: Critical Art and the Dangers of Transparency," in *Law and the Visible*, edited by A. Sarat, L. Douglas, and M. M. Umphrey (Amherst: University of Massachusetts Press, 2021).

1. Brucato, "New Transparency"; Han, *Transparency Society*; Hetherington, *Guerrilla Auditors*; Monahan, "Surveillance and Terrorism."

2. Giddens, *Consequences of Modernity*; Porter, *Trust in Numbers*; Scott, *Seeing Like a State*.

3. Atilla Hallsby observes that the rise in transparency discourses can be traced to mid-twentieth-century concerns with increasingly secretive US institutions. Moreover, he links this discourse to cybernetic models of communication that would see noise or friction as corrupting: "Transparency also reflects techniques of transmission in which information is allowed to traverse from one person to another without resistance, such as from sender to receiver, or from an elected representative to the represented. A transparent exchange between sender and receiver, would mean that a message passes from one pole to the other uninhibited, or without loss of fidelity." In my framing, which aligns with Hallsby's, the valorization of transparency as idealized transmission would occlude the politics of the systems and rituals of transmission. Hallsby, "Psychoanalysis against Wikileaks," 69.

4. Taylor, *Archive and the Repertoire*.

5. Foucault, *History of Sexuality*, 1.

6. Beauchamp, *Going Stealth*, 49, 48.

7. Harding, *Performance, Transparency, and the Cultures of Surveillance*, 5.

8. On a parallel track, Morrison posits that "surveillance artists make visible the archival drive of surveillance and work to enrich and redirect its repertoire." Morrison, *Discipline and Desire*, 25.

9. As Daniela Agostinho, Catherine D'Ignazio, Annie Ring, Nanna Bonde Thylstrup, and Kristin Veel posit in their impressive research project on archival uncertainty, "Critiques of archival reason and practice . . . show that the piecing together of information

is not a neutral pursuit, both capture and exclusion have important ethical consequences, and archives are always contested sites of power, knowledge, possibility, and aspiration." Agostinho et al., "Uncertain Archives," 425.

10. Hetherington, *Guerrilla Auditors*.

11. Sekula, "Body and the Archive."

12. Foucault, *Archaeology of Knowledge*; Foucault, *Order of Things*.

13. Foucault, *Discipline and Punish*; Foucault, "Life of Infamous Men."

14. Foucault, *Archaeology of Knowledge*, 129.

15. Derrida, "Archive Fever," 11, cited in Manoff, "Theories of the Archive from across the Disciplines."

16. Manoff, "Theories of the Archive from across the Disciplines."

17. Le Goff, *History and Memory*; Osborne, "Ordinariness of the Archive"; see also Scott, *Seeing Like a State*.

18. Richards, *Imperial Archive*; Spivak, "Rani of Sirmur." It is important to remember the central role of the geographical and anthropological sciences in constructing these imperial maps and archives. More than simply saying that the social sciences have been complicit in egregious state practices, as some form of cautionary tale, it would be better to face the fact that the social sciences and their theoretical frameworks emerged in conjunction with—and within—the modern state, in the service of its military and capitalistic interests, and to question the extent to which that legacy continues to shape scholarly inquiry and assessment of its value today. Duncan, "Complicity and Resistance in the Colonial Archive"; Marcus, "Once and Future Ethnographic Archive"; Price, *Cold War Anthropology*; Richards, *Imperial Archive*.

19. Bowker and Star, *Sorting Things Out*; Lyon, "Identification Practices."

20. Koehler, *Stasi*; Lyon, "Identification Practices"; Osborne, "Ordinariness of the Archive"; see also McCoy, *Policing America's Empire*.

21. Lynch, "Archives in Formation."

22. Take, as one authoritative example, a passage from the International Council on Archives's *Universal Declaration on Archives*: archives "play an essential role in the development of societies by safeguarding and contributing to individual and community memory. Open access to archives enriches our knowledge of human society, promotes democracy, protects citizens' rights and enhances the quality of life." Gilliland and McKemmish, "Role of Participatory Archives in Furthering Human Rights, Reconciliation and Recovery," 1.

23. Joyce, "Politics of the Liberal Archive."

24. Joyce, "Politics of the Liberal Archive." For a treatment of this "public police" phenomenon in a historical context, see Reeves, *Citizen Spies*.

25. Joyce, "Politics of the Liberal Archive," 36.

26. Osborne, "Ordinariness of the Archive."

27. Osborne, "Ordinariness of the Archive," 59.

28. Sekula, "Body and the Archive."

29. Coombe, "Is There a Cultural Studies of Law?," 57.

30. Lazarus-Black and Hirsch, *Contested States*; Merry, "Rights Talk and the Experience of Law"; Crenshaw, "Demarginalizing the Intersection of Race and Sex."

31. Calavita, *Invitation to Law and Society*.

32. Cohen, "Studying Law Studying Surveillance," 92.

33. Crenshaw, "Demarginalizing the Intersection of Race and Sex"; Mills, *Racial Contract*; Monahan, "Privatization Cultures and the Racial Order."

34. Halpern, *Beautiful Data*, 21.

35. Andrejevic, "Surveillance in the Big Data Era."

36. Halpern, *Beautiful Data*; McCosker and Wilken, "Rethinking 'Big Data' as Visual Knowledge."

37. Deleuze, "Diagram"; McCosker and Wilken, "Rethinking 'Big Data' as Visual Knowledge."

38. Radomes are microwave radar units encased in a protective dome structure to insulate them from the elements and from scrutiny. Wood, "Territoriality and Identity at Raf Menwith Hill."

39. Sohn, "Trevor Paglen Plumbs the Internet."

40. Greenwald, *No Place to Hide*; Sohn, "Trevor Paglen Plumbs the Internet."

41. Quoted in Weiner, "Prying Eyes," 54.

42. Paglen, *Blank Spots on the Map*, 280, 277.

43. Gilliom and Monahan, *Supervision*; Paglen, *Blank Spots on the Map*.

44. One important counterpoint was with Paglen's photographs of a "black site" detention facility in Afghanistan. When the US government tried to prevent Majid Khan—a US legal resident who was subjected to extraordinary rendition and tortured by the CIA—from obtaining legal counsel because he might reveal secret information about his treatment, Paglen's published photographs were cited by the Center for Constitutional Rights as legal evidence that the site in question was not, in fact, secret. Davis, *9.5 Theses on Art and Class*; Weiner, "Prying Eyes."

45. Weiner, "Prying Eyes."

46. Quoted in Weiner, "Prying Eyes," 56, 60.

47. Potolsky, *National Security Sublime*, 101.

48. Potolsky describes creative work like Paglen's as operating in the register of "the national security sublime," which "brings out both the immense scope of the national security state and the difficulty of understanding it by traditional means, proffering an aesthetic solution to a nearly intractable problem of interpretation." Potolsky, *National Security Sublime*, 5. Then again, according to some observers of audiences at Paglen's exhibits, the "art-seeking class" in attendance seems more interested in the social event of consuming art than the politics: "Those who lingered were drawn to the video installation's lush images and pulsing soundscape, although many glanced away period- ically at their phones, texting and e-mailing and posting photos, as though they hadn't quite got the message." Sohn, "Trevor Paglen Plumbs the Internet."

49. Van Houtryve, "Blue Sky Days."

50. Begley, "Plain Sight."

51. These secretive yet suspected surveillance actions reproduced an aura of anxiety for Muslim American communities and sometimes included the coercive recruitment of community insiders. Inderpal Grewal explains: "In 2002, the FBI as well as the New York City police began to carry out surveillance on Muslim mosques and neighbor-

hoods. Some of this surveillance involved using demographic information to 'map' neighborhoods and carry out video surveillance and tracking of individuals, as well as using digital technologies to gather information and to monitor activities of individuals. It also included recruiting community members who were asked to spy on friends and family and to surf websites connected with their networks in order to report their findings to the FBI." Grewal, *Saving the Security State*, 149.

52. Begley, "Plain Sight."

53. Begley's collage also highlights the *volume* of the police archive in a way that individual images could not connote.

54. This responsibilizing motif can be seen in full force at one of Trevor Paglen's exhibits with the implementation of a Tor node for anonymous web browsing. Hill, "Art That Shows Us What Mass Surveillance Actually Looks Like"; Kafer, "Wi-Fi Defiance." Museumgoers can *choose* the anonymous network for their internet activity and thereby make a small, individualized contribution to the protection of privacy in society. The fact that an institution (the museum) provides such a node is perhaps more consequential as a symbolic statement that could be replicated by other institutions. That said, the emphasis on threats to privacy, as opposed to other social problems facilitated by surveillance, aligns well, of course, with the individualizing slant of the liberal archive. Monahan, "Regulating Belonging."

55. Barocas and Selbst, "Big Data's Disparate Impact"; Gandy, *Coming to Terms with Chance*; Gillespie, "Relevance of Algorithms"; Pasquale, *Black Box Society*.

56. Amicelle, "Towards a 'New' Political Anatomy of Financial Surveillance"; Amoore, *Politics of Possibility*; Ball et al., *Private Security State*; Regan and Monahan, "Beyond Counterterrorism."

57. Boyle and Haggerty, "Spectacular Security"; Hayes, "Surveillance-Industrial Complex"; Monahan, *Surveillance in the Time of Insecurity*. Through the law the state also protects the ecology for corporate data practices and profits as seen, for instance, with the refuge created for copyright law in online environments. Postigo, *Digital Rights Movement*; Cohen, *Configuring the Networked Self*; Gillespie, *Wired Shut*.

58. Cirio, "Street Ghosts." Chris Ingraham and Allison Rowland have written about complementary artistic efforts to stage unreal tableaux vivants (living images) for Google Street View cameras, including events like emergency childbirths and crime scenes, in order to resist the reductive frames of Google archives by "performing imperceptibility." Ingraham and Rowland, "Performing Imperceptibility."

59. By returning to Google's original image, the man does not seem to be gardening, after all, but instead performing some kind of maintenance work around a fire hydrant. Cirio, "Album Archive." The image is true to the Google original but easy to misread— or read differently—as the context fluctuates. The discrepancies highlight the vital role of framing and the necessary interpretive dimension of reading photographs. Meaning is always fluid, never fixed.

60. *Data doubles* are abstract and partial representations of individual bodies in data, usually acted upon instrumentally by institutions. Haggerty and Ericson, "Surveillant Assemblage."

61. This is not to say that the digital does not degrade too, as can be noted with frantic efforts to translate digital content before media disintegrate or protocols become obsolete. Blanchette, "Material History of Bits."

62. Wiedenhöfer, "WALLonWALL."

63. Wiedenhöfer, "WALLonWALL."

64. Relatedly, in his reflections on Northern Ireland, Nils Zurawski observes the dual nature of surveillance in that context: "The practice of external surveillance was closely connected to acts of violence and deeply embedded in the way the conflict was carried out, while internal surveillance was about control, policing and discipline. All this upheld a system of communal deterrence that to this day structures many aspects of life and political discourse in Northern Ireland." Zurawski, "'I Know Where You Live!,'" 499.

65. Wiedenhöfer, "WALLonWALL."

66. Peter Geoghegan, "Will Belfast Ever Have a Berlin Wall Moment and Tear Down Its 'Peace Walls?,'" *Guardian*, September 29, 2015, accessed September 28, 2020, www .theguardian.com/cities/2015/sep/29/belfast-berlin-wall-moment-permanent-peace -walls; Steven Grattan, "Northern Ireland Still Divided by Peace Walls 20 Years after Conflict," *World*, January 14, 2020, accessed September 28, 2020, www.pri.org/stories /2020-01-14/northern-ireland-still-divided-peace-walls-20-years-after-conflict.

67. James Angelos, "Will Brexit Bring the Troubles Back to Northern Ireland?," *New York Times*, December 30, 2019, accessed September 28, 2020, www.nytimes.com/2019 /12/30/magazine/brexit-northern-ireland.html; Geoghegan, "Will Belfast Ever Have a Berlin Wall Moment?"; McGrade, "Story behind Northern Ireland's Peace Walls."

68. Angelos, "Will Brexit Bring the Troubles Back?"; Grattan, "Northern Ireland Still Divided by Peace Walls."

69. The Ulster Defense Association was a violent pro-British "loyalist" or "Unionist" group that was responsible for hundreds of killings during the Troubles. Angelos, "Will Brexit Bring the Troubles Back?"

70. Angelos, "Will Brexit Bring the Troubles Back?"

71. Hammerand, "New Town."

72. Compare Marwick, "To Catch a Predator?"; Shade, "Contested Spaces"; Steeves, "Online Surveillance in Canadian Schools."

73. Dubrofsky and Magnet, *Feminist Surveillance Studies*; Monahan, "Dreams of Control at a Distance"; Koskela, "'Gaze without Eyes'"; Koskela, "Video Surveillance, Gender, and the Safety of Public Urban Space"; Koskela, "'You Shouldn't Wear That Body'"; van der Meulen and Heynen, *Expanding the Gaze*.

74. *Discrimination by abstraction* refers to "the ways that technological systems, especially those that produce representations of data, strip away social context, leaving a disembodied and highly abstract depiction of the world and of what matters in it. The act of filtering out bodies and social contexts facilitates a kind of [masculine] control at a distance that is the hallmark of modern surveillance systems." Monahan, "Dreams of Control at a Distance," 289.

75. Eubanks, *Automating Inequality*; Shapiro, "Predictive Policing for Reform?"; Shapiro, "Street-Level."

76. My emphasis here is upon *normative* white subjecthood, so I am not making broad claims about white individuals' insulation from police or state surveillance. See, as an important counterpoint, or as an exception that proves the rule, John Gilliom's powerful study of state surveillance of white welfare mothers in the US Midwest. Gilliom, *Overseers of the Poor*.

77. Andrejevic, *iSpy*; Steeves, "Hide and Seek"; Zuboff, *Age of Surveillance Capitalism*.

78. Clive Thompson, "The Visible Man: An FBI Target Puts His Whole Life Online," *Wired*, May 22, 2007, accessed June 12, 2017, www.wired.com/2007/05/ps -transparency.

79. Elahi, "FBI, Here I Am!"

80. Elahi, "Thousand Little Brothers."

81. Hogue, "Performing, Translating, Fashioning"; Morrison, *Discipline and Desire*.

82. Hall, Monahan, and Reeves, "Surveillance and Performance." See also Hall, *Transparent Traveler*, 16.

83. Brunton and Nissenbaum have explored and theorized tactics such as this as forms of "obfuscation." Brunton and Nissenbaum, *Obfuscation*.

84. Elahi, "I Share Everything."

85. Elahi, "Prism"; Tim Smith, "Hasan Elahi Addresses Surveillance in Multilayered Exhibit at C. Grimaldis Gallery," *Baltimore Sun*, May 24, 2016, accessed June 12, 2017, www.baltimoresun.com/entertainment/arts/artsmash/bs-ae-arts-story-0527-20160526 -story.html.

86. Elahi, "Thousand Little Brothers."

87. Elahi, "Thousand Little Brothers."

88. Greenwald, *No Place to Hide*.

89. Spieker, *Big Archive*, 3.

90. Sturken and Cartwright, *Practices of Looking*; Doane, "Indexicality."

91. Crary, "Techniques of the Observer"; Gates, "Cultural Labor of Surveillance."

92. Rose, *Visual Methodologies*.

93. Tagg, *Disciplinary Frame*, xxviii.

94. Hall, *Transparent Traveler*, 19.

95. Although the emphasis in this chapter is on artistic destabilizations of state and corporate transparency efforts, appeals to transparency can also be seen in efforts to document, comprehend, and collectively process traumatic events such as mass shootings. As what I read to be a complementary articulation of "crisis vision," Kelly Gates incisively describes media forensic efforts (for example, to document the actions of shooters leading up to their attacks) as performing a similar sublimating function: "A forensic sensibility has become a defining feature of the contemporary structure of feeling in the political cultures of places formerly known as liberal democracies. What better way to assuage the anxieties of extreme violence than through a combination of media-forensic analysis and reality-based dramatic narration? The appeal of a false forensic certainty seems like a fitting, if circumscribed, response to the intensifying anxieties associated with social fragmentation, economic precarity, and toxic politics— the totality of the contemporary crisis." Gates, "Media Evidence and Forensic Journal- ism," 407.

96. Forms of state and corporate rationality merged in the management of the Holocaust. As David Lyon relates, "In Germany, where . . . the administration of the Holocaust represents the apogee of modernist rationality, International Business Machines (IBM) was recruited to provide the technical infrastructure for genocidal identification." Lyon, "Identification Practices," 46. For an overview of the relation of the state to bureaucratic and scientific identification techniques, see Monahan and Murakami Wood, "Identity and Identification."

97. Monahan, *Surveillance in the Time of Insecurity*.

98. Giddens, *Nation-State and Violence*, 341.

99. Birchall et al., "Openness and Opacity," 4.

CHAPTER THREE. **Complicity**

A form of chapter 3 was published as "Ways of Being Seen: Surveillance Art and the Interpellation of Viewing Subjects," *Cultural Studies* vol. 32, no. 4 (2018).

1. Bertrand and Bridle, *Watched*; Brighenti, "Artveillance"; Levin, Frohne, and Weibel, *Ctrl [Space]*; Morrison, *Discipline and Desire*.

2. Andrejevic, "Surveillance in the Big Data Era"; Degli Esposti, "When Big Data Meets Dataveillance"; Pasquale, *Black Box Society*; Barocas and Selbst, "Big Data's Disparate Impact"; Matzner, "Beyond Data as Representation." Sarah Brayne offers a helpful definition of *big data* that captures the concept's vernacular expansion while retaining much of its technical specificity: "Big data is a *data environment* made possible by the mass digitization of information and associated with the use of advanced analytics, including network analysis and machine learning algorithms." Brayne, *Predict and Surveil*, 3.

3. Berger, *Ways of Seeing*.

4. Foucault, *Discipline and Punish*; Lianos, "Social Control after Foucault"; Murakami Wood, "Beyond the Panopticon?"

5. Deleuze, "Postscript on the Societies of Control"; Haggerty and Ericson, "Surveillant Assemblage."

6. Amoore, "Biometric Borders"; Salter, "Passports, Mobility, and Security."

7. Althusser, "Ideology and Ideological State Apparatuses."

8. Hage, "Affective Politics of Racial Mis-interpellation," 121–22.

9. Mills, *Racial Contract*, 53.

10. Fanon, *Black Skin, White Masks*, 93.

11. Mills, *Racial Contract*, 83.

12. Hall, "Problem of Ideology," 64.

13. Mitchell, *Picture Theory*; Purvis and Hunt, "Discourse, Ideology."

14. Pajnik and Lesjak-Tušek, "Observing Discourses of Advertising"; Sturken and Cartwright, *Practices of Looking*; Wenner, "On the Limits of the New and the Lasting Power of the Mediasport Interpellation."

15. Mitchell, *Picture Theory*, 75. See also Doy, *Picturing the Self*.

16. Mirzoeff, *Watching Babylon*.

17. Sturken and Cartwright, *Practices of Looking*.

18. Fiske, "Culture, Ideology, Interpellation," 1270.

19. Butler, "Conscience Doth Make Subjects of Us All"; Grossberg, "Cultural Studies and/in New Worlds"; Hall, "Signification, Representation, Ideology."

20. Butler, "Conscience Doth Make Subjects of Us All," 25.

21. Charland, "Constitutive Rhetoric."

22. Rancière, *Politics of Aesthetics*.

23. Rancière, *Dissensus*, 36.

24. Birchall, "Aesthetics of the Secret."

25. Rancière, *Politics of Aesthetics*.

26. Rancière, *Politics of Aesthetics*; Sayers, "Jacques Rancière (2004) The Politics of Aesthetics."

27. For example, Poitras, *Astro Noise*; Poitras, *Citizenfour*.

28. Birchall, "Aesthetics of the Secret."

29. Birchall, "Aesthetics of the Secret."

30. Bishop, *Artificial Hells*, 2.

31. Bishop, *Artificial Hells*; Perucci, "What the Fuck Is That?"

32. Bishop, *Artificial Hells*, 275.

33. *#NotABugSplat* is an international project with representatives in the United States and Pakistan. D&AD, "Not a Bug Splat"; #NotABugSplat, "#Notabugsplat." I am grateful to Zac Parker for bringing this project to my attention.

34. D&AD, "Not a Bug Splat."

35. Sophia Saifi, "Not a 'Bug Splat': Artists Give Drone Victims a Face in Pakistan," CNN, April 9, 2014, accessed January 8, 2017, www.cnn.com/2014/04/09/world/asia /pakistan-drones-not-a-bug-splat.

36. #NotABugSplat, "#Notabugsplat."

37. Saifi, "Not a 'Bug Splat.'"

38. Gusterson, *Drone*.

39. Kindervater, "Emergence of Lethal Surveillance"; Niva, "Disappearing Violence"; Parks and Kaplan, *Life in the Age of Drone Warfare*.

40. Abu-Lughod, *Do Muslim Women Need Saving?*; Puar, *Terrorist Assemblages*; Wall, "Philanthropic Soldiers, Practical Orientalism, and the Occupation of Iraq."

41. Spivak, "Can the Subaltern Speak?"

42. Selod, *Forever Suspect*; Zine, "Between Orientalism and Fundamentalism."

43. Selod, *Forever Suspect*, 5.

44. Saifi, "Not a 'Bug Splat.'"

45. Gregory, "From a View to a Kill."

46. The emphasis on girls in need of saving is a rhetorical device that reproduces a set of implied binaries: between adults and children, men and women, Western and Other. It suggests that there is no innocence or humanity in adults, especially not in men, who in this frame cannot inspire empathy, only fear.

47. Bureau of Investigative Journalism, "CIA Drone Strikes in Pakistan, 2004 to Present."

48. As outlined in the book's introduction, it might be tempting for scholars with progressive leanings to celebrate anti-surveillance artworks because of their implied opposition to state and corporate control structures, but I am more interested in exploring how such works construct subjects, structure relations, and assert values. In short, this is a project of cultural critique that attempts to grasp the contemporary "problem space" diagnosed and responded to by critical surveillance art.

49. Wall and Monahan, "Surveillance and Violence from Afar."

50. Parks, "Zeroing In."

51. Morozov, *To Save Everything, Click Here.*

52. Kolesnikoff, "Defamiliarization." Similarly, in their interviews with critical surveillance artists, Luke Stark and Kate Crawford found that "tactics of defamiliarization were matched with the desire [on the part of artists] to produce a strong emotional response. Many of the artists . . . claimed they wanted audiences to confront their relationship to technology when presented with their artwork: forcing a kind of friction and reflection was central to the ethical impact these artists sought rather than producing the 'right' emotional effect." Stark and Crawford, "Work of Art in the Age of Artificial Intelligence," 446.

53. Mitchell, *Landscape and Power*, 2.

54. Barrell, *Dark Side of the Landscape*; Gustafsson, "Foresight, Hindsight and State Secrecy in the American West"; Mitchell, *Landscape and Power.*

55. Marx, *Machine in the Garden.*

56. Mitchell, *Landscape and Power*, 2.

57. Bishop, *Artificial Hells.*

58. Crary, *Suspensions of Perception.*

59. Amoore, *Politics of Possibility*; Gilliom and Monahan, *Supervision*; Lyon, *Surveillance Studies.*

60. Graham and Wood, "Digitizing Surveillance"; Nissenbaum, *Privacy in Context*; Staples, *Everyday Surveillance.*

61. Andrejevic, "Surveillance in the Big Data Era"; Lyon, "Surveillance, Snowden, and Big Data"; Mayer-Schönberger and Cukier, *Big Data.*

62. Depoorter, "Jaywalking"; Greenberg, "Turning Live Surveillance Feeds into Unsettling Works of Art."

63. Fuchs, "Web 2.0, Prosumption, and Surveillance"; Monahan, "Built to Lie"; Mosco, *To the Cloud.*

64. Depoorter, "Jaywalking." Although these were perhaps unintentional, one could read the spelling and grammatical errors as subtle critiques of the fallibility of surveillance systems, which can generate and act on "noise" with material effects for targets.

65. This installation is part of a larger suite of projects called *Sheriff Software.* Depoorter, "Sheriff Software."

66. See Gunders, "'Here's Lookin' at You,'" for reflections on how interpellative functions are delegated to CCTV in other contexts as well.

67. Koskela, "'Don't Mess with Texas!'"; Sandhu and Haggerty, "Private Eyes."

68. Debatty, "Sheriff Software"; Murakami Wood, "Surveillance in the World City"; Trottier, "Crowdsourcing CCTV Surveillance on the Internet."

69. Musheno, Levine, and Palumbo, "Television Surveillance and Crime Prevention."

70. Indeed, in the contemporary context, platform-based residential surveillance systems, such as Amazon's Ring or Google's Nest, facilitate discriminatory practices on the part of community members who become primed to scout for bodies "out of place." When coupled with social-networking platforms like Nextdoor, Rahim Kurwa argues, the systems contribute to the erection of "digitally gated communities" that reproduce earlier forms of racial segregation. Furthermore, as Lauren Bridges has shown in her research on Amazon's Ring system, through private agreements the system is accessible to many police departments without a warrant, thereby further entrenching the police in neighborhood segregation efforts. Kurwa, "Building the Digitally Gated Community"; Bridges, "Infrastructural Obfuscation."

71. One might also compare Depoorter's installation to psychological experiments like Stanley Milgram's study, where subjects were enrolled as supposed research assistants who believed they were administering electrical shocks to participants in another room. A key difference is that Depoorter's piece is not measuring individuals' compliance with authority directives, as was the case with Milgram's study, but is instead generating technological valences toward intervention (such as the big red button that invites pushing) and harnessing discomfort to engender awareness, introspection, and a sense of human connection. Milgram, "Behavioral Study of Obedience."

72. Downey, "Lives of Others"; Haney and Zimbardo, "Past and Future of US Prison Policy"; Harding, *Performance, Transparency, and the Cultures of Surveillance*; Griggs, "Coverage of the Stanford Prison Experiment in Introductory Psychology Textbooks."

73. Le Texier, "Debunking the Stanford Prison Experiment."

74. Downey, "Lives of Others," 75.

75. Harding, *Performance, Transparency, and the Cultures of Surveillance*, 131.

76. Harding, *Performance, Transparency, and the Cultures of Surveillance*, 121. See also Miller, "Jeremy Bentham's Panoptic Device."

CHAPTER FOUR. **Violence**

1. Bourgois delineates, as well, additional forms of violence: "Direct Political: Targeted physical violence and terror administered by official authorities and those opposing it, such as military repression, police torture, and armed resistance . . . [and] Everyday: Daily practices and expressions of violence on a micro-interactional level: interpersonal, domestic and delinquent." Bourgois, "Continuum of Violence in War and Peace," 426.

2. Mirzoeff, *Right to Look*; Gandy, *Coming to Terms with Chance*.

3. Monahan, "Regulating Belonging"; Sekula, "Body and the Archive."

4. Ticktin, *Casualties of Care*; Topak, "Humanitarian and Human Rights Surveillance."

5. Besteman, *Making Refuge*; Guerette, *Migration, Culture Conflict, Crime and Terrorism*; Philo, Briant, and Donald, *Bad News for Refugees*.

6. Abraham, "Migrant Surveillance"; Ranjan, "Migrant Surveillance and State Power"; Monahan, "Regulating Belonging."

7. Paul Collier and Alexander Betts, "Why Denying Refugees the Right to Work Is a Catastrophic Error," *Guardian*, March 22, 2017, accessed October 28, 2018, www .theguardian.com/world/2017/mar/22/why-denying-refugees-the-right-to-work-is-a -catastrophic-error.

8. Wike, Stokes, and Simmons, "Europeans Fear Wave of Refugees Will Mean More Terrorism, Fewer Jobs."

9. UNHCR, "Figures at a Glance."

10. Feldman, "On Cultural Anesthesia," 207.

11. Invisibility can also enable and mask exercises of *everyday violence* on vulnerable others—for instance, forms of intimate partner abuse and femicide. Weil, "Making Femicide Visible."

12. Demos, *Migrant Image*, 4.

13. Poloni, "Displacement Island."

14. Cuttitta, "'Borderizing' the Island Setting and Narratives of the Lampedusa 'Border Play'"; Wright, "Lampedusa's Gaze."

15. Poloni, "Displacement Island."

16. Holert, "From the Archives of Invisibility," 1.

17. In dramatic contrast to Poloni's *Displacement Island*, which provides only fleeting traces of refugees, artist Ai Weiwei staged a graphic re-creation of the now iconic 2015 image of the three-year-old drowned Syrian boy, Alan Kurdi, lying facedown and lifeless on a Turkish beach. In Weiwei's reproduction in 2016, he struck the same pose as the toddler, lying on a rocky shore with his head facing the lapping waves and his arms awkwardly positioned at his sides. Whereas the original photograph, in Homi Bhabha's words, "abruptly brought the plight of the long living hell of millions of refugees to the world's moral attention and captured the global imagination," the black-and-white photo of Weiwei's performance strove to rekindle that collective shock and memory. Predictably, it also produced some intense backlash, with critics decrying it as "'callous,' 'careerist,' and even 'egotistical victim porn,'" illustrating, as Katarzyna Marciniak relates, "the point that approaching artistic representations of trauma is always highly contentious, overdetermined, and aporetic." Schulze-Engler, Malreddy, and Karugia, "'Even the Dead Have Human Rights,'" 8; Marciniak, "'Opening a Certain Poetic Space,'" 2–3.

18. Holert, "From the Archives of Invisibility."

19. Poloni, "Displacement Island," 75.

20. "Castaway 'Was Thrown Overboard,'" BBC News, April 21, 2006, accessed October 28, 2018, http://news.bbc.co.uk/2/hi/europe/4930792.stm.

21. SKMU, "SKMU Sørlandets Kunstmuseum—Hanne Nielsen & Birgit Johnsen"; Nielsen and Johnsen, "Drifting."

22. "Homeless Londoner Found on Raft off Norway," United Press International, May 4, 2006, accessed October 28, 2018, www.upi.com/Homeless-Londoner-found-on -raft-off-Norway/77151146774244.

23. SKMU, "SKMU Sørlandets Kunstmuseum—Hanne Nielsen & Birgit Johnsen"; Falch, "Drifting."

24. Magelssen, "White-Skinned Gods," 32.

25. Monahan, "Regulating Belonging"; Nwabuzo and Schaeder, "Racism and Discrimination in the Context of Migration in Europe"; Pouilly, "Refugee Women and Children Face Heightened Risk of Sexual Violence amid Tensions and Overcrowding at Reception Facilities on Greek Islands." This is not to suggest that women and children are the only ones subjected to sexual violence. For instance, a United Nations report found that many Syrian boys and men have been victims of sexual violence, especially—but certainly not only—"gay, bisexual, transgender and intersex individuals." UNHCR, "UNHCR Study Uncovers Shocking Sexual Violence against Syrian Refugee Boys, Men."

26. Williams, *Culture & Society: 1780–1950*, 299–300.

27. In a similar vein, James Bridle's *Seamless Transitions* reproduces exact replicas of immigrant detention facilities to encourage critical contemplation by viewers. Bridle, "Seamless Transitions."

28. Downey, "Ethics of Engagement"; Bishop, *Artificial Hells*; Canclini, *Art beyond Itself*.

29. Möntmann, "Community Service."

30. Rogers, "Capital Implications"; Heidenreich, "Santiago Sierra."

31. Downey, "Ethics of Engagement."

32. Alÿs, "When Faith Moves Mountains."

33. Möntmann, "Community Service," n.p.

34. Möntmann, "Community Service."

35. Downey, "Ethics of Engagement," 603.

36. Downey, "Ethics of Engagement."

37. Sierra, "Línea De 160 Cm Tatuada Sobre 4 Personas."

38. Quoted in Spiegler, "When Human Beings Are the Canvas."

39. Tate Museum, "Santiago Sierra." Explicating his general approach to confronting art consumers, Sierra says, "My role in this game is to press my finger on the sore places and create uncomfortable situations for people who want to have fun in the gallery." Quoted in Spiegler, "When Human Beings Are the Canvas," 97.

40. Tate Museum, "Santiago Sierra."

41. As Simone Weil observes, a force is anything "that turns anybody who is subjected to it into a thing. Exercised to the limit, it turns man into a thing in the most literal sense: it makes a corpse out of him." Weil, "Iliad, or the Poem of Force," 6.

42. Bishop, "Delegated Performance."

43. The title of this work refers to Horace McCoy's Depression-era novel *They Shoot Horses, Don't They?*, which was adapted as a popular film in 1969. In both works the characters are encouraged to participate in a dance marathon to win prize money, but they push themselves to the point of death (for some) and are exploited and swindled along the way. Richmond, "A Time to Mourn and a Time to Dance."

44. Tate Museum, "Phil Collins."

45. Phil Collins, "The Truth about Reality TV," *Telegraph*, August 22, 2006, accessed October 28, 2018, www.telegraph.co.uk/culture/art/3654759/The-truth-about-reality-TV .html.

46. Compare Duffy, *(Not) Getting Paid to Do What You Love*; and Marwick, *Status Update*.

47. Coupe, "Watchtower."

48. Coupe, "Artist Interview."

49. Andrejevic, "Estranged Free Labor"; Fuchs, "Web 2.0, Prosumption, and Surveillance."

50. Coupe, "Watchtower."

51. Levina, "Whiteness and the Joys of Cruelty," 75.

52. In this vein, for example, Arizona sheriff Joe Arpaio notoriously required male inmates to wear pink underwear, and he installed a "jail cam" allowing outsiders to view prisoners over the internet. Lynch, "Punishing Images"; Jim Hill, "Arizona Criminals Find Jail Too in-'Tents,'" CNN, July 27, 1999, www.cnn.com/US/9907/27/tough .sheriff.

53. Goldman, "Trending Now."

54. Magnet and Rodgers, "Stripping for the State"; Beauchamp, "Artful Concealment and Strategic Visibility"; Currah and Moore, "'We Won't Know Who You Are.'"

55. Goldman, "Trending Now"; Julie Deardorff, "Shame Returns as Punishment," *Chicago Tribune*, April 12, 2000, accessed October 28, 2018, www.chicagotribune.com /news/ct-xpm-2000-04-12-0004120235-story.html.

56. Such cruelty ramifies especially harshly upon people who do not conform to normative gender expectations. For instance, 2020 was the "deadliest year on record" for transgender and gender-nonconforming individuals, with at least thirty-seven violent deaths in the United States. One can speculate that the crisis-vision crucible of the global pandemic and radicalized white supremacy exacerbated existing intolerance to bring about such deadly outcomes. Roberts, "Marking the Deadliest Year on Record, HRC Releases Report on Violence against Transgender and Gender Non-Conforming People."

57. Goldman, "Trending Now."

58. Kealey, "Patterns of Punishment"; Ziel, "Eighteenth Century Public Humiliation Penalties in Twenty-First Century America."

59. Friedman, *Crime and Punishment in American History*; Goldman, "Trending Now."

60. United States v. Gementera.

61. Ziel, "Eighteenth Century Public Humiliation Penalties in Twenty-First Century America"; Whitman, "What Is Wrong with Inflicting Shame Sanctions."

62. Trottier, "Coming to Terms with Shame"; Marwick, Fontaine, and boyd, "'Nobody Sees It, Nobody Gets Mad.'"

63. Kochel, Wilson, and Mastrofski, "Effect of Suspect Race on Officers' Arrest Decisions."

64. Gandy, *Coming to Terms with Chance*.

65. Cirio, "Obscurity."

66. Birchall, *Shareveillance*, 45.

67. Thomas B. Edsall, "The Expanding World of Poverty Capitalism," *New York Times*, August 26, 2014, accessed March 29, 2016, www.nytimes.com/2014/08/27/opinion /thomas-edsall-the-expanding-world-of-poverty-capitalism.html; Monahan, "Regulating Belonging."

68. Cirio, "Obscurity."

69. Blanchette and Johnson, "Data Retention and the Panoptic Society"; Bennett, "Right to Be Forgotten."

70. Quoted in Pangburn, "Artist Blurs More Than 15 Million Mugshots to Protect Your Right to Privacy."

71. Marwick, "Scandal or Sex Crime?"; Citron, *Hate Crimes in Cyberspace.*

72. Goldman, "Trending Now," 439.

73. Silva, "Having the Time of Our Lives," 79. See also Levina, "Whiteness and the Joys of Cruelty."

74. "First they came for the Communists / And I did not speak out / Because I was not a Communist / Then they came for the Socialists / And I did not speak out / Because I was not a Socialist / Then they came for the trade unionists / And I did not speak out / Because I was not a trade unionist / Then they came for the Jews / And I did not speak out / Because I was not a Jew / Then they came for me / And there was no one left / To speak out for me." Niemöller, "First They Came."

75. Haslund-Christensen, "Who's Next?"

76. Furthermore, particularly with respect to the US context, Mia Fischer argues that state violence against gender-nonconforming individuals emerges from a similar modality to that which I describe as crisis vision: "Dominant representations of trans people as deceptive, deviant, and threatening continue to permeate mass-mediated discourses and are used to justify and frequently normalize state-sanctioned violence against gender-nonconforming populations." Fischer, *Terrorizing Gender*, 6.

77. Fischer, *Terrorizing Gender*, 170.

78. Doane, "Indexical and the Concept of Medium Specificity"; Crary, *Techniques of the Observer.*

79. One can see the dangers of this modality most clearly in celebrations of the work of photojournalists producing photographic representations of atrocity. In her book *The Cruel Radiance*, Susie Linfield, for instance, betrays a steadfast belief in the empirical accuracy and evidentiary importance of visual documents, as well as a problematic universalist frame of "human rights" through which audiences can supposedly achieve agreement. The unreflexive insensitivity of this position comes through most clearly when Linfield interprets an image of Iraqi women grieving the violent death of a relative; as she says of her emotional reaction, "I felt impatience, even anger: rather than embracing these mourners, I wanted to shake them. . . . I doubt that such sorrows [of women like those depicted] will even begin to abate until the many women in the many cemeteries stop wailing and praising and instead demand entry, as active citizens, into the world." Linfield, *Cruel Radiance*, 27. Such an articulation probably reveals more about Linfield's privilege and politics than about the specific image or the context of its making, but it does illustrate the dangers of subordinating ethics to efficacy, of relationships to results. By casting people as in need of saving, or worse in need of

self-saving, they can become further objectified and victimized, pawns in the particular struggles deemed most important to artists, critics, or academics.

80. Canclini, *Art beyond Itself*, 169. Susan Sontag similarly challenges the presumed efficacy of representations of atrocity: "In a world in which photography is brilliantly at the service of consumerist manipulations, no effect of a photograph of a doleful scene can be taken for granted." Sontag, *Regarding the Pain of Others*, 79–80.

81. This implied promise of the liberal order performs symbolic violence by conditioning subjects to accept externally imposed assessments of their social positions, along what I have called a "continuum of threat." It works by enfolding subjects in a mythology of universal rights. As Denise Ferreira da Silva explains, "Without some assumption of a universal (in terms of equality and/or transcendence), it is inconceivable that free (self-determined) persons or collectives would accept being represented by somebody or something other than themselves." da Silva, "Reading Art as Confrontation," 2.

82. Nguyen, *Gift of Freedom*; Puar, *Terrorist Assemblages*; Weheliye, *Habeas Viscus*.

CHAPTER FIVE. Disruption

Portions of chapter 5 appeared as "The Arresting Gaze: Artistic Disruptions of Antiblack Surveillance," *International Journal of Cultural Studies* vol. 23, no. 4 (2020).

1. Gandy, *Coming to Terms with Chance*; Lyon, *Surveillance Society*; Mirzoeff, *Right to Look*.

2. Dubrofsky and Magnet, *Feminist Surveillance Studies*.

3. Andrejevic, "Surveillance in the Big Data Era"; Magnet, *When Biometrics Fail*; Staples, *Everyday Surveillance*.

4. Monahan, "Dreams of Control at a Distance." Compare Haraway, *Simians, Cyborgs, and Women*.

5. Wall and Linnemann, "Staring Down the State." See also Berry for an account of how alleged "reckless eyeballing" of white women by black men has been used as an invitation for white male retaliation. Berry, "'Reckless Eyeballing.'"

6. Gilroy, "Art of Darkness."

7. Gilroy, "Cruciality and the Frog's Perspective"; Gilroy, *Black Atlantic*.

8. Hall, "Black Diaspora Artists in Britain," 23.

9. Mercer, "Stuart Hall and the Visual Arts," 82.

10. Bishop, *Artificial Hells*; Watts, *Hearing the Hurt*.

11. Sharpe, *In the Wake*, 3.

12. Carbado, "From Stopping Black People to Killing Black People"; Hirschfield, "Lethal Policing"; Silva, *Brown Threat*.

13. Monahan, "Regulating Belonging"; Varvin, "Our Relations to Refugees"; Winokur and Kashi, "They Came Here Seeking Freedom and Were Imprisoned Instead."

14. Sawyer and Wagner, "Mass Incarceration."

15. NAACP, "Criminal Justice Fact Sheet."

16. Hartman, *Lose Your Mother*, 6.

17. Center on Budget and Policy Priorities, "Tracking the COVID-19 Recession's Effects on Food, Housing, and Employment Hardships"; French and Monahan, "Disease Surveillance"; Maria Godoy and Daniel Wood, "What Do Coronavirus Racial Disparities Look Like State by State?," NPR, May 30, 2020, accessed July 14, 2020, www.npr.org/sections/health-shots/2020/05/30/865413079/what-do-coronavirus-racial-disparities-look-like-state-by-state; Grineski et al., "Hazardous Air Pollutants and Flooding"; Sharpe, *In the Wake*; Williams, "Turning the Tide."

18. Lowe, *Intimacies of Four Continents*, 6.

19. Benjamin, *Race after Technology*.

20. My position is informed by Alexander Weheliye's critique of the conceptual limitations of resistance and agency: "As explanatory tools, these concepts [resistance and agency] have a tendency to blind us, whether through strenuous denials or exalted celebrations of their existence, to the manifold occurrences of freedom in zones of indistinction. As modes of analyzing and imagining the practices of the oppressed in the face of extreme violence . . . resistance and agency assume full, self-present, and coherent subjects working against something or someone. . . . Why are formations of the oppressed deemed liberatory only if they resist hegemony and/or exhibit the full agency of the oppressed? What deformations of freedom become possible in the absence of resistance and agency?" Weheliye, *Habeas Viscus*, 2.

21. Spillers, "Mama's Baby, Papa's Maybe," 67–68.

22. Weheliye, *Habeas Viscus*, 43–44.

23. This can be read against variants of Afro-pessimism, such as those developed by Frank Wilderson, that view liberal social orders as necessarily reproductive of black (social) death without any possibility for resolution or fundamental alteration. The reason for this, as Wilderson explains, is that rather than existing in a state of conflict, where solutions might be posed, society is defined by a rubric of antagonism that not only precludes resolution "but entails the obliteration of one of the positions." Wilderson, *Red, White & Black*, 5.

24. Weheliye, *Habeas Viscus*, 12.

25. Lorde, *Sister Outsider*, 74, 28.

26. Sharpe, *In the Wake*, 14, 18.

27. Katherine McKittrick poetically describes this potential: "Liberation is an already existing and unfinished and unmet possibility, laced with creative labor, that emerges from the ongoing collaborative expression of black humanity and black livingness." McKittrick, *Dear Science and Other Stories*, 13.

28. Browne, *Dark Matters*, 21.

29. Fair, "Surveilling Social Difference."

30. Browne, *Dark Matters*.

31. Glasbeek, Alam, and Roots, "Seeing and Not-Seeing," 333.

32. Ober, "Recasting the Past."

33. Culp, "Afro-pessimism as Aesthetic Blackness?," 8.

34. See Browne, *Dark Matters*.

35. Culp, "Afro-pessimism as Aesthetic Blackness?," 8.

36. Ober, "Recasting the Past."

37. Hartman, *Scenes of Subjection*. See also Weheliye, *Habeas Viscus*, 91.

38. Armond Towns detects similar legacies at play with respect to academic discourse: "As a Black man, the way that I can dialogue with a person, regardless of their race, is always predicated on the racial violence of chattel slavery—which is to say English was necessarily whipped into one of my ancestors on a plantation, until today none of that ancestor's relatives can speak anything else. I write and speak in blood, despite promises of the recognition of 'everyone's' humanity." Towns, "'What Do We Wanna Be?,'" 78.

39. Hall, *Transparent Traveler*.

40. Weheliye, *Habeas Viscus*, 3.

41. Hartman and Wilderson, "Position of the Unthought," 184–85, quoted in Danylevich, "Beyond Thinking."

42. American artist Scott Tyler chose the name Dread Scott in obvious reference to Dred Scott, the nineteenth-century black slave whose lawsuit for freedom was infamously denied by the US Supreme Court on the basis that people of African descent could never qualify for US citizenship. Dubin, *Arresting Images*.

43. Chappell, "College Apologizes after Native American Students' Visit Is Sidelined by Police"; Doug Criss and Amir Vera, "Three Black People Checked Out of Their Airbnb Rental. Then Someone Called the Police on Them," CNN, May 10, 2018, accessed August 8, 2018, www.cnn.com/2018/05/07/us/airbnb-police-called-trnd/index.html; Carla Herreria, "Woman Calls Police on Black Family for Bbqing at a Lake in Oakland," *Huffington Post*, May 11, 2018, accessed August 8, 2018, www.huffingtonpost.com/entry/woman-calls-police-oakland-barbecue_us_5af50125e4b00d7e4c18f741.

44. Dread Scott's *Stop* project was partially supported by the Rush Philanthropic Arts Foundation and other contributors. Scott, "Stop."

45. In Hall's terminology, this can be read as a form of transcoding that recalibrates the relationship of (white) viewers to black images and introduces moments of productive tension wherein reflexivity and a recognition of complicity could emerge. Hall, *Representation*; see also Mercer, "Stuart Hall and the Visual Arts."

46. Boyle and Haggerty, "Spectacular Security."

47. Scott, "Stop."

48. Weheliye, *Habeas Viscus*, 11.

49. Wesley Lowery, "Aren't More White People Than Black People Killed by Police? Yes, but No," *Washington Post*, July 11, 2016, accessed August 8, 2018, www.washingtonpost.com/news/post-nation/wp/2016/07/11/arent-more-white-people-than-black-people-killed-by-police-yes-but-no/.

50. Goodwin, "Professional Vision."

51. Goodwin, "Professional Vision"; Nix et al., "Bird's Eye View of Civilians Killed by Police in 2015."

52. Chin and Wells, "Blue Wall of Silence as Evidence of Bias and Motive to Lie"; Huq and McAdams, "Litigating the Blue Wall of Silence."

53. Jotham Sederstrom, "Museum Exhibit in Brooklyn on Police Shootings Draws Fire from Police Union," *New York Daily News*, February 29, 2008, accessed August 8,

2018, www.nydailynews.com/news/museum-exhibit-brooklyn-police-shootings-draws
-fire-police-union-article-1.306295.

54. According to a newspaper story discussing the reaction to Scott's *Blue Wall of Violence*, the Council on the Arts and the city Department of Cultural Affairs did designate $68,000 for the museum, but these funds were not used to directly support Scott's exhibition. Sederstrom, "Museum Exhibit in Brooklyn on Police Shootings." See also Ben Muessig, "Cops: Art Show Is 'Brutal' to Us," *Brooklyn Paper*, March 8, 2008, accessed August 8, 2018, www.brooklynpaper.com/stories/31/10/31_10_cops_art_show _is_brutal.html.

55. Quoted in Muessig, "Cops."

56. Harding, *Performance, Transparency, and the Cultures of Surveillance*.

57. Bloch, "Art of #BlackLivesMatter."

58. Lorde, *Sister Outsider*.

59. Mirror Casket Project, "Mirror Casket Project."

60. Bloch, "Art of #BlackLivesMatter"; Mirror Casket Project, "Mirror Casket Project."

61. Bloch, "Art of #BlackLivesMatter"; NWF Mail, "We Are Human, Too."

62. Mirror Casket Project, "Mirror Casket Project."

63. Sexton, "Ruse of Engagement," 49.

64. Mills, *Racial Contract*.

65. Weheliye, *Habeas Viscus*, 90. Pornotroping and surveillance are two viewing logics that work in concert to enforce racial hierarchies in contemporary Western societies. Pornotroping normalizes racial hierarchies through tacit reference to a hidden social register, within which one can imagine his or her assigned place. Surveillance both constitutes and enforces racial hierarchies through its application. In that contemporary surveillance apparatuses impose differential forms of visibility and control based upon one's social position, they segment out populations and seek to hold them in their prescribed places. In conjunction, the normalizing of racial hierarchies (via pornotroping) and the policing of racial hierarchies (via surveillance) solidify cultural and social dimensions of racism.

66. Sharpe relates something similar in her description of the "work" done by images of black suffering, ranging from depictions of lynchings to police beatings to death by neglect: "These images work to confirm the status, location, and already held opinions within dominant ideology about those exhibitions of spectacular Black bodies whose meanings then remain unchanged. . . . Such repetitions often work to solidify and make continuous the colonial project of violence." Sharpe, *In the Wake*, 116–17.

67. Nicole Fuller, Ted Phillips, Maria Alvarez, Anthony M. Destefano, and Will James, "'Millions March NYC,' Protesting Grand Jury Decision in Eric Garner Death, Ends in Manhattan," *Newsday*, December 13, 2014, accessed August 13, 2018, www .newsday.com/news/new-york/millions-march-nyc-protesting-grand-jury-decision-in -eric-garner-death-begins-in-manhattan-1.9711149.

68. Bloch, "Art of #BlackLivesMatter"; Matt Sledge and Braden Goyette, "Tens of Thousands March on NYPD Headquarters to Protest Police Killings," *Huffington Post*,

December 13, 2014, accessed August 13, 2018, www.huffingtonpost.com/2014/12/13 /millions-march-nyc_n_6320348.html.

69. Hartman, *Scenes of Subjection*, 60.

70. Some of the performance venues for *What Remains* included Danspace Project in New York, the Museum of Contemporary Art in Chicago, and the Walker Art Center in Minneapolis. The primary analysis in this section is of a full video screening of the dance, not of in-person attendance by the author. Rawls, "What Remains."

71. Quoted in Gallagher-Ross, "In Progress."

72. Siobhan Burke, "Claudia Rankine and Will Rawls: Surveillance and the Black Experience," *New York Times*, April 25, 2017, accessed August 13, 2018, www.nytimes .com/2017/04/25/arts/dance/claudia-rankine-will-rawls-surveillance.html.

73. Burke, "Claudia Rankine and Will Rawls."

74. Rawls, "What Remains."

75. Rankine, "Some Years There Exists a Wanting to Escape."

76. Fanon, *Black Skin, White Masks*.

77. Glissant, *Poetics of Relation*.

78. Under the rubric of "gestures of concern," Chris Ingraham has expressed a similar investment in collective, and often mundane, acts of being together: "Worlds [that people] would like to imagine as worthy of being shared . . . need to be created again and again through performed enactments of their creative sustenance. . . . Gestures of concern . . . build affect worlds as replenishable commonwealths consisting in the activity of sharing concerns that may be too great to resolve, though the ongoing activity of holding open a space for raising the common as a question fortifies a feeling that things are good enough for now (if only just)." Ingraham, *Gestures of Concern*, 161–62.

79. Phelan, *Unmarked*.

80. Taylor, *Archive and the Repertoire*.

81. Towns, "Toward a Black Media Philosophy," 870.

Conclusion

1. Lateral or peer surveillance, though not necessarily valenced toward data extraction, is similarly premised on asymmetrical power relations and performances of control. For instance, the monitoring of an acquaintance or coworker on social media is not surveillance in and of itself; it becomes "surveillance" at the moment when information from that monitoring is applied to influence the behavior or actions of others. It is surveillance when and if power asymmetries are exploited. Because these forms of surveillance may occur between parties occupying similar social positions or having comparable status within institutions, they draw attention to the ways in which all surveillance is contingent and contextually dependent. One does not have to possess institutional authority in order to engage in or be a part of surveillance-facilitated acts of control. The same observation would hold, of course, for articulations of *sousveillance*, or so-called surveillance from below. Gilliom and Monahan, *Supervision*;

Monahan and Murakami Wood, "Resistance and Opposition"; Monahan, "Counter-Surveillance as Political Intervention?"

2. Rancière, *Politics of Aesthetics*.

3. Harding, *Performance, Transparency, and the Cultures of Surveillance*, 55.

4. Ellison, *Invisible Man*.

5. Mills, *Blackness Visible*, 116–17.

6. Drawing on Stuart Hall, Simone Browne describes this as a process of "epidermalization," whereby race becomes inscribed upon the skin, stripping humanity from black bodies while making them legible for others: "It is the making of the black body as out of place, an attempt to deny its capacity for humanness, which makes for the productive power of epidermalization." Browne, *Dark Matters*, 98.

7. Du Bois, *Souls of Black Folk*, 45; see also Mills, *Blackness Visible*, 10–11.

8. Siobhan Burke, "Claudia Rankine and Will Rawls: Surveillance and the Black Experience," *New York Times*, April 25, 2017, accessed August 13, 2018, www.nytimes.com /2017/04/25/arts/dance/claudia-rankine-will-rawls-surveillance.html.

9. Monahan, "Privatization Cultures and the Racial Order."

10. Scher, "Security by Julia."

11. It is no coincidence that this coalescence occurred alongside the institutionalization of surveillance studies as a transdisciplinary field. Surveillance studies scholars and artists have been in conversation from the outset, even if they have not always shared the same orbit. The field is built upon such cross-fertilizations. As David Murakami Wood and I relate in our overview of the field's formation, "The field's defining feature is its search for commonalities among tensions in disciplinary approaches to surveillance. This is the reason we prefer to call surveillance studies a 'transdisciplinary field.' It draws its strength and forms its identity from shared general concerns and productive frictions among disciplines, all the while fostering departures and innovations." Monahan and Murakami Wood, *Surveillance Studies*, xxi.

12. Monahan, *Surveillance in the Time of Insecurity*.

13. Andrejevic, *Infoglut*; Marwick and Lewis, "Media Manipulation and Disinformation Online"; Eli Pariser, "How the Net Traps Us All in Our Own Little Bubbles," *Guardian*, June 12, 2011, www.guardian.co.uk/technology/2011/jun/12/google -personalisation-internet-data-filtering?cat=technology&type=article; Partin and Marwick, "Construction of Alternative Facts."

14. Crary, *Techniques of the Observer*; Crary, *Suspensions of Perception*.

15. Glissant, *Poetics of Relation*, 190.

16. Glissant, *Poetics of Relation*, 190 (emphasis added).

17. Weheliye, *Habeas Viscus*, 2.

18. Søilen, "Safe Is a Wonderful Feeling," 181.

19. I am intentionally referencing the concept of "lines of flight," as developed by Gilles Deleuze and Félix Guattari, which signifies "movements of deterritorialization and destratification. . . . Lines of flight, for their part, never consist in running away from the world but rather in causing runoffs, as when you drill a hole in a pipe; there is no social system that does not leak from all directions, even if it makes its segments increasingly rigid in order to seal the lines of flight. . . . It is on lines of flight that new

weapons are invented, to be turned against the heavy arms of the State." Deleuze and Guattari, *A Thousand Plateaus*, 3, 204. See also Bogard, although his elision of lines of flight with resistance has been criticized by Caluya for its inattention to the creative capacity of such movement. Bogard, "Surveillance Assemblages and Lines of Flight"; Caluya, "Post-Panoptic Society?"

Abraham, Roshan. "Migrant Surveillance: How the Federal Government Monitors Asylum Seekers." CUNY Graduate School of Journalism, 2016. Accessed October 28, 2018. https://academicworks.cuny.edu/cgi/viewcontent.cgi?article=1181&context=gj_etds.

Abu-Lughod, Lila. *Do Muslim Women Need Saving?* Cambridge, MA: Harvard University Press, 2013.

Agamben, Giorgio. *Homo Sacer: Sovereign Power and Bare Life*. Stanford, CA: Stanford University Press, 1998.

Agostinho, Daniela, Catherine D'Ignazio, Annie Ring, Nanna Bonde Thylstrup, and Kristin Veel. "Uncertain Archives: Approaching the Unknowns, Errors, and Vulnerabilities of Big Data through Cultural Theories of the Archive." *Surveillance & Society* 17, no. 3/4 (2019): 422–41.

Althusser, Louis. "Ideology and Ideological State Apparatuses." In *Literary Theory: An Anthology*, edited by Julie Rivkin and Michael Ryan, 693–702. Malden, MA: Blackwell, 2004.

Alÿs, Francis. "When Faith Moves Mountains." 2002. Accessed October 28, 2018. http://francisalys.com/when-faith-moves-mountains.

Amicelle, Anthony. "Towards a 'New' Political Anatomy of Financial Surveillance." *Security Dialogue* 42, no. 2 (2011): 161–78.

Amoore, Louise. "Biometric Borders: Governing Mobilities in the War on Terror." *Political Geography* 25, no. 3 (2006): 336–51.

Amoore, Louise. *The Politics of Possibility: Risk and Security beyond Probability*. Durham, NC: Duke University Press, 2013.

Andrejevic, Mark. "Estranged Free Labor." In *Digital Labor: The Internet as Playground and Factory*, edited by Trebor Scholz, 149–64. New York: Routledge, 2013.

Andrejevic, Mark. *Infoglut: How Too Much Information Is Changing the Way We Think and Know*. New York: Routledge, 2013.

Andrejevic, Mark. *iSpy: Surveillance and Power in the Interactive Era*. Lawrence: University Press of Kansas, 2007.

Andrejevic, Mark. "Surveillance in the Big Data Era." In *Emerging Pervasive Information and Communication Technologies (PICT)*, edited by Kenneth D. Pimple, 55–69. New York: Springer, 2014.

Andrejevic, Mark. "Whither-Ing Critique." *Communication and Critical/Cultural Studies* 10, nos. 2–3 (2013): 222–28.

Ball, Kirstie. "Organization, Surveillance and the Body: Towards a Politics of Resistance." *Organization* 12, no. 1 (2005): 89–108.

Ball, Kirstie, Ana Canhoto, Elizabeth Daniel, Sally Dibb, Maureen Meadows, and Keith Spiller. *The Private Security State? Surveillance, Consumer Data and the War on Terror.* Copenhagen: Copenhagen Business School Press, 2015.

Barnard-Wills, David. *Surveillance and Identity: Discourse, Subjectivity and the State.* Burlington, VT: Ashgate, 2012.

Barnard-Wills, Katherine, and David Barnard-Wills. "Invisible Surveillance in Visual Art." *Surveillance & Society* 10, no. 3/4 (2012): 204–14.

Barocas, Solon, and Andrew D. Selbst. "Big Data's Disparate Impact." *California Law Review* 104, no. 3 (2016): 671–732.

Barrell, John. *The Dark Side of the Landscape: The Rural Poor in English Painting 1730–1840.* Cambridge: Cambridge University Press, 1980.

Baskin, Danielle. "Facial ID Respirator Masks." 2020. Accessed September 14, 2020. https://faceidmasks.com.

Baskin, Danielle. "Made This Service. . . ." Twitter, February 15, 2020. Accessed September 14, 2020. https://twitter.com/djbaskin/status/1228798382598000640.

Beauchamp, Toby. "Artful Concealment and Strategic Visibility: Transgender Bodies and U.S. State Surveillance after 9/11." *Surveillance & Society* 6, no. 4 (2009): 356–66.

Beauchamp, Toby. *Going Stealth: Transgender Politics and U.S. Surveillance Practices.* Durham, NC: Duke University Press, 2019.

Begley, Josh. "Plain Sight: The Visual Vernacular of NYPD Surveillance." Open Society Foundations, 2014. Accessed June 11, 2017. www.opensocietyfoundations.org/moving-walls/22/plain-sight-visual-vernacular-nypd-surveillance.

Bell, Charlotte. "The Inner City and the 'Hoodie.'" *Wasafiri* 28, no. 4 (2013): 38–44.

Benjamin, Ruha. *Race after Technology: Abolitionist Tools for the New Jim Code.* Medford, MA: Polity, 2019.

Bennett, Steven C. "The Right to Be Forgotten: Reconciling EU and US Perspectives." *Berkeley Journal of International Law* 30 (2012): 161–95.

Berger, John. *Ways of Seeing.* London: British Broadcasting Corporation and Penguin Books, 1972.

Bering, Jesse. "There's Something Queer about That Face." *Scientific American*, February 23, 2009. Accessed May 25, 2014. www.scientificamerican.com/blog/post/something-queer-about-that-face.

Berlant, Lauren Gail. *Cruel Optimism.* Durham, NC: Duke University Press, 2011.

Berry, Mary Frances. "'Reckless Eyeballing': The Matt Ingram Case and the Denial of African American Sexual Freedom." *Journal of African American History* 93, no. 2 (2008): 223–34.

Bertrand, Ann-Christin, and James Bridle, eds. *Watched! Surveillance, Art and Photography.* Köln: Walther König, 2016.

Besteman, Catherine. *Making Refuge: Somali Bantu Refugees and Lewiston, Maine.* Durham, NC: Duke University Press, 2016.

Birchall, Clare. "Aesthetics of the Secret." *New Formations* 83 (2014): 25–46.

Birchall, Clare. *Radical Secrecy: The Ends of Transparency in Datafied America.* Minneapolis: University of Minnesota Press, 2021.

Birchall, Clare. *Shareveillance: The Dangers of Openly Sharing and Covertly Collecting Data.* Minneapolis: University of Minnesota Press, 2017.

Birchall, Clare, Francien Broekhuizen, Simon Dawes, Danai Mikelli, and Poppy Wilde. "Openness and Opacity: An Interview with Clare Birchall." *Networking Knowledge: Journal of the MeCCSA Postgraduate Network* 9, no. 1 (2016).

Bishop, Claire. *Artificial Hells: Participatory Art and the Politics of Spectatorship.* London: Verso, 2012.

Bishop, Claire. "Delegated Performance: Outsourcing Authenticity." *October* 140 (2012): 91–112.

Blanchette, Jean-François. "A Material History of Bits." *Journal of the Association for Information Science and Technology* 62, no. 6 (2011): 1042–57.

Blanchette, Jean-François, and Deborah G. Johnson. "Data Retention and the Panoptic Society: The Social Benefits of Forgetfulness." *Information Society* 18, no. 1 (2002): 33–45.

Blas, Zach. "Facial Weaponization Suite (2011–Present)." 2014. Accessed May 25, 2014. www.zachblas.info/projects/facial-weaponization-suite.

Blas, Zach. "Informatic Opacity." In *Posthuman Glossary*, edited by Rosi Braidotti and Maria Hlavajova, 198–99. London: Bloomsbury Academic, 2018.

Bloch, Nadine. "The Art of #BlackLivesMatter." Waging Nonviolence, January 8, 2015. Accessed August 8, 2018. https://wagingnonviolence.org/feature/art-blacklivesmatter.

Bogard, William. "Surveillance Assemblages and Lines of Flight." In *Theorizing Surveillance: The Panopticon and Beyond*, edited by David Lyon, 97–122. Cullompton, UK: Willan, 2006.

Bourgois, Philippe. "The Continuum of Violence in War and Peace: Post–Cold War Lessons from El Salvador." In *Violence in War and Peace*, edited by Nancy Scheper-Hughes and Philippe Bourgois, 425–34. Malden, MA: Blackwell, 2004.

Bowker, Geoffrey C., and Susan Leigh Star. *Sorting Things Out: Classification and Its Consequences.* Cambridge, MA: MIT Press, 1999.

Boyle, Philip, and Kevin D. Haggerty. "Spectacular Security: Mega-events and the Security Complex." *International Political Sociology* 3, no. 3 (2009): 257–74.

Brayne, Sarah. *Predict and Surveil: Data, Discretion, and the Future of Policing.* New York: Oxford University Press, 2021.

Bridges, Lauren. "Infrastructural Obfuscation: Unpacking the Carceral Logics of the Ring Surveillant Assemblage." *Information, Communication & Society* 24, no. 6 (2021): 830–49.

Bridle, James. "Seamless Transitions." In *Watched! Surveillance, Art and Photography*, edited by Ann-Christin Bertrand and James Bridle, 188–89. Köln: Walther König, 2016.

Brighenti, Andrea Mubi. "Artveillance: At the Crossroads of Art and Surveillance." *Surveillance & Society* 7, no. 2 (2010): 137–48.

Brighenti, Andrea Mubi. "Visibility: A Category for the Social Sciences." *Current Sociology* 55, no. 3 (2007): 323–42.

Browne, Simone. *Dark Matters: On the Surveillance of Blackness*. Durham, NC: Duke University Press, 2015.

Browne, Simone. "Digital Epidermalization: Race, Identity and Biometrics." *Critical Sociology* 36, no. 1 (2010): 131–50.

Brucato, Ben. "The New Transparency: Police Violence in the Context of Ubiquitous Surveillance." *Media and Communication* 3, no. 3 (2015): 39–55.

Bruce, La Marr Jurelle. *How to Go Mad without Losing Your Mind: Madness and Black Radical Creativity*. Durham, NC: Duke University Press, 2020.

Brunton, Finn, and Helen Nissenbaum. *Obfuscation: A User's Guide for Privacy and Protest*. Cambridge, MA: MIT Press, 2015.

Bureau of Investigative Journalism. "CIA Drone Strikes in Pakistan, 2004 to Present." 2016. Accessed December 28, 2016. https://docs.google.com/spreadsheets/d/1NAfjFonM-Tn7fziqiv33HlGto9wgLZDSCP-BQaux51w/edit?pref=2&pli=1#gid=694046452.

Butler, Judith. *Bodies That Matter: On the Discursive Limits of "Sex."* New York: Routledge, 1993.

Butler, Judith. "Conscience Doth Make Subjects of Us All." *Yale French Studies* 88 (1995): 6–26.

Butler, Judith. *Gender Trouble: Feminism and the Subversion of Identity*. New York: Routledge, 1990.

Cahill, Susan. "Visual Art, Corporeal Economies, and the 'New Normal' of Surveillant Policing in the War on Terror." *Surveillance & Society* 17, no. 3/4 (2018): 252–66.

Calavita, Kitty. *Invitation to Law and Society: An Introduction to the Study of Real Law*. Chicago: University of Chicago Press, 2010.

Caluya, Gilbert. "The Post-Panoptic Society? Reassessing Foucault in Surveillance Studies." *Social Identities* 16, no. 5 (2010): 621–33.

Ca'Macana. "The Old Tradition of Disguise: A Brief History of Venetian Masks." *Ca'Macana Venezia*, October 15, 2013. Accessed May 25, 2014. www.camacana.com/a-brief-history-of-venetian-masks.

Canclini, Néstor García. *Art beyond Itself: Anthropology for a Society without a Story Line*. Durham, NC: Duke University Press, 2014.

Carbado, Devon W. "From Stopping Black People to Killing Black People: The Fourth Amendment Pathways to Police Violence." *California Law Review* 105, no. 1 (2017): 125–64.

Cartwright, Lisa. *Screening the Body: Tracing Medicine's Visual Culture*. Minneapolis: University of Minnesota Press, 1995.

Castells, Manuel. *The Power of Identity*. Malden, MA: Blackwell, 1997.

Celis, Claudio. "Critical Surveillance Art in the Age of Machine Vision and Algorithmic Governmentality: Three Case Studies." *Surveillance & Society* 18, no. 3 (2020): 295–311.

Chappell, Bill. "College Apologizes after Native American Students' Visit Is Sidelined by Police." NPR, May 4, 2018. Accessed August 8, 2018. www.npr.org/sections /thetwo-way/2018/05/04/608533284/college-apologizes-after-native-american -students-visit-is-sidelined-by-police.

Charland, Maurice. "Constitutive Rhetoric: The Case of the Peuple Quebecois." *Quarterly Journal of Speech* 73, no. 2 (1987): 133–50.

Chen, Angela. "How Coronavirus Turned the 'Dystopian Joke' of FaceID Masks into a Reality." MIT *Technology Review*, February 29, 2020. Accessed September 14, 2020. www.technologyreview.com/2020/02/29/905599/how-coronavirus-turned-the -dystopian-joke-of-faceid-masks-into-a-reality.

Chin, Gabriel J., and Scott C. Wells. "The Blue Wall of Silence as Evidence of Bias and Motive to Lie: A New Approach to Police Perjury." *University of Pittsburgh Law Review* 59 (1997): 233–99.

Cirio, Paolo. "Album Archive: Street Ghosts—Public." 2013. Accessed June 12, 2017. https://get.google.com/albumarchive/101628793830161569774/album/AF1QipP66 ok3UiNs8t4wovmvBOSJgHTfspSw7IOgLZNV/AF1QipPQVd9svwHBqIC2RZTv5R -gobERYJFjdm2ckOiY.

Cirio, Paolo. "Obscurity." 2016. Accessed January 15, 2017. https://obscurity.online.

Cirio, Paolo. "Street Ghosts." Open Society Foundations, 2014. Accessed June 12, 2017. www.opensocietyfoundations.org/moving-walls/22/street-ghosts.

Citron, Danielle Keats. *Hate Crimes in Cyberspace*. Cambridge, MA: Harvard University Press, 2014.

Cohen, Julie E. *Configuring the Networked Self: Law, Code, and the Play of Everyday Practice*. New Haven, CT: Yale University Press, 2012.

Cohen, Julie E. "Studying Law Studying Surveillance." *Surveillance & Society* 13, no. 1 (2015): 91–101.

Cole, Simon A. *Suspect Identities: A History of Fingerprinting and Criminal Identification*. Cambridge, MA: Harvard University Press, 2001.

Coll, Sami. "Power, Knowledge, and the Subjects of Privacy: Understanding Privacy as the Ally of Surveillance." *Information, Communication & Society* 17, no. 10 (2014): 1250–63.

Coombe, Rosemary. "Is There a Cultural Studies of Law?" In *A Companion to Cultural Studies*, edited by Toby Miller, 36–62. Malden, MA: Blackwell, 2001.

Coupe, James. "Artist Interview: James Coupe, Creator of 'Watchtower: A Machine for Living.'" *Blink*, August 12, 2018. Accessed October 28, 2018. https://medium.com /surveillance-and-society/artist-interview-james-coupe-creator-of-watchtower-a -machine-for-living-abcc321a8b57.

Coupe, James. "Watchtower (a Machine for Living)." 2017. Accessed October 28, 2018. http://jamescoupe.com/?p=2339.

Cowen, Deborah. *The Deadly Life of Logistics: Mapping Violence in Global Trade*. Minneapolis: University of Minnesota Press, 2014.

Crary, Jonathan. *Suspensions of Perception: Attention, Spectacle, and Modern Culture*. Cambridge, MA: MIT Press, 1999.

Crary, Jonathan. "Techniques of the Observer." *October* 45 (1988): 3–35.

Crary, Jonathan. *Techniques of the Observer: On Vision and Modernity in the Nineteenth Century*. Cambridge, MA: MIT Press, 1992.

Crenshaw, Kimberlé. "Demarginalizing the Intersection of Race and Sex: A Black Feminist Critique of Antidiscrimination Doctrine, Feminist Theory and Antiracist Politics." *University of Chicago Legal Forum* 1989 (1989): 139–67.

Culp, Andrew. "Afro-Pessimism as Aesthetic Blackness? [Putting the Pessimism in Afro-Pessimism]." *Philofiction*, January 8, 2016. Accessed August 8, 2018. https://non.copyriot.com/afro-pessimism-as-aesthetic-blackness-putting-the-pessimism-in-afro-pessimism.

Currah, Paisley, and Lisa Jean Moore. "'We Won't Know Who You Are': Contesting Sex Designations in New York City Birth Certificates." *Hypatia* 24, no. 3 (2009): 113–35.

Cuttitta, Paolo. "'Borderizing' the Island Setting and Narratives of the Lampedusa 'Border Play.'" *ACME: An International E-Journal for Critical Geographies* 13, no. 2 (2014).

da Silva, Denise Ferreira. "Reading Art as Confrontation." *E-flux Journal* 65 (2015): 1–6.

D&AD. "Not a Bug Splat." 2015. Accessed January 8, 2017. www.dandad.org/awards/professional/2015/white-pencil-creativity-for-good/24225/not-a-bug-splat.

Danylevich, Theodora. "Beyond Thinking: Black Flesh as *Meat Patties* and *The End of Eating Everything*." *Rhizomes* 29 (2016). www.rhizomes.net/issue29/danylevich/index.html.

Daston, Lorraine, and Peter Galison. "The Image of Objectivity." *Representations* 40 (1992): 81–128.

Davis, Ben. *9.5 Theses on Art and Class*. Chicago: Haymarket, 2013.

De Villiers, Nicholas. *Opacity and the Closet: Queer Tactics in Foucault, Barthes, and Warhol*. Minneapolis: University of Minnesota Press, 2012.

Debatty, Régine. "Sheriff Software: The Games That Allow You to Play Traffic Cop for Real." We Make Money Not Art, November 19, 2015. Accessed January 2, 2017. http://we-make-money-not-art.com/sheriff-software-the-games-that-allow-you-to-play-traffic-cop-for-real.

Degli Esposti, Sara. "When Big Data Meets Dataveillance: The Hidden Side of Analytics." *Surveillance & Society* 12, no. 2 (2014): 209–25.

Deleuze, Gilles. "The Diagram." In *The Deleuze Reader*, edited by Constantin V. Boundas, 193–200. New York: Columbia University Press, 1993.

Deleuze, Gilles. "Postscript on the Societies of Control." *October* 59 (Winter 1992): 3–7.

Deleuze, Gilles, and Félix Guattari. *A Thousand Plateaus: Capitalism and Schizophrenia*. Translated by Brian Massumi. Minneapolis: University of Minnesota Press, 1987.

Demos, T. J. *The Migrant Image*. Durham, NC: Duke University Press, 2013.

Depoorter, Dries. "Jaywalking." 2015. Accessed January 2, 2017. http://driesdepoorter.be/jaywalking.

Depoorter, Dries. "Sheriff Software." 2015. Accessed January 2, 2017. http://driesdepoorter.be/sheriffsoftware.

Derrida, Jacques. "Archive Fever: A Freudian Impression." *Diacritics* 25, no. 2 (1995): 9–63.

Derrida, Jacques. *Limited Inc*. Translated by Samuel Weber and Jeffrey Mehlman. Evanston, IL: Northwestern University Press, 1988.

Doane, Mary Ann. "The Indexical and the Concept of Medium Specificity." *differences* 18, no. 1 (2007): 128–52.

Doane, Mary Ann. "Indexicality: Trace and Sign: Introduction." *differences* 18, no. 1 (2007): 1–6.

Downey, Anthony. "An Ethics of Engagement: Collaborative Art Practices and the Return of the Ethnographer." *Third Text* 23, no. 5 (2009): 593–603.

Downey, Anthony. "The Lives of Others: Artur Zmijewski's 'Repetition,' the Stanford Prison Experiment, and the Ethics of Surveillance." In *Conspiracy Dwellings: Surveillance in Contemporary Art*, edited by Outi Remes and Pam Skelton, 67–81. Newcastle upon Tyne, UK: Cambridge Scholars Publishing, 2010.

Doy, Gen. *Picturing the Self: Changing Views of the Subject in Visual Culture*. London: I. B. Tauris, 2005.

Du Bois, W. E. B. *The Souls of Black Folk*. New York: New American Library, 1969.

Dubin, Steven C. *Arresting Images: Impolitic Art and Uncivil Actions*. New York: Routledge, 1992.

Dubrofsky, Rachel E. "Surveillance on Reality Television and Facebook: From Authenticity to Flowing Data." *Communication Theory* 21, no. 2 (2011): 111–29.

Dubrofsky, Rachel E., and Shoshana Amielle Magnet, eds. *Feminist Surveillance Studies*. Durham, NC: Duke University Press, 2015.

Dubrofsky, Rachel E., and Emily D. Ryalls. "The Hunger Games: Performing Not-Performing to Authenticate Femininity and Whiteness." *Critical Studies in Media Communication* 31, no. 5 (2014): 395–409.

Duffy, Brooke Erin. *(Not) Getting Paid to Do What You Love: Gender, Social Media, and Aspirational Work*. New Haven, CT: Yale University Press, 2017.

Dumit, Joseph. *Picturing Personhood: Brain Scans and Biomedical Identity*. Princeton, NJ: Princeton University Press, 2004.

Duncan, James. "Complicity and Resistance in the Colonial Archive: Some Issues of Method and Theory in Historical Geography." *Historical Geography* 27 (1999): 119–28.

Eagleton, Terry. *The Ideology of the Aesthetic*. Oxford: Blackwell, 1990.

Elahi, Hasan. "FBI, Here I Am!" TEDGlobal, July 2011. Accessed June 12, 2017. www.ted.com/talks/hasan_elahi.

Elahi, Hasan. "I Share Everything. Or Do I?" Ideas.TED.com, July 1, 2014. Accessed June 12, 2017. http://ideas.ted.com/i-share-everything-or-do-i.

Elahi, Hasan. "Prism." 2015. Accessed June 12, 2017. http://elahi.umd.edu/elahi_prism.php.

Elahi, Hasan. "Thousand Little Brothers." Open Society Foundations, 2014. Accessed December 26, 2016. www.opensocietyfoundations.org/moving-walls/22/thousand-little-brothers.

Ellison, Ralph. *Invisible Man*. New York: Vintage, 1995.

Eubanks, Virginia. *Automating Inequality: How High-Tech Tools Profile, Police, and Punish the Poor*. New York: St. Martin's, 2017.

Eubanks, Virginia. "Technologies of Citizenship: Surveillance and Political Learning in the Welfare System." In *Surveillance and Security: Technological Politics and Power in Everyday Life*, edited by Torin Monahan, 89–107. New York: Routledge, 2006.

Fair, Freda L. "Surveilling Social Difference: Black Women's 'Alley Work' in Industrializing Minneapolis." *Surveillance & Society* 15, no. 5 (2017): 655–75.

Falch, Frank. "Drifting. Hanne Nielsen & Birgit Johnsen." Sørlandets Kunstmuseum, 2014. Accessed October 28, 2018. http://videoraum.dk/uploads/drifting-hanne-nielsen-birgit-johnsen-by-frank-falch-s-rlandets-kunstmuseum-uk.pdf.

Fang, Karen. *Arresting Cinema: Surveillance in Hong Kong Film.* Stanford, CA: Stanford University Press, 2017.

Fanon, Frantz. *Black Skin, White Masks.* New York: Grove, 1952.

Feldman, Allen. "On Cultural Anesthesia: From Desert Storm to Rodney King." In *Violence in War and Peace,* edited by Nancy Scheper-Hughes and Philippe Bourgois, 207–16. Malden, MA: Blackwell, 2004.

Fernandez, Luis A., and Laura Huey. "Is Resistance Futile? Thoughts on Resisting Surveillance." *Surveillance & Society* 6, no. 3 (2009): 198–202.

Fischer, Mia. *Terrorizing Gender: Transgender Visibility and the Surveillance Practices of the US Security State.* Lincoln: University of Nebraska Press, 2019.

Fisher, Jill A., ed. *Gender and the Science of Difference: Cultural Politics of Contemporary Science and Medicine.* New Brunswick, NJ: Rutgers University Press, 2011.

Fisher, Jill A. "Tattooing the Body, Marking Culture." *Body & Society* 8, no. 4 (2002): 91–107.

Fiske, John. "Culture, Ideology, Interpellation." In *Literary Theory: An Anthology,* edited by Julie Rivkin and Michael Ryan, 1268–73. Malden, MA: Blackwell, 2004.

Foucault, Michel. *The Archaeology of Knowledge and the Discourse on Language.* Translated by A. M. Sheridan Smith. New York: Pantheon, 1972.

Foucault, Michel. *Discipline and Punish: The Birth of the Prison.* New York: Vintage, 1977.

Foucault, Michel. *The History of Sexuality: An Introduction,* vol. 1. New York: Vintage, 1978.

Foucault, Michel. "The Life of Infamous Men." In *Michel Foucault: Power, Truth, Strategy,* edited by Paul Foss and Meaghan Morris, 76–91. Sydney: Feral, 1979.

Foucault, Michel. *The Order of Things: An Archaeology of the Human Sciences.* New York: Vintage, 1970.

Foucault, Michel. *"Society Must Be Defended": Lectures at the College De France, 1975–76.* Translated by David Macey. New York: Picador, 2003.

French, Martin, and Torin Monahan. "Dis-ease Surveillance: How Might Surveillance Studies Address Covid-19?" *Surveillance & Society* 18, no. 1 (2020): 1–11.

Friedman, Lawrence. *Crime and Punishment in American History.* New York: Basic Books, 1993.

Fuchs, Christian. "Web 2.0, Prosumption, and Surveillance." *Surveillance & Society* 8, no. 3 (2011): 288–309.

Fyfe, Gordon, and John Law. "Introduction: On the Invisibility of the Visual." In *Picturing Power: Visual Depiction and Social Relations,* 1–14. London: Routledge, 1988.

Gallagher-Ross, Anna. "In Progress: An Interview with John Lucas, Claudia Rankine, and Will Rawls of 'What Remains.'" We're Watching, 2017. Accessed August 13, 2018.

http://blogs.bard.edu/wearewatching/2017/02/23/in-process-an-interview-with-john
-lucas-claudia-rankine-and-will-rawls-of-what-remains.

Gandy, Oscar H., Jr. *Coming to Terms with Chance: Engaging Rational Discrimination and Cumulative Disadvantage.* Burlington, VT: Ashgate, 2009.

Gandy, Oscar H., Jr. *The Panoptic Sort: A Political Economy of Personal Information.* Boulder, CO: Westview, 1993.

Gates, Kelly. "The Cultural Labor of Surveillance: Video Forensics, Computational Objectivity, and the Production of Visual Evidence." *Social Semiotics* 23, no. 2 (2013): 242–60.

Gates, Kelly. "Media Evidence and Forensic Journalism." *Surveillance & Society* 18, no. 3 (2020): 403–8.

Gates, Kelly. *Our Biometric Future: Facial Recognition Technology and the Culture of Surveillance.* New York: New York University Press, 2011.

Giddens, Anthony. *The Consequences of Modernity.* Stanford, CA: Stanford University Press, 1990.

Giddens, Anthony. *The Nation-State and Violence.* Vol. 2, *A Contemporary Critique of Historical Materialism.* Berkeley: University of California Press, 1987.

Gillespie, Tarleton. "The Relevance of Algorithms." In *Media Technologies: Essays on Communication, Materiality, and Society,* edited by Tarleton Gillespie, Pablo J. Boczkowski, and Kirsten A. Foot, 167–93. Cambridge, MA: MIT Press, 2014.

Gillespie, Tarleton. *Wired Shut: Copyright and the Shape of Digital Culture.* Cambridge, MA: MIT Press, 2007.

Gilliland, Anne J., and Sue McKemmish. "The Role of Participatory Archives in Furthering Human Rights, Reconciliation and Recovery." *Atlanti: Review for Modern Archival Theory and Practice* 24 (2014): 78–88.

Gilliom, John. *Overseers of the Poor: Surveillance, Resistance, and the Limits of Privacy.* Chicago: University of Chicago Press, 2001.

Gilliom, John, and Torin Monahan. *Supervision: An Introduction to the Surveillance Society.* Chicago: University of Chicago Press, 2013.

Gilroy, Paul. "Art of Darkness: Black Art and the Problem of Belonging to England." *Third Text* 4, no. 10 (1990): 45–52.

Gilroy, Paul. *The Black Atlantic: Modernity and Double Consciousness.* New York: Verso, 1993.

Gilroy, Paul. "Cruciality and the Frog's Perspective." *Third Text* 2, no. 5 (1988): 33–44.

Glasbeek, Amanda, Mariful Alam, and Katrin Roots. "Seeing and Not-Seeing: Race and Body-Worn Cameras in Canada." *Surveillance & Society* 18, no. 3 (2020): 328–42.

Glissant, Édouard. *Poetics of Relation.* Translated by Betsy Wing. Ann Arbor: University of Michigan Press, 1997.

Goffman, Erving. *The Presentation of Self in Everyday Life.* London: Allen Lane, 1969.

Goldman, Lauren M. "Trending Now: The Use of Social Media Websites in Public Shaming Punishments." *American Criminal Law Review* 52 (2015): 415–51.

Goodman, Amy. "Yes Men Hoax on BBC Reminds World of Dow Chemical's Refusal to Take Responsibility for Bhopal Disaster." Democracy Now, December 6, 2004.

Accessed October 6, 2014. www.democracynow.org/2004/12/6/yes_men_hoax_on
_bbc_reminds.

Goodwin, Charles. "Professional Vision." *American Anthropologist* 96, no. 3 (1994):
606–33.

Graham, Stephen. *Cities under Siege: The New Military Urbanism*. London: Verso, 2010.

Graham, Stephen. *Vertical: The City from Satellites to Bunkers*. New York: Verso, 2016.

Graham, Stephen, and David Wood. "Digitizing Surveillance: Categorization, Space,
Inequality." *Critical Social Policy* 23, no. 2 (2003): 227–48.

Greenberg, Andy. "Turning Live Surveillance Feeds into Unsettling Works of Art."
Wired, March 25, 2016. www.wired.com/2016/03/turning-live-surveillance-feeds
-unsettling-works-art.

Greenwald, Glenn. *No Place to Hide: Edward Snowden, the NSA, and the U.S. Surveillance
State*. New York: Metropolitan, 2014.

Gregory, Derek. "From a View to a Kill: Drones and Late Modern War." *Theory, Culture
& Society* 28, nos. 7–8 (2011): 188–215.

Grewal, Inderpal. *Saving the Security State: Exceptional Citizens in Twenty-First-Century
America*. Durham, NC: Duke University Press, 2017.

Griggs, Richard A. "Coverage of the Stanford Prison Experiment in Introductory Psychology Textbooks." *Teaching of Psychology* 41, no. 3 (2014): 195–203.

Grinberg, Daniel. "Tracking Movements: Black Activism, Aerial Surveillance, and
Transparency Optics." *Media, Culture & Society* 41, no. 3 (2019): 294–316.

Grineski, Sara, Timothy W. Collins, Jayajit Chakraborty, and Marilyn Montgomery.
"Hazardous Air Pollutants and Flooding: A Comparative Interurban Study of Environmental Injustice." *GeoJournal* 80, no. 1 (2015): 145–58.

Grossberg, Lawrence. "Cultural Studies and/in New Worlds." *Critical Studies in Mass
Communication* 10, no. 1 (1993): 1–22.

Guerette, Rob T., and Joshua D. Freilich, eds. *Migration, Culture Conflict, Crime and
Terrorism*. London: Routledge, 2016.

Gunders, John. "'Here's Lookin' at You': Video Surveillance and the Interpellated Body."
Social Alternatives 19, no. 1 (2000): 22–25.

Gustafsson, Henrik. "Foresight, Hindsight and State Secrecy in the American West:
The Geopolitical Aesthetics of Trevor Paglen." *Journal of Visual Culture* 12, no. 1
(2013): 148–64.

Gusterson, Hugh. *Drone: Remote Control Warfare*. London: MIT Press, 2016.

Hage, Ghassan. "The Affective Politics of Racial Mis-interpellation." *Theory, Culture &
Society* 27, nos. 7–8 (2011): 112–29.

Haggerty, Kevin D., and Richard V. Ericson. "The Surveillant Assemblage." *British Journal of Sociology* 51, no. 4 (2000): 605–22.

Hall, Rachel. "Of Ziploc Bags and Black Holes: The Aesthetics of Transparency in the
War on Terror." *Communication Review* 10, no. 4 (2007): 319–46.

Hall, Rachel. *The Transparent Traveler: The Performance and Culture of Airport Security*.
Durham, NC: Duke University Press, 2015.

Hall, Rachel, Torin Monahan, and Joshua Reeves. "Surveillance and Performance."
Surveillance & Society 14, no. 2 (2016): 154–67.

Hall, Stuart. "Black Diaspora Artists in Britain: Three 'Moments' in Post-War History." *History Workshop Journal* 61, no. 1 (2006): 1–24.

Hall, Stuart. "The Problem of Ideology: Marxism without Guarantees." In *Marx 100 Years On*, edited by Betty Matthews, 57–85. London: Lawrence & Wishart, 1983.

Hall, Stuart. *Representation: Cultural Representations and Signifying Practices*. London: Sage, 1997.

Hall, Stuart. "Signification, Representation, Ideology: Althusser and the Post-structuralist Debates." *Critical Studies in Mass Communication* 2, no. 2 (1985): 91–114.

Hallsby, Atilla. "Psychoanalysis against Wikileaks: Resisting the Demand for Transparency." *Review of Communication* 20, no. 1 (2020): 69–86.

Halpern, Orit. *Beautiful Data: A History of Vision and Reason since 1945*. Durham, NC: Duke University Press, 2014.

Hammerand, Andrew. "The New Town." Open Society Foundations, 2014. Accessed June 12, 2017. www.opensocietyfoundations.org/moving-walls/22/new-town.

Han, Byung-Chul. *The Transparency Society*. Stanford, CA: Stanford University Press, 2015.

Haney, Craig, and Philip Zimbardo. "The Past and Future of US Prison Policy: Twenty-Five Years after the Stanford Prison Experiment." *American Psychologist* 53, no. 7 (1998): 709–24.

Haraway, Donna J. *Simians, Cyborgs, and Women: The Reinvention of Nature*. New York: Routledge, 1991.

Harcourt, Bernard E. *Exposed: Desire and Disobedience in the Digital Age*. Cambridge, MA: Harvard University Press, 2015.

Harding, James M. *Performance, Transparency, and the Cultures of Surveillance*. Ann Arbor: University of Michigan Press, 2018.

Harding, Sandra G., ed. *The "Racial" Economy of Science: Toward a Democratic Future*. Bloomington: Indiana University Press, 1993.

Hartman, Saidiya. *Lose Your Mother: A Journey Along the Atlantic Slave Route*. New York: Farrar, Straus and Giroux, 2007.

Hartman, Saidiya V. *Scenes of Subjection: Terror, Slavery, and Self-Making in Nineteenth-Century America*. New York: Oxford University Press, 1997.

Hartman, Saidiya V., and Frank B. Wilderson. "The Position of the Unthought." *Qui Parle* 13, no. 2 (2003): 183–201.

Harvey, Adam. "cv Dazzle: Camouflage from Face Detection." 2013. Accessed December 23, 2013. http://cvdazzle.com.

Harvey, Adam. "How to Hide from Machines." *DIS Magazine* (2013). Accessed December 23, 2013. http://dismagazine.com/dystopia/evolved-lifestyles/8115/anti-surveillance-how-to-hide-from-machines.

Haslund-Christensen, Charlotte. "Who's Next?," 2012. Accessed October 31, 2018. www.charlottehaslund.com/works/index-grid.php?whos_next.

Haslund-Christensen, Charlotte. "Who's Next?" *Printed Matter*, 2012. Accessed October 31, 2018. www.printedmatter.org/catalog/31605.

Hayes, Ben. "The Surveillance-Industrial Complex." In *Routledge Handbook of Surveillance Studies*, edited by Kirstie Ball, Kevin D. Haggerty, and David Lyon, 167–75. London: Routledge, 2012.

Heidenreich, Stefan. "Santiago Sierra." *Frieze*, March 3, 2001. Accessed October 28, 2018. https://frieze.com/article/santiago-sierra.

Hetherington, Kregg. *Guerrilla Auditors: The Politics of Transparency in Neoliberal Paraguay*. Durham, NC: Duke University Press, 2011.

Hill, Kashmir. "Art That Shows Us What Mass Surveillance Actually Looks Like." *Fusion*, September 20, 2015. Accessed December 26, 2016. http://fusion.net/story/199240/trevor-paglen-art-shows-what-mass-surveillance-looks-like.

Hirschfield, Paul J. "Lethal Policing: Making Sense of American Exceptionalism." *Sociological Forum* 30, no. 4 (2015): 1109–17.

Hogue, Simon. "Performing, Translating, Fashioning: Spectatorship in the Surveillant World." *Surveillance & Society* 14, no. 2 (2016): 168–83.

Holert, Tom. "From the Archives of Invisibility: Marco Poloni's Displacement Island and the Visuality of the Border Regime." Supplement to "Displacement Island," 2013. Accessed October 28, 2018. www.theanalogueislandbureau.net/pdf/tom_holert_from_the_archives_of_invisibility_marco_poloni_s_displacement_island_and_the_visuality_of_the_border_regime_2013.pdf.

hooks, bell. "The Oppositional Gaze: Black Female Spectators." In *Black Looks: Race and Representation*, 115–31. Boston: South End, 1992.

Huey, Laura, Kevin Walby, and Aaron Doyle. "Cop Watching in the Downtown Eastside: Exploring the Use of (Counter)Surveillance as a Tool of Resistance." In *Surveillance and Security: Technological Politics and Power in Everyday Life*, edited by Torin Monahan, 149–65. New York: Routledge, 2006.

Huq, Aziz Z., and Richard H. McAdams. "Litigating the Blue Wall of Silence: How to Challenge the Police Privilege to Delay Investigation." *University of Chicago Legal Forum* (2016): 213–53.

Ingraham, Chris. *Gestures of Concern*. Durham, NC: Duke University Press, 2020.

Ingraham, Chris, and Allison Rowland. "Performing Imperceptibility: Google Street View and the Tableau Vivant." *Surveillance & Society* 14, no. 2 (2016): 211–26.

Joyce, Kelly A. *Magnetic Appeal: MRI and the Myth of Transparency*. Ithaca, NY: Cornell University Press, 2008.

Joyce, Patrick. "The Politics of the Liberal Archive." *History of the Human Sciences* 12, no. 2 (1999): 35–49.

Juris, Jeffrey S. *Networking Futures: The Movements against Corporate Globalization*. Durham, NC: Duke University Press, 2008.

Kafer, Gary. "Wi-Fi Defiance: Autonomy in the Information Age." *Qui Parle* 27, no. 1 (2018): 199–231.

Kapadia, Ronak K. *Insurgent Aesthetics: Security and the Queer Life of the Forever War*. Durham, NC: Duke University Press, 2019.

Kealey, Linda. "Patterns of Punishment: Massachusetts in the Eighteenth Century." *American Journal of Legal History* 30, no. 2 (1986): 163–86.

Kindervater, Katharine Hall. "The Emergence of Lethal Surveillance: Watching and Killing in the History of Drone Technology." *Security Dialogue* 47, no. 3 (2016): 223–38.

Kochel, Tammy Rinehart, David B. Wilson, and Stephen D. Mastrofski. "Effect of Suspect Race on Officers' Arrest Decisions." *Criminology* 49, no. 2 (2011): 473–512.

Koehler, John O. *Stasi: The Untold Story of the East German Secret Police*. Boulder, CO: Westview, 1999.

Kolesnikoff, Nina. "Defamiliarization." In *Encyclopedia of Contemporary Literary Theory: Approaches, Scholars, Terms*, edited by Irena R. Makaryk, 528–29. Toronto: University of Toronto Press, 1993.

Koskela, Hille. "'Don't Mess with Texas!': Texas Virtual Border Watch Program and the (Botched) Politics of Responsibilization." *Crime, Media, Culture* 7, no. 1 (2011): 49–66.

Koskela, Hille. "'The Gaze without Eyes': Video-Surveillance and the Changing Nature of Urban Space." *Progress in Human Geography* 24, no. 2 (2000): 243–65.

Koskela, Hille. "Hijacking Surveillance? The New Moral Landscapes of Amateur Photographing." In *Technologies of Insecurity: The Surveillance of Everyday Life*, edited by Katja Franko Aas, Helene Oppen Gundhus, and Heidi Mork Lomell, 147–67. New York: Routledge-Cavendish, 2009.

Koskela, Hille. "Video Surveillance, Gender, and the Safety of Public Urban Space: 'Peeping Tom' Goes High Tech?" *Urban Geography* 23, no. 3 (2002): 257–78.

Koskela, Hille. "'You Shouldn't Wear That Body': The Problematic of Surveillance and Gender." In *Routledge Handbook of Surveillance Studies*, edited by Kirstie Ball, Kevin D. Haggerty and David Lyon, 49–56. London: Routledge, 2012.

Kreiss, Daniel, and Shannon C. Mcgregor. "The 'Arbiters of What Our Voters See': Facebook and Google's Struggle with Policy, Process, and Enforcement around Political Advertising." *Political Communication* 36, no. 4 (2019): 1–24.

Kurwa, Rahim. "Building the Digitally Gated Community: The Case of Nextdoor." *Surveillance & Society* 17, no. 1/2 (2019): 111–17.

Lazarus-Black, Mindie, and Susan F. Hirsch, eds. *Contested States: Law, Hegemony, and Resistance*. New York: Routledge, 1994.

Le Goff, Jacques. *History and Memory*. New York: Columbia University Press, 1992.

Le Texier, T. "Debunking the Stanford Prison Experiment." *American Psychologist* 74, no. 7 (2019): 823–39.

Lefait, Sébastien. *Surveillance on Screen: Monitoring Contemporary Films and Television Programs*. Lanham, MD: Scarecrow, 2013.

Lévi-Strauss, Claude. *Structural Anthropology*. Translated by Claire Jacobson and Brooke Grundfest Schoepf. New York: Basic Books, 1963.

Levin, Thomas Y., Ursula Frohne, and Peter Weibel, eds. *Ctrl [Space]: Rhetorics of Surveillance from Bentham to Big Brother*. Cambridge, MA: MIT Press, 2002.

Levina, Marina. "Whiteness and the Joys of Cruelty." *Communication and Critical/Cultural Studies* 15, no. 1 (2018): 73–78.

Lewis, Randolph. *Under Surveillance: Being Watched in Modern America*. Austin: University of Texas Press, 2017.

Lianos, Michalis. "Social Control after Foucault." *Surveillance & Society* 1, no. 3 (2003): 412–30.

Linfield, Susie. *The Cruel Radiance: Photography and Political Violence*. Chicago: University of Chicago Press, 2011.

Lorde, Audre. *Sister Outsider: Essays and Speeches*. Berkeley, CA: Crossing, 2007.

Lowe, Lisa. *The Intimacies of Four Continents*. Durham, NC: Duke University Press, 2015.

Lynch, Michael. "Archives in Formation: Privileged Spaces, Popular Archives and Paper Trails." *History of the Human Sciences* 12, no. 2 (1999): 65–87.

Lynch, Mona. "Punishing Images: Jail Cam and the Changing Penal Enterprise." *Punishment & Society* 6, no. 3 (2004): 255–70.

Lyon, David. "Identification Practices: State Formation, Crime Control, Colonialism and War." In *Technologies of Insecurity: The Surveillance of Everyday Life*, edited by Katja Franko Aas, Helene Oppen Gundhus, and Heidi Mork Lomell, 42–58. New York: Routledge-Cavendish, 2009.

Lyon, David. *Identifying Citizens: ID Cards as Surveillance*. Cambridge, UK: Polity, 2009.

Lyon, David. *Surveillance after Snowden*. Malden, MA: Polity, 2015.

Lyon, David, ed. *Surveillance as Social Sorting: Privacy, Risk, and Digital Discrimination*. New York: Routledge, 2003.

Lyon, David. "Surveillance, Snowden, and Big Data: Capacities, Consequences, Critique." *Big Data & Society* 1, no. 2 (2014): 1–13.

Lyon, David. *Surveillance Society: Monitoring Everyday Life*. Buckingham, UK: Open University, 2001.

Lyon, David. *Surveillance Studies: An Overview*. Cambridge, UK: Polity, 2007.

Magelssen, Scott. "White-Skinned Gods: Thor Heyerdahl, the Kon-Tiki Museum, and the Racial Theory of Polynesian Origins." *TDR/The Drama Review* 60, no. 1 (2016): 25–49.

Magnet, Shoshana Amielle. *When Biometrics Fail: Gender, Race, and the Technology of Identity*. Durham, NC: Duke University Press, 2011.

Magnet, Shoshana, and Tara Rodgers. "Stripping for the State: Whole Body Imaging Technologies and the Surveillance of Othered Bodies." *Feminist Media Studies* 12, no. 1 (2012): 101–18.

Mann, Steve. "'Reflectionism' and 'Diffusionism.'" In *Ctrl [Space]: Rhetorics of Surveillance from Bentham to Big Brother*, edited by Thomas Y. Levin, Ursula Frohne, and Peter Weibel, 530–43. Cambridge, MA: MIT Press, 2002.

Mann, Steve, Jason Nolan, and Barry Wellman. "Sousveillance: Inventing and Using Wearable Computing Devices for Data Collection in Surveillance Environments." *Surveillance & Society* 1, no. 3 (2003): 331–55.

Manoff, Marlene. "Theories of the Archive from across the Disciplines." *portal: Libraries and the Academy* 4, no. 1 (2004): 9–25.

Marciniak, Katarzyna. "'Opening a Certain Poetic Space': What Can Art Do for Refugees?" *Media Fields Journal* 12 (2017): 1–11.

Marcus, George E. "The Once and Future Ethnographic Archive." *History of the Human Sciences* 11, no. 4 (1998): 49–64.

Marwick, Alice E. "Scandal or Sex Crime? Gendered Privacy and the Celebrity Nude Photo Leaks." *Ethics and Information Technology* 19, no. 3 (2017): 177–91.

Marwick, Alice E. *Status Update: Celebrity, Publicity, and Branding in the Social Media Age*. New Haven, CT: Yale University Press, 2013.

Marwick, Alice E. "To Catch a Predator? The MySpace Moral Panic." *First Monday* 13, no. 6 (2008). https://doi.org/10.5210/fm.v13i6.2152.

Marwick, Alice E. "Why Do People Share Fake News? A Sociotechnical Model of Media Effects." *Georgetown Law Technology Review* 2, no. 2 (2018): 474–512.

Marwick, Alice, Claire Fontaine, and danah boyd. "'Nobody Sees It, Nobody Gets Mad': Social Media, Privacy, and Personal Responsibility among Low-SES Youth." *Social Media+Society* 3, no. 2 (2017): 1–14.

Marwick, Alice, and Rebecca Lewis. "Media Manipulation and Disinformation Online." Data & Society Research Institute, 2017.

Marx, Gary T. *Undercover: Police Surveillance in America*. Berkeley: University of California Press, 1988.

Marx, Leo. *The Machine in the Garden: Technology and the Pastoral Ideal in America*. London: Oxford University Press, 1964.

Mason, Corinne, and Shoshana Magnet. "Surveillance Studies and Violence against Women." *Surveillance & Society* 10, no. 2 (2012): 105–18.

Mattelart, Armand. *The Globalization of Surveillance*. Translated by Susan Taponier and James A. Cohen. Malden, MA: Polity, 2010.

Matzner, Tobias. "Beyond Data as Representation: The Performativity of Big Data in Surveillance." *Surveillance & Society* 14, no. 2 (2016): 197–210.

Mayer-Schönberger, Viktor, and Kenneth Cukier. *Big Data: A Revolution That Will Transform How We Live, Work, and Think*. Boston: Houghton Mifflin Harcourt, 2013.

Mbembe, Achille. "Necropolitics." *Public Culture* 51, no. 1 (2003): 11–40.

McCosker, Anthony, and Rowan Wilken. "Rethinking 'Big Data' as Visual Knowledge: The Sublime and the Diagrammatic in Data Visualisation." *Visual Studies* 29, no. 2 (2014): 155–64.

McCoy, Alfred W. *Policing America's Empire: The United States, the Philippines, and the Rise of the Surveillance State*. Madison: University of Wisconsin Press, 2009.

McGrade, Niall. "The Story behind Northern Ireland's Peace Walls." *Culture Trip*, August 22, 2017. Accessed September 28, 2020. https://theculturetrip.com/europe/united-kingdom/northern-ireland/articles/the-story-behind-northern-irelands-peace-walls.

McGrath, John E. *Loving Big Brother: Performance, Privacy and Surveillance Space*. New York: Routledge, 2004.

McKittrick, Katherine. *Dear Science and Other Stories*. Durham, NC: Duke University Press, 2021.

Medel, China. "Transactional Seeing and Becoming Flesh." *Third Text* 30, nos. 5–6 (2017): 420–36.

Mercer, Kobena. "Stuart Hall and the Visual Arts." *Small Axe: A Caribbean Journal of Criticism* 19, no. 1 (2015): 78–87.

Merchant, Carolyn. *The Death of Nature: Women, Ecology, and the Scientific Revolution*. San Francisco: Harper & Row, 1980.

Merry, Sally Engle. "Rights Talk and the Experience of Law: Implementing Women's Human Rights to Protection from Violence." *Human Rights Quarterly* 25, no. 2 (2003): 343–81.

Meyer, Robinson. "Avoid Facial Detection Algorithms . . . with a T-Shirt." *Atlantic*, October 3, 2013. Accessed December 23, 2013. www.theatlantic.com/technology /archive/2013/10/avoid-facial-detection-algorithms-with-a-t-shirt/280253.

Milgram, Stanley. "Behavioral Study of Obedience." *Journal of Abnormal and Social Psychology* 67, no. 4 (1963): 371–78.

Miller, Jacques-Alain. "Jeremy Bentham's Panoptic Device." *October* 41 (1987): 3–29.

Mills, Charles W. *Blackness Visible: Essays on Philosophy and Race*. Ithaca, NY: Cornell University Press, 1998.

Mills, Charles W. *The Racial Contract*. Ithaca, NY: Cornell University Press, 1997.

Mirror Casket Project. "The Mirror Casket Project: About." 2018. Accessed August 13, 2018. http://mirrorcasket.com/aboutus.

Mirzoeff, Nicholas. *The Right to Look: A Counterhistory of Visuality*. Durham, NC: Duke University Press, 2011.

Mirzoeff, Nicholas. *Watching Babylon: The War in Iraq and Global Visual Culture*. New York: Routledge, 2005.

Mitchell, W. J. T. *Landscape and Power*. 2nd ed. Chicago: University of Chicago Press, 2002.

Mitchell, W. J. T. *Picture Theory: Essays on Verbal and Visual Representation*. Chicago: University of Chicago Press, 1994.

Monahan, Torin. "Built to Lie: Investigating Technologies of Deception, Surveillance, and Control." *Information Society* 32, no. 4 (2016): 229–40.

Monahan, Torin. "Counter-Surveillance as Political Intervention?" *Social Semiotics* 16, no. 4 (2006): 515–34.

Monahan, Torin. "Dreams of Control at a Distance: Gender, Surveillance, and Social Control." *Cultural Studies <=> Critical Methodologies* 9, no. 2 (2009): 286–305.

Monahan, Torin. "Privatization Cultures and the Racial Order: A Dispatch from the US." In *Private Influences, Privatization, and Criminal Justice in Canada*, edited by Alex Luscombe, Kevin Walby, and Derek Silva. Vancouver: University of British Columbia Press, forthcoming.

Monahan, Torin. "Reckoning with Covid, Racial Violence, and the Perilous Pursuit of Transparency." *Surveillance & Society* 19 (2021): 1–10.

Monahan, Torin. "Regulating Belonging: Surveillance, Inequality, and the Cultural Production of Abjection." *Journal of Cultural Economy* 10, no. 2 (2017): 191–206.

Monahan, Torin. "Surveillance and Inequality." *Surveillance & Society* 5, no. 3 (2008): 217–26.

Monahan, Torin. "Surveillance and Terrorism." In *Routledge Handbook of Surveillance Studies*, edited by Kirstie Ball, Kevin D. Haggerty, and David Lyon, 285–91. London: Routledge, 2012.

Monahan, Torin. "Surveillance as Cultural Practice." *Sociological Quarterly* 52, no. 4 (2011): 495–508.

Monahan, Torin. *Surveillance in the Time of Insecurity*. New Brunswick, NJ: Rutgers University Press, 2010.

Monahan, Torin, and David Murakami Wood. "Identity and Identification." In *Surveillance Studies: A Reader*, edited by Torin Monahan and David Murakami Wood, 93–95. New York: Oxford University Press, 2018.

Monahan, Torin, and David Murakami Wood. "Introduction: Surveillance Studies as a Transdisciplinary Endeavor." In *Surveillance Studies: A Reader*, edited by Torin Monahan and David Murakami Wood, xix–xxxiv. New York: Oxford University Press, 2018.

Monahan, Torin, and David Murakami Wood. "Resistance and Opposition." In *Surveillance Studies: A Reader*, edited by Torin Monahan and David Murakami Wood, 331–33. New York: Oxford University Press, 2018.

Monahan, Torin, and David Murakami Wood, eds. *Surveillance Studies: A Reader*. New York: Oxford University Press, 2018.

Möntmann, Nina. "Community Service." *Frieze*, October 1, 2006. Accessed October 28, 2018. https://frieze.com/article/community-service.

Moore, Lisa Jean, and Paisley Currah. "Legally Sexed: Birth Certificates and Transgender Citizens." In *Feminist Surveillance Studies*, edited by Rachel E. Dubrofsky and Shoshana Amielle Magnet, 58–76. Durham, NC: Duke University Press, 2015.

Morozov, Evgeny. *To Save Everything, Click Here: The Folly of Technological Solutionism*. New York: PublicAffairs, 2013.

Morrison, Elise. *Discipline and Desire: Surveillance Technologies in Performance*. Ann Arbor: University of Michigan Press, 2016.

Mosco, Vincent. *To the Cloud: Big Data in a Turbulent World*. New York: Paradigm, 2014.

Mulvey, Laura. "Visual Pleasure and Narrative Cinema." *Screen* 16, no. 3 (1975): 6–18.

Murakami Wood, David. "Beyond the Panopticon? Foucault and Surveillance Studies." In *Space, Knowledge and Power: Foucault and Geography*, edited by Jeremy W. Crampton and Stuart Elden, 245–63. Burlington, VT: Ashgate, 2007.

Murakami Wood, David. "Surveillance in the World City." In *International Handbook of Globalization and World Cities*, edited by Ben Derudder, Michael Hoyler, Peter J. Taylor, and Frank Witlox, 336–46. Northampton, MA: Edward Elgar, 2012.

Murakami Wood, David, and Kirstie Ball. "Brandscapes of Control? Surveillance, Marketing and the Co-construction of Subjectivity and Space in Neo-liberal Capitalism." *Marketing Theory* 13, no. 1 (2013): 47–67.

Murakami Wood, David (ed.), Kirstie Ball, David Lyon, Clive Norris, and Charles Raab. *A Report on the Surveillance Society*. Wilmslow, UK: Office of the Information Commissioner, 2006.

Musheno, Michael C., James P. Levine, and Denis J. Palumbo. "Television Surveillance and Crime Prevention: Evaluating an Attempt to Create Defensible Space in Public Housing." *Social Science Quarterly* 58, no. 4 (1978): 647–56.

Musser, Amber Jamilla. *Sensual Excess: Queer Femininity and Brown Jouissance*. New York: New York University Press, 2018.

NAACP. "Criminal Justice Fact Sheet." National Association for the Advancement of Colored People, 2018. Accessed August 8, 2018. www.naacp.org/criminal-justice-fact -sheet.

Nguyen, Mimi Thi. *The Gift of Freedom: War, Debt, and Other Refugee Passages*. Durham, NC: Duke University Press, 2012.

Nguyen, Mimi Thi. "The Hoodie as Sign, Screen, Expectation, and Force." *Signs* 40, no. 4 (2015): 791–816.

Nielsen, Hanne, and Birgit Johnsen. "Drifting." *Videoraum*, 2014. Accessed October 28, 2018. http://videoraum.dk/en/works/drifting.

Niemöller, Martin. "First They Came." 1946. Accessed August 16, 2019. www.hmd.org .uk/resource/first-they-came-by-pastor-martin-niemoller.

Nissenbaum, Helen Fay. *Privacy in Context: Technology, Policy, and the Integrity of Social Life*. Stanford, CA: Stanford Law Books, 2010.

Niva, Steve. "Disappearing Violence: JSOC and the Pentagon's New Cartography of Networked Warfare." *Security Dialogue* 44, no. 3 (2013): 185–202.

Nix, Justin, Bradley A. Campbell, Edward H. Byers, and Geoffrey P. Alpert. "A Bird's Eye View of Civilians Killed by Police in 2015: Further Evidence of Implicit Bias." *Criminology & Public Policy* 16, no. 1 (2017): 309–40.

Noble, Safiya Umoja. *Algorithms of Oppression: How Search Engines Reinforce Racism*. New York: New York University Press, 2018.

Noisebridge. "Anti Surveillance Fashion Show." November 13, 2012. Accessed May 25, 2014. www.noisebridge.net/wiki/Anti_Surveillance_Fashion_Show.

#NotABugSplat. "#Notabugsplat: A Giant Art Installation Targets Predator Drone Operators." 2014. Accessed January 8, 2017. https://notabugsplat.com.

Nwabuzo, Ojeaku, and Lisa Schaeder. "Racism and Discrimination in the Context of Migration in Europe." European Commission, March 31, 2017. Accessed October 28, 2018. https://ec.europa.eu/migrant-integration/librarydoc/racism-and -discrimination-in-the-context-of-migration-in-europe-1.

NWF Mail. "We Are Human, Too." YouTube, October 14, 2014. Accessed August 13, 2018. www.youtube.com/watch?v=gnc1xCLAkEg#t=77.

Ober, Cara. "Recasting the Past: Hank Willis Thomas in South Africa." BmoreArt, July 10, 2014. Accessed August 8, 2018. www.bmoreart.com/2014/07/recasting-the -past-hank-willis-thomas-in-south-africa.html.

Osborne, Thomas. "The Ordinariness of the Archive." *History of the Human Sciences* 12, no. 2 (1999): 51–64.

Paglen, Trevor. *Blank Spots on the Map: The Dark Geography of the Pentagon's Secret World*. New York: Dutton, 2009.

Paglen, Trevor, and Rebecca Solnit. *Invisible: Covert Operations and Classified Land-scapes*. New York: Aperture, 2010.

Pajnik, Mojca, and Petra Lesjak-Tušek. "Observing Discourses of Advertising: Mobitel's Interpellation of Potential Consumers." *Journal of Communication Inquiry* 26, no. 3 (2002): 277–99.

Pallitto, Robert M. *Bargaining with the Machine: Technology, Surveillance, and the Social Contract*. Lawrence: University of Kansas Press, 2020.

Pangburn, DJ. "An Artist Blurs More Than 15 Million Mugshots to Protect Your Right to Privacy." Good, May 6, 2016. www.good.is/articles/your-mugshot-does-not-have-to-be-forever.

Parks, Lisa. "Zeroing In: Overhead Imagery, Infrastructure Ruins, and Datalands in Afghanistan and Iraq." In The Visual Culture Reader, 3rd ed., edited by Nicholas Mirzoeff, 196–206. New York: Routledge, 2012.

Parks, Lisa, and Caren Kaplan, eds. Life in the Age of Drone Warfare. Durham, NC: Duke University Press, 2017.

Partin, William Clyde, and Alice Emily Marwick. "The Construction of Alternative Facts: Dark Participation and Knowledge Production in the Qanon Conspiracy." AoIR Selected Papers of Internet Research (2020). https://doi.org/10.5210/spir.v2020i0.11302.

Pasquale, Frank. The Black Box Society: The Secret Algorithms That Control Money and Information. Cambridge, MA: Harvard University Press, 2015.

Patton, Jason W. "Protecting Privacy in Public? Surveillance Technologies and the Value of Public Places." Ethics and Information Technology 2 (2000): 181–87.

Perucci, Tony. "What the Fuck Is That? The Poetics of Ruptural Performance." Liminalities: A Journal of Performance Studies 5, no. 3 (2009): 1–18.

Pfaffenberger, Bryan. "Technological Dramas." Science, Technology, and Human Values 17, no. 3 (1992): 282–312.

Phelan, Peggy. Unmarked: The Politics of Performance. New York: Routledge, 1993.

Philo, Greg, Emma Briant, and Pauline Donald. Bad News for Refugees. New York: Pluto, 2013.

Piper, Adrian. Out of Order, Out of Sight: Selected Writings in Meta-Art, 1968–1992, vol. 1. Cambridge, MA: MIT Press, 1996.

Poitras, Laura, ed. Astro Noise: A Survival Guide for Living under Total Surveillance. New York: Whitney Museum of American Art, 2016.

Poitras, Laura. Citizenfour. HBO Films, Participant Media and Praxis Films. Radius-TWC, October 10, 2014.

Poloni, Marco. "Displacement Island." In Watched! Surveillance, Art and Photography, edited by Ann-Christin Bertrand and James Bridle, 74–79. Köln: Walther König, 2016.

Poloni, Marco. "Displacement Island: Press Release." Campagne Première, 2013. Accessed October 28, 2018. www.campagne-premiere.com/exhibitions/marco-poloni/displacement-island/press-release.

Poole, Deborah. Vision, Race, and Modernity: A Visual Economy of the Andean Image World. Princeton, NJ: Princeton University Press, 1997.

Porter, Theodore M. Trust in Numbers: The Pursuit of Objectivity in Science and Public Life. Princeton, NJ: Princeton University Press, 1995.

Postigo, Hector. The Digital Rights Movement: The Role of Technology in Subverting Digital Copyright. Cambridge, MA: MIT Press, 2012.

Potolsky, Matthew. The National Security Sublime: On the Aesthetics of Government Secrecy. New York: Routledge, 2019.

Pouilly, Cécile. "Refugee Women and Children Face Heightened Risk of Sexual Violence amid Tensions and Overcrowding at Reception Facilities on Greek Islands."

United Nations High Commissioner for Refugees, February 9, 2018. Accessed
   October 28, 2018. www.unhcr.org/en-us/news/briefing/2018/2/5a7d67c4b/refugee
   -women-children-face-heightened-risk-sexual-violence-amid-tensions.html.
Price, David H. *Cold War Anthropology: The CIA, the Pentagon, and the Growth of Dual Use
   Anthropology*. Durham, NC: Duke University Press, 2016.
Prior, Thomas. "Anonymous vs. Steubenville." *Rolling Stone*, November 27, 2013.
   Accessed May 25, 2014. www.rollingstone.com/culture/news/anonymous-vs
   -steubenville-20131127.
Puar, Jasbir K. *Terrorist Assemblages: Homonationalism in Queer Times*. Durham, NC:
   Duke University Press, 2007.
Purvis, Trevor, and Alan Hunt. "Discourse, Ideology, Discourse, Ideology, Discourse,
   Ideology. . . ." *British Journal of Sociology* 44, no. 3 (1993): 473–99.
Queer Technologies. "Queer Technologies: Facial Weaponization Suite Information
   Session & Demonstration." Vimeo, 2011. Accessed May 25, 2014. http://vimeo.com
   /26812338.
Rancière, Jacques. *Dissensus: On Politics and Aesthetics*. Translated by Steve Corcoran.
   London: Continuum, 2010.
Rancière, Jacques. *The Politics of Aesthetics: The Distribution of the Sensible*. New York:
   Continuum, 2006.
Ranjan, Devika. "Migrant Surveillance and State Power: Electronic Tagging of Asylum-
   Seekers in the UK." PhD diss., University of Cambridge, 2018.
Rankine, Claudia. "Some Years There Exists a Wanting to Escape. . . ." Poetry Foun-
   dation, 2014. Accessed August 13, 2018. www.poetryfoundation.org/poems/57799
   /citizen-some-years-there-exists-a-wanting-to-escape.
Rawls, Will. "What Remains: Full Performance." Vimeo, 2017. Accessed August 13,
   2018. https://vimeo.com/226027745.
Reeves, Joshua. *Citizen Spies: The Long Rise of America's Surveillance Society*. New York:
   New York University Press, 2017.
Reeves, Joshua, and Jeremy Packer. "Police Media: The Governance of Territory, Speed,
   and Communication." *Communication and Critical/Cultural Studies* 10, no. 4 (2013):
   359–84.
Regan, Priscilla M., and Torin Monahan. "Beyond Counterterrorism: Data Sharing,
   Privacy, and Organizational Histories of DHS Fusion Centers." *International Journal of
   E-Politics* 4, no. 3 (2013): 1–14.
Rho, Hye Jin, Hayley Brown, and Shawn Fremstad. *A Basic Demographic Profile of Work-
   ers in Frontline Industries*. Center for Economic and Policy Research (April 2020).
   https://cepr.net/a-basic-demographic-profile-of-workers-in-frontline-industries.
Richards, Thomas. *The Imperial Archive: Knowledge and the Fantasy of Empire*. New
   York: Verso, 1993.
Richmond, Lee J. "A Time to Mourn and a Time to Dance: Horace Mccoy's 'They Shoot
   Horses, Don't They?'" *Twentieth Century Literature* 17, no. 2 (1971): 91–100.
Roberts, Madeleine. "Marking the Deadliest Year on Record, HRC Releases Report on
   Violence against Transgender and Gender Non-Conforming People." Human Rights
   Campaign, November 19, 2020. Accessed September 7, 2021. www.hrc.org/press

-releases/marking-the-deadliest-year-on-record-hrc-releases-report-on-violence
-against-transgender-and-gender-non-conforming-people.

Rogers, Kenneth. "Capital Implications: The Function of Labor in the Video Art of Juan Devis and Yoshua Okón." *Social Identities* 15, no. 3 (2009): 331–49.

Rose, Gillian. *Visual Methodologies: An Introduction to Researching with Visual Materials.* 3rd ed. Thousand Oaks, CA: Sage, 2012.

Rule, Nicholas O., Nalini Ambady, Reginald B. Adams Jr., and C. Neil Macrae. "Accuracy and Awareness in the Perception and Categorization of Male Sexual Orientation." *Journal of Personality and Social Psychology* 95, no. 5 (2008): 1019–28.

Salter, Mark B. "Passports, Mobility, and Security: How Smart Can the Border Be?" *International Studies Perspectives* 5, no. 1 (2004): 71–91.

Sandhu, Ajay, and Kevin D. Haggerty. "Private Eyes: Private Policing and Surveillance." In *Routledge Handbook of Private Security Studies*, edited by Rita Abrahamsen and Anna Leander, 100–108. New York: Routledge, 2016.

Saunders, Barry F. CT *Suite: The Work of Diagnosis in the Age of Noninvasive Cutting.* Durham, NC: Duke University Press, 2008.

Sawyer, Wendy, and Peter Wagner. "Mass Incarceration: The Whole Pie 2020." Prison Policy Initiative, March 24, 2020. Accessed August 8, 2018. www.prisonpolicy.org /reports/pie2020.html.

Sayers, Sean. "Jacques Rancière (2004) The Politics of Aesthetics: The Distribution of the Sensible." *Culture Machine*, 2005. https://culturemachine.net/reviews/ranciere -the-politics-of-aesthetics-sayers.

Scheper-Hughes, Nancy, and Philippe Bourgois. "Introduction: Making Sense of Violence." In *Violence in War and Peace*, edited by Nancy Scheper-Hughes and Philippe Bourgois, 1–31. Malden, MA: Blackwell, 2004.

Scher, Julia. "Security by Julia." 2020. Accessed October 24, 2020. www.juliascher.com.

Schulze-Engler, Frank, Pavan Kumar Malreddy, and John Njenga Karugia. "'Even the Dead Have Human Rights': A Conversation with Homi K. Bhabha." *Journal of Postcolonial Writing* 54, no. 5 (2018): 702–16.

Schwartz, Joan M., and Terry Cook. "Archives, Records, and Power: The Making of Modern Memory." *Archival Science* 2 (2002): 1–19.

Scott, Dread. "Stop." 2012. Accessed August 8, 2018. www.dreadscott.net/works/stop.

Scott, James C. *Seeing Like a State: How Certain Schemes to Improve the Human Condition Have Failed.* New Haven, CT: Yale University Press, 1998.

Sekula, Allan. "The Body and the Archive." *October* 39 (1986): 3–64.

Selod, Saher. *Forever Suspect: Racialized Surveillance of Muslim Americans in the War on Terror.* New Brunswick, NJ: Rutgers University Press, 2018.

Selvaggio, Leo. "URME Surveillance: Indiegogo Campaign." Vimeo, 2014. Accessed May 25, 2014. http://vimeo.com/90828804.

Selvaggio, Leonardo. "URME Surveillance: Performing Privilege in the Face of Automation." *International Journal of Performance Arts and Digital Media* 11, no. 2 (2015): 165–84.

Sexton, Jared. *Amalgamation Schemes: Antiblackness and the Critique of Multiracialism.* Minneapolis: University of Minnesota Press, 2008.

Sexton, Jared. "The Ruse of Engagement: Black Masculinity and the Cinema of Policing." *American Quarterly* 61, no. 1 (2009): 39–63.

Shade, Leslie Regan. "Contested Spaces: Protecting or Inhibiting Girls Online?" In
Growing Up Online, edited by Sandra Weber and Shanly Dixon, 229–47. New York:
Springer, 2007.

Shapin, Steven. *A Social History of Truth: Civility and Science in Seventeenth-Century
England*. Chicago: University of Chicago Press, 1994.

Shapiro, Aaron. "Predictive Policing for Reform? Indeterminacy and Intervention in
Big Data Policing." *Surveillance & Society* 17, no. 3/4 (2019): 456–72.

Shapiro, Aaron. "Street-Level: Google Street View's Abstraction by Datafication." *New
Media & Society* 20, no. 3 (2018): 1201–19.

Sharpe, Christina. *In the Wake: On Blackness and Being*. Durham, NC: Duke University
Press, 2016.

Shaw, Sophie. "When Fashion Speaks: Slogan T-Shirts Give Way to Political Face
Masks." CR *Fashion Book*, June 9, 2020. Accessed September 17, 2020. www
.crfashionbook.com/fashion/a32804002/slogan-t-shirts-political-face-masks.

Sheehan, Angela. "Noisebridge Anti/Surveillance Fashion Show." YouTube, May 29,
2010. Accessed May 25, 2014. www.youtube.com/watch?v=7mbsI2UXA8U.

Shell, Hanna Rose. *Hide and Seek: Camouflage, Photography, and the Media of Reconnais-
sance*. New York: Zone, 2012.

Sierra, Santiago. "Línea De 160 Cm Tatuada Sobre 4 Personas." YouTube, June 20, 2012.
Accessed October 28, 2018. www.youtube.com/watch?reload=9&v=w7P9YMwIfxc.

Silva, Kumarini. *Brown Threat: Identification in the Security State*. Minneapolis: University of Minnesota Press, 2016.

Silva, Kumarini. "Having the Time of Our Lives: Love-Cruelty as Patriotic Impulse."
Communication and Critical/Cultural Studies 15, no. 1 (2018): 79–84.

Simon, Stephanie. "Suspicious Encounters: Ordinary Preemption and the Securitization of Photography." *Security Dialogue* 43, no. 2 (2012): 157–73.

SKMU. "SKMU Sørlandets Kunstmuseum—Hanne Nielsen & Birgit Johnsen:
Drifting." *e-flux*, January 19, 2017. Accessed October 28, 2018. www.e-flux.com
/announcements/82699/hanne-nielsen-birgit-johnsen-drifting.

Sohn, Tim. "Trevor Paglen Plumbs the Internet." *New Yorker*, September 22, 2015.
Accessed June 11, 2017. www.newyorker.com/tech/elements/trevor-paglen-plumbs
-the-internet-at-metro-pictures-gallery.

Søilen, Karen Louise Grova. "Safe Is a Wonderful Feeling: Atmospheres of Surveillance
and Contemporary Art." *Surveillance & Society* 18, no. 2 (2020): 170–84.

Sontag, Susan. *Regarding the Pain of Others*. New York: Picador, 2003.

Spiegler, Marc. "When Human Beings Are the Canvas." *ARTnews*, June 2003, 94–97.

Spieker, Sven. *The Big Archive: Art from Bureaucracy*. Cambridge, MA: MIT Press, 2008.

Spillers, Hortense J. "Mama's Baby, Papa's Maybe: An American Grammar Book." *diacritics* 17, no. 2 (1987): 65–81.

Spivak, Gayatri Chakravorty. "Can the Subaltern Speak?" In *Marxism and the Interpretation of Culture*, edited by Cary Nelson and Lawrence Grossberg, 271–313. Bas-
ingstoke, UK: Macmillan Education, 1988.

Spivak, Gayatri Chakravorty. "The Rani of Sirmur: An Essay in Reading the Archives." *History and Theory* 24, no. 3 (1985): 247–72.

Staples, William G. *Everyday Surveillance: Vigilance and Visibility in Postmodern Life.* 2nd ed. Lanham, MD: Rowman & Littlefield, 2014.

Stark, Luke, and Kate Crawford. "The Work of Art in the Age of Artificial Intelligence: What Artists Can Teach Us About the Ethics of Data Practice." *Surveillance & Society* 17, no. 3/4 (2019): 442–55.

Steeves, Valerie. "Hide and Seek: Surveillance of Young People on the Internet." In *Routledge Handbook of Surveillance Studies*, edited by Kirstie Ball, Kevin D. Haggerty, and David Lyon, 352–59. London: Routledge, 2012.

Steeves, Valerie. "Online Surveillance in Canadian Schools." In *Schools under Surveillance: Cultures of Control in Public Education*, edited by Torin Monahan and Rodolfo D. Torres, 87–103. New Brunswick, NJ: Rutgers University Press, 2010.

Sturken, Marita, and Lisa Cartwright. *Practices of Looking: An Introduction to Visual Culture.* 2nd ed. Oxford: Oxford University Press, 2009.

Suárez-Krabbe, Julia. "The Other Side of the Story: Human Rights, Race, and Gender from a Transatlantic Perspective." In *Decolonizing Enlightenment: Transnational Justice, Human Rights and Democracy in a Postcolonial World*, edited by Nikita Dhawan, 211–26. Opladen, Germany: Barbara Budrich, 2014.

Surveillance Camera Players. *We Know You Are Watching.* Self-published, Factory School: Southpaw Culture, 2006.

Tagg, John. *The Disciplinary Frame: Photographic Truths and the Capture of Meaning.* Minneapolis: University of Minnesota Press, 2009.

Tate Museum. "Phil Collins: They Shoot Horses." Tate, 2004. Accessed October 28, 2018. www.tate.org.uk/art/artworks/collins-they-shoot-horses-t12030.

Tate Museum. "Santiago Sierra: Performance and Controversy." *TateShots*, April 21, 2008. Accessed October 28, 2018. www.tate.org.uk/art/artists/santiago-sierra-6878 /santiago-sierra-performance-and-controversy#.

Taylor, Diana. *The Archive and the Repertoire: Performing Cultural Memory in the Americas.* Durham, NC: Duke University Press, 2003.

Terrall, Mary. "Gendered Spaces, Gendered Audiences: Inside and Outside the Paris Academy of Sciences." *Configurations* 2 (1995): 207–32.

Terry, Jennifer. *An American Obsession: Science, Medicine, and Homosexuality in Modern Society.* Chicago: University of Chicago Press, 1999.

Ticktin, Miriam Iris. *Casualties of Care: Immigration and the Politics of Humanitarianism in France.* Berkeley: University of California Press, 2011.

Tiffany, Kaitlyn. "How 'Karen' Became a Coronavirus Villain." *Atlantic*, May 6, 2020. Accessed September 17, 2020. www.theatlantic.com/technology/archive/2020/05 /coronavirus-karen-memes-reddit-twitter-carolyn-goodman/611104.

Topak, Özgün E. "Humanitarian and Human Rights Surveillance: The Challenge to Border Surveillance and Invisibility?" *Surveillance & Society* 17, no. 3/4 (2019): 382–404.

Towns, Armond R. "Toward a Black Media Philosophy." *Cultural Studies* 34, no. 6 (2020): 851–73.

Towns, Armond R. "'What Do We Wanna Be?' Black Radical Imagination and the Ends of the World." *Communication and Critical/Cultural Studies* 17, no. 1 (2020): 75–80.

"Tracking the Covid-19 Recession's Effects on Food, Housing, and Employment Hardships." Center on Budget and Policy Priorities, September 16, 2020. Accessed September 17, 2020. www.cbpp.org/research/poverty-and-inequality/tracking-the -covid-19-recessions-effects-on-food-housing-and.

Treichler, Paula A., Lisa Cartwright, and Constance Penley. "Introduction: Paradoxes of Visibility." In *The Visible Woman: Imaging Technologies, Gender, and Science*, edited by Paula Treichler, Lisa Cartwright, and Constance Penley, 1–17. New York: New York University Press, 1998.

Trottier, Daniel. "Coming to Terms with Shame: Exploring Mediated Visibility against Transgressions." *Surveillance & Society* 16, no. 2 (2018): 170–82.

Trottier, Daniel. "Crowdsourcing CCTV Surveillance on the Internet." *Information, Communication & Society* 17, no. 5 (2014): 609–26.

Trump, Donald J. "Remarks by President Trump in Press Briefing." September 16, 2020. Accessed September 17, 2020. www.whitehouse.gov/briefings-statements/remarks -president-trump-press-briefing-september-16-2020.

Turner, Victor. *Dramas, Fields, and Metaphors: Symbolic Action in Human Society*. Ithaca, NY: Cornell University Press, 1974.

Tuttle, Ross, and Erin Schneider. "Stopped-and-Frisked: 'For Being a F**king Mutt.'" *Nation*, October 8, 2012. Accessed May 25, 2014. www.thenation.com/article/170413 /stopped-and-frisked-being-fking-mutt-video#axzz2YU9ugp4y.

UNHCR. "Figures at a Glance." United Nations High Commissioner for Refugees, 2018. Accessed October 28, 2018. www.unhcr.org/en-us/figures-at-a-glance.html.

UNHCR. "UNHCR Study Uncovers Shocking Sexual Violence against Syrian Refugee Boys, Men." United Nations High Commissioner for Refugees, December 6, 2017. Accessed October 28, 2018. www.unhcr.org/en-us/news/press/2017/12/5a27a6594 /unhcr-study-uncovers-shocking-sexual-violence-against-syrian-refugee-boys.html.

"United States v. Gementera, 379 F.3d 596 (9th Cir.)." 2004. https://law.justia.com /cases/federal/appellate-courts/F3/379/596/475040.

van der Meulen, Emily, and Robert Heynen, eds. *Expanding the Gaze: Gender and the Politics of Surveillance*. Toronto: University of Toronto Press, 2016.

van der Ploeg, Irma. "The Illegal Body: 'Eurodac' and the Politics of Biometric Identification." *Ethics and Information Technology* 1 (1999): 295–302.

Van Dijck, José. *The Transparent Body: A Cultural Analysis of Medical Imaging*. Seattle: University of Washington Press, 2005.

van Houtryve, Tomas. "Blue Sky Days." Open Society Foundations, 2014. Accessed June 11, 2017. www.opensocietyfoundations.org/moving-walls/22/blue-sky-days.

Varvin, Sverre. "Our Relations to Refugees: Between Compassion and Dehumanization." *American Journal of Psychoanalysis* 77, no. 4 (2017): 359–77.

Wacquant, Loïc. *Punishing the Poor: The Neoliberal Government of Social Insecurity*. Durham, NC: Duke University Press, 2009.

Wacquant, Loïc J. D. "Toward a Social Praxeology: The Structure and Logic of Bourdieu's Sociology." In *An Invitation to Reflexive Sociology*, edited by Pierre Bourdieu and Loïc J. D. Wacquant, 1–59. Chicago: University of Chicago Press, 1992.

Wall, Tyler. "Philanthropic Soldiers, Practical Orientalism, and the Occupation of Iraq." *Identities* 18, no. 5 (2011): 481–501.

Wall, Tyler. "Unmanning the Police Manhunt: Vertical Security as Pacification." *Socialist Studies* 9, no. 2 (2013): 32–56.

Wall, Tyler, and Travis Linnemann. "Staring Down the State: Police Power, Visual Economies, and the 'War on Cameras.'" *Crime, Media, Culture* 10, no. 2 (2014): 133–49.

Wall, Tyler, and Torin Monahan. "Surveillance and Violence from Afar: The Politics of Drones and Liminal Security-Scapes." *Theoretical Criminology* 15, no. 3 (2011): 239–54.

Watts, Eric King. *Hearing the Hurt: Rhetoric, Aesthetics, and Politics of the New Negro Movement*. Tuscaloosa: University Alabama Press, 2012.

Weheliye, Alexander G. *Habeas Viscus: Racializing Assemblages, Biopolitics, and Black Feminist Theories of the Human*. Durham, NC: Duke University Press, 2014.

Weil, Shalva. "Making Femicide Visible." *Current Sociology* 64, no. 7 (2016): 1124–37.

Weil, Simone. "The Iliad, or the Poem of Force." *Chicago Review* 18, no. 2 (1965): 5–30.

Weiner, Jonah. "Prying Eyes." *New Yorker*, October 22, 2012, 54–61. Accessed June 11, 2017. www.newyorker.com/magazine/2012/10/22/prying-eyes.

Wenner, Lawrence A. "On the Limits of the New and the Lasting Power of the Mediasport Interpellation." *Television & New Media* 15, no. 8 (2014): 732–40.

Whitman, James Q. "What Is Wrong with Inflicting Shame Sanctions." *Yale Law Journal* 107 (1998): 1055–92.

Wiedenhöfer, Kai. "WALLonWALL." 2019. Accessed September 28, 2020. www.wallonwall.org/?p=668.

Wiedenhöfer, Kai. "WALLonWALL: Belfast '19." 2019. Accessed September 28, 2020. www.wallonwall.org/?p=668.

Wike, Richard, Bruce Stokes, and Katie Simmons. "Europeans Fear Wave of Refugees Will Mean More Terrorism, Fewer Jobs." Pew Research Center, July 11, 2016. Accessed October 28, 2018. www.pewglobal.org/2016/07/11/europeans-fear-wave-of-refugees-will-mean-more-terrorism-fewer-jobs.

Wilderson, Frank B., III. *Red, White & Black: Cinema and the Structure of U.S. Antagonisms*. Durham, NC: Duke University Press, 2010.

Williams, Angela. "Turning the Tide: Recognizing Climate Change Refugees in International Law." *Law & Policy* 30, no. 4 (2008): 502–29.

Williams, Raymond. *Culture & Society: 1780–1950*. New York: Columbia University Press, 1983.

Winner, Langdon. *The Whale and the Reactor: A Search for Limits in an Age of High Technology*. Chicago: University of Chicago Press, 1986.

Winokur, Julie, and Ed Kashi. "They Came Here Seeking Freedom and Were Imprisoned Instead. Look at Their Faces." *Mother Jones*, March 23, 2018. Accessed

August 8, 2018. www.motherjones.com/politics/2018/03/they-came-here-seeking -freedom-and-were-imprisoned-instead-look-at-their-faces.

Wise, J. Macgregor. *Surveillance and Film*. New York: Bloomsbury, 2016.

Wood, David. "Territoriality and Identity at Raf Menwith Hill." In *Architectures: Modernism and After*, edited by Andrew Ballantyne, 142–62. Malden, MA: Blackwell, 2004.

Woods, Heather Suzanne. "Anonymous, Steubenville, and the Politics of Visibility: Questions of Virality and Exposure in the Case of #Oprollredroll and #Occupysteubenville." *Feminist Media Studies* 14, no. 6 (2014): 1096–98.

Woods, Heather Suzanne. "Asking More of Siri and Alexa: Feminine Persona in Service of Surveillance Capitalism." *Critical Studies in Media Communication* 35, no. 4 (2018): 334–49.

Wright, Jordana, Amanda Glasbeek, and Emily van der Meulen. "Securing the Home: Gender, CCTV and the Hybridized Space of Apartment Buildings." *Theoretical Criminology* 19, no. 1 (2015): 95–111.

Wright, Simona. "Lampedusa's Gaze: Messages from the Outpost of Europe." *Italica* 91, no. 4 (2014): 775–802.

Ziel, Paul. "Eighteenth Century Public Humiliation Penalties in Twenty-First Century America: The Shameful Return of Scarlet Letter Punishments in US v. Gementera." *BYU Journal of Public Law* 19 (2004): 499–522.

Zimmer, Catherine. *Surveillance Cinema*. New York: New York University Press, 2015.

Zine, Jasmin. "Between Orientalism and Fundamentalism: The Politics of Muslim Women's Feminist Engagement." *Muslim World Journal of Human Rights* 3, no. 1 (2006): 1–24.

Zuboff, Shoshana. *The Age of Surveillance Capitalism: The Fight for a Human Future at the New Frontier of Power*. New York: PublicAffairs, 2019.

Zurawski, Nils. "'I Know Where You Live!'—Aspects of Watching, Surveillance and Social Control in a Conflict Zone (Northern Ireland)." *Surveillance & Society* 2, no. 4 (2005): 498–512.

INDEX

objectification, 8, 11, 45, 70, 91; of laborers, 98–106, 113–14; of women, 36–37, 149n31

objectivity, 7, 11, 20, 91–92

Obscurity, 107–9, 146

160 cm Line Tattooed on Four People, 99–101

One Nation Under CCTV, 1–3, 4

opacity, 17, 19, 25, 55, 72, 80, 112, 158n88; aesthetics of, 143–44; archives and, 60–61, 63, 67; collective, 20, 145; in CV Dazzle works, 26–28; dehumanization and, 15, 91; in *Facial Weaponization Suite*, 34; glitches in, 151n58, 152n63; in *Jaywalking*, 86–87; performances of, 14, 74; privacy contrasted with, 14, 150n50; rights to, 14, 41, 67; transparency contrasted with, 14, 68, 88–89, 151n59; in URME *Project*, 31–32

oppression, 6, 14–15, 25, 116

order, 106; ideological, 73, 75; racial, 13, 42, 71, 115, 136, 140, 144

Orientalism, 78

Osborne, Thomas, 47–48

Other, the (social designation), 12, 17, 24, 28–29, 41, 92; dehumanization of, 15, 144; tropes surrounding, 76–77

oversaturation, archival, 62–67

Packer, Jeremy, 157n78

Paglen, Trevor, 51–53, 54–55, 157n86

paintings, 10, 71, 79–80

Pakistan, 75, 78, 146

Palestine, 58, 101–2

panopticon, 86

panoramic images, 1, 51, 58

Pantaleo, Daniel, 130

participatory art, 27, 74–75, 99–106; *Jaywalking* as, 83–87; *#NotABugSplat* as, 75–79

patriarchy, 13, 118–19

peer surveillance, 176n1

Penley, Constance, 148n20

people of color, 12, 31, 132, 137–38, 145

perceived threats, 6, 9, 157n58

performances, 11, 16, 39, 44, 152n63, 154n34, 156n75; by Elahi, 62–67; exploitation, 98–106; of identity, 31, 34; *Mirror Casket Project*, 128–30; of opacity, 14, 74; participatory art, 74–75; of transparency, 22; *What Remains* as, 132–37

personhood, 8, 90. *See also* liberal subjects/personhood

Peru, 96, 98

Peshawar, Pakistan, 75–76, 78

Philadelphia, Pennsylvania, 128

photography, 36–37, 113–14, 121–22, 161n59, 171n79, 172n80; black-and-white, 67–68, 78, 168n17; blurriness in, 51–52, 54, 56, 59–60; of borders, 56, 58–59; by Elahi, 62–67; mugshot, 110–12; by Paglen, 51–53, 160n44; by Poloni, 92–94, 97; by van Houtryve, 53–54

Piper, Adrian, 17

Plain Sight, 53–54

plantations, slavery, 9, 24, 119, 131–32, 174n38

platforms, digital, 3–4, 103–4, 167n70

play, 4, 24, 27, 36–37, 38–39

poetry, 110, 119, 133, 171n74

police, 5, 31, 39–40, 47, 61, 161n53, 167n70; black men killed by, 121, 128, 149n28; filming of, 40, 157n78; in *Jaywalking*, 83–87; mugshots, 106–11; in *One Nation Under CCTV*, 1, 2; photographic evidence used by, 66; threats and, 126, 157n58; violence, 12, 21, 42, 123–32; in *Who's Next?*, 110–12. *See also* violence, police

politics, of archives, 44, 45–49

Poloni, Marco, 92–94, 97

Poole, Deborah, 149n36

populism, 25, 142

pornotrope/pornotroping, 8, 12–13, 130, 136, 175n65

Postcode Criminals project, 123, 125

postmodernism, 25

Potolsky, Matthew, 52, 160n48

poverty capitalism, 108

power, 8, 9, 17, 20, 38, 45, 46, 176n1; of biometric systems, 28; of evidence, 66; hierarchical, 14; in URME *Project*, 30–32; of visibility, 40, 115, 128

precarity, 12, 36

Prism, 63–64

privacy, 4, 12, 39, 108, 156n75, 161n54; facial recognition and, 29–30; in *The New Town*, 59–61; opacity contrasted with, 14, 150n50; rights to, 32–33, 66

privilege, 12, 17, 91, 142, 171n79; of artists, 18, 97–98, 100–101; avoidance as, 22; male, 30–31. *See also* white privilege profiling, racial, 9, 54, 62

prostitutes, 90–91, 99–101, 102–3

Protestants, 58, 106–7

protests, 16, 21, 29, 128–31

Prude, Daniel, 149n28

public, 47, 53, 85; awareness, 23, 29, 39; shaming, 106–12; spaces, 39, 55–56, 58, 79–83

Quebec sovereignty movement, 72–73

queerness, 33–35

race, 148n25, 177n6

racial, 49, 116–20, 167n70; order, 13, 42, 71, 115, 136, 140, 144; profiling, 9, 54, 62; subjugation, 13, 15, 23, 123, 139; violence, 21, 41, 46, 174n38

racialization, 5, 12–13, 45, 138, 143; archives reinforcing, 19, 50; of bodies, 12–13, 28, 53, 122; gendered, 76–77; hierarchies, 8, 17, 70–71, 117, 139–40, 174n65; of identities, 24, 48, 97–98; interpellation as, 70–71, 91–92; of threats, 28, 77; of violence, 21, 41, 46, 75–79, 116–20, 174n38

racial justice movement, 22–23

racism, 19, 70–71, 93, 108, 117, 139; antiblack, 8–9, 23, 120, 128, 132, 140; of police, 123–32

radomes, 51, 160n38

Raise Up, 120–23, 137

Ramallah, Palestine, 101–2

ramifications, 18, 48, 142, 149n31; of slavery, 118–19; of surveillance, 4, 16, 29

Rancière, Jacques, 6, 38, 40, 73, 147n14

Rankine, Claudia, 132–38, 140–41, 144

rapes, 156n60, 157n83

rationality, 49, 108, 164n96; scientific, 11, 13, 43

Rawls, Will, 132–38, 144

realism, 55–56, 65–66, 68, 91, 113–14

redlining, digital, 61

Reeves, Joshua, 31, 157n78

refugees, 90; crises, 17–18, 91–98, 113–14; detention centers for, 91–94, 96, 169n27; in *Displacement Island*, 168n17; in #NotABugSplat, 75–79

regimes, visibility, 6, 8–9, 11, 12, 16, 18, 74

Repetition (film), 85

residential surveillance, 167n70

resistance, 23, 38, 118, 152n63, 157n83, 173n30; through avoidance, 26–28; tactics, 39–40

responsibilization, 18–19, 25–26, 99, 144, 161n54; of audiences, 74–75, 86–89; collective, 69, 85, 89, 145; of individuals, 4–5, 12, 37, 156n69

rights, 17, 24, 118, 139; to be forgotten, 108, 112; to hide, 25, 34, 39–40; human, 91, 110–11, 113–14, 142, 153n10, 171n79; to opacity, 14, 41, 67; to privacy, 32–33, 66

Ring, Amazon, 167n70

Ring, Annie, 158n9

Roots, Katrin, 120

Rwanda, 46

Scenes of Subjection (Hartman), 122, 131

Scheper-Hughes, Nancy, 90

Scher, Julia, 141

Schwartz, Joan M., 43

science, prejudices in, 7, 34–35

scientific, 148n20; knowledge, 7, 9–10, 34–35; rationality, 11, 13, 43

scientific revolution, 7, 43, 140

Scott, Dread (Scott Tyler), 123–27, 137–38, 175n54

Scott, Walter, 128

Seattle, 103–4

security sublime, 160n48

segregation, racial, 167n70

Sekula, Allan, 46, 48

self-branding, 27, 121

self-reflexivity, 87–89

Selvaggio, Leo, 29–32, 34

settler colonialism, 117, 123

Seurat, Georges, 10

sexism, 28, 32

Sexton, Jared, 8, 129

sexual: assault, 37, 40; violence, 97, 169n25

sexualizing/sexualization, 8, 37

sex workers, 90–91, 99–101, 102–3, 120

shame/shaming, 106–12, 108

Sharpe, Christina, 116–17, 119, 137, 175n66

Shell, Hanna Rose, 153n7

Shoreditch, London, 85

Sierra, Santiago, 98–102, 104, 113–14, 169n39

signifiers, 15–16, 22, 34, 38–39, 77, 148n25

Silva, Kumarini, 109–10

skin color, 17, 77, 96–97, 99, 123–25, 177n6

slavery, 8–9; legacy of, 116–23, 121, 174n38; plantations, 9, 24, 119, 131–32; *What Remains* addressing, 132–37

Twitter, 155n55
Tyler, Scott. *See* Scott, Dread (Scott Tyler)

UK (United Kingdom), 1–3, 139
Ulster Defense Association, 58–59, 162n69
uncertainty, 13, 15, 58–59, 67, 145, 158n9
United Kingdom (UK), 1–3, 139
United Nations, 169n25
United States (US), 21, 27, 77, 119, 158n3, 170n56, 171n76; drones used by, 75–79; government, 5, 49, 55, 142, 160n44; hate crimes in, 112; on immigration, 139; incarceration in, 117; legacies of slavery and, 116–21; shaming in, 106–7
universal threats, 4–5, 18–19
upskirt photography, 36–37
URME Project, 29–32, 34
US. *See* United States
US-Mexico border, 58, 85

Veel, Kristin, 158n9
Vega, Elizabeth, 128–30
victims, 25, 75–79, 90, 93, 117; of exploitation, 98–106
videos, 120, 160n51, 176n70; *Drifting* as, 17, 94–97, 146; by Scott, D., 123–25, 137, 145; by Selvaggio, 29–30
Villiers, Nicholas de, 151n59
violence, 5, 17, 28, 75–79, 150n50; antiblack, 8–9, 23, 120, 128–29, 132, 140; artistic frame of, 19–20, 90–91, 113–14, 142; dehumanizing, 14–15, 117–19; invisibility of, 111–12, 169n11; police, 12, 21, 42, 123–32; sexual, 97, 169n25; state, 18, 171n76; structural, 90–92, 97–99, 108, 113–14; symbolic, 38, 54, 90–91, 101, 106, 108, 113–14, 172n81; visibility as, 7, 10, 89–90, 99–106; against women, 25, 36–37
violence, racialized, 21, 41, 46, 75–79, 116–20, 174n38
visibility/visualizations, 4, 13, 18, 50–55, 107–12, 148n20; power of, 40, 115, 128; regimes, 6, 8–9, 11, 12, 16, 18, 74; state projects, 6, 20, 24, 38; violence and, 7, 10, 89–90, 99–106
visual economies, 9–10, 13, 77, 93, 149n36
voyeurism, 25, 60–61, 109
vulnerabilities, 4, 38, 60–61, 90, 142

Wacquant, Loïc J. D., 43
wakes/wake work (metaphor), 116–17, 119, 125, 132, 136–37, 175n66
Walby, Kevin, 157n83
Wall, Tyler, 157n78
WALLonWALL, 56, 58–59
War on Terror, 3, 67, 76–78, 86
Watchmen (HBO show), 22
Watchtower (A Machine for Living), 103–6, 114
Ways of Seeing (Berger), 69
webcams, 59–60, 81, 170n72
websites, 62–63, 107–9
Weheliye, Alexander, 118–19, 122, 125, 130, 144, 173n20, 175n65
Weil, Simone, 169n41
Weiner, Jonah, 52
What Remains, 132–37, 176n70
white gaze, 132, 140–41
whiteness, 42, 122, 132, 142, 148n25; refugees and, 77, 96–97
white people, 22, 60–61, 92–94, 120, 123; as audiences, 132–33, 138, 174n45. *See also* subjecthood/subjects, white
white privilege, 19, 23, 25, 28, 154n34; COVID-19 pandemic and, 22, 42; in URME Project, 31–32
white supremacy, 8, 13, 21–23, 71, 86, 115, 122
Who's Next?, 110–12
Wiedenhöfer, Kai, 56, 58–59
Wilderson, Frank, 8, 148n25, 173n23
Williams, Raymond, 97
Wilson, Darren, 128
Wise, J. Macgregor, 150
women, 32, 38, 77, 156n60, 169n25, 171n79; in *160 cm Line Tattooed on Four People*, 99–101; objectification of, 36–37, 149n31; scientific prejudices against, 7, 34–35; violence against, 25, 36–37
Woods, Heather, 157n83
workers/labor, 21, 98–106, 113–14, 117–18

xenophobia, 17, 21

zero-tolerance policing, 125
Zimbardo, Philip, 85–86
Zimmerman, George, 41
Żmijewski, Artur, 85–86, 98
Zurawski, Nils, 162n64

www.ingramcontent.com/pod-product-compliance
Lightning Source LLC
Chambersburg PA
CBHW051212170526
45166CB00005B/1860